THE
FUTURE
OF
CHINA

THE FUTURE OF CHINA

After Mao

ROSS TERRILL

DELACORTE PRESS/NEW YORK

Published by
Delacorte Press
1 Dag Hammarskjold Plaza
New York, N.Y. 10017

Manufactured in the United States of America
First printing

Designed by Oksana Kushnir

Library of Congress Cataloging in Publication Data

Terrill, Ross.
The future of China.
Includes index.
1. China—Politics and government—1976-
2. China—Foreign relations—1976-   I. Title.
DS779.26.T48   951.05   78-1896
ISBN 0-440-02499-4

EVENTS OF 1976 AND 1977

1976 (Year of the Dragon)

January	Death of Chou En-lai
	Republication of two poems written by Mao Tse-tung on the eve of the Cultural Revolution
February	Richard Nixon revisits China
	Press carries strongly anti-Soviet articles
	Hua Kuo-feng becomes acting premier
March	Veiled attacks on Teng Hsiao-p'ing fill the press, as do ultra-leftist articles of all kinds
April	Massive demonstration in Peking's main square
	Teng is dismissed from all posts
	Hua is named premier
May	Mao's meetings with the prime ministers of Singapore and Pakistan are his last ever with foreigners
June	Gang of Four are prominent in many spheres
July	Death of Chu Te
	Strong earthquake in the Tangshan area
September	Death of Mao Tse-tung
October	Fall of the Gang of Four
	Plans are announced for Mao Memorial Hall and Volume V of Mao's *Selected Works*

Hua is named Mao's successor as chairman of the CCP

Military press lauds Hua

November   Gang of Four vilified up and down the nation

Sino-Soviet polemics ease and Moscow's chief border negotiator returns to Peking

China completes its twenty-first nuclear test, and its fourth during 1976

December   Republication of Mao's speech "On the Ten Great Relationships"

1977 (Year of the Snake)

January   Extensive commemoration of first anniversary of Chou's death

People's Daily for the first time prints a quotation of Hua in a box on page one

February   Greater diversity is becoming apparent in the performing arts

April   National Conference on Industry

Publication of Volume V of Mao's *Selected Works*

May   Soviet polemics against China resume in full force

Carter declares China "a key force for global peace"

July   Teng is restored to all his posts

National Conference on Foreign Trade

August   Secretary Vance visits China

Tenth CCP Congress confirms the new Hua-Yeh-Teng leadership and crystalizes

.

TERMS AND NAMES

CCP	Communist Party of China
Chang Ch'un-ch'iao	Shanghai politician who was the most distinguished member of the Gang of Four; born about 1912, he rose to high posts including vice-premier and was a theorist of note
Chiang Ch'ing	Third and last wife of Mao, born in 1910, part of the militant Gang of Four
Ch'in Shih Huang	Strong-man emperor who unified China 2100 years ago
Cultural Revolution left	The Gang of Four and others, many of them young, who rose to prominence in 1966–67 and continued in the 1970s to support policies often considered ultra-leftist
Gang of Four	Quartet of ultra-leftists, including Mao's wife, who rose to power in the Cultural Revolution and were crushed within weeks of Mao's death in the fall of 1976
"goulash communism"	Khrushchev's maxim in a speech at Budapest to the effect that a socialist government could be tested by whether or not it provided the people with a good plate of goulash

Great Leap Forward Accelerated drive toward socialism begun in the spring of 1958, only partially successful

Hua Kuo-feng Supreme leader of China after succeeding Mao as Chairman of the CCP in October 1976. Born in 1921 in Shansi Province, Hua spent most of his career in Hunan Province until he entered the national scene in 1969. In 1975 he became Minister of Public Security and in early 1976 he succeeded Chou En-lai as premier.

Legalism Science of power evolved by China's *realpolitik* tradition of amoral administrators, going back more than 2000 years

Liberation The revolution of 1949

Liu Shao-ch'i Major Chinese leader who rose to be head of state and Mao's heir apparent in the 1960s, until he became the prime target of the Cultural Revolution ("China's Khrushchev"). He died in obscurity in 1973 at the age of 75.

"On the Ten Great Relationships" A brilliant and enduring state-of-the-union speech given by Mao in 1956

"people's war" Unofficial summation of the type of warfare Mao and the PLA came to believe in after developing it so

	successfully against Japan and Chiang Kai-shek: the whole society is mobilized, men are valued over weapons, the enemy is lured in and then surrounded, social policy is given almost equal stress with military policy, and the army moves among the people as fish swim in water
PLA	People's Liberation Army—the Chinese armed forces
PRC	People's Republic of China
Shanghai Communiqué	Charter of Sino-American detente signed by Richard Nixon and Chou En-lai in February 1972
Story of the Marshes	Historical novel of peasant revolt in the Sung Dynasty (960–1279), also translated under the titles *Water Margin* and *All Men Are Brothers*.
Teng Hsiao-p'ing	Major Chinese leader, born in Szechwan in 1904, purged in 1967 and again in 1976 but today third in the Peking regime
Unit 8341	Elite Peking military unit with special political responsibilities
wall poster	A message, generally written by hand in large characters—the Chinese term *da zi bao* means "big-character poster"—and pasted on a wall; sometimes officially inspired and sometimes not

Wang Hung-wen — Shanghai cotton-mill worker who rose with the abruptness of a "helicopter" in the Cultural Revolution and fell in 1976 as the youngest (born 1935) of the Gang of Four

"With you in charge I have no worries" — A note in six Chinese characters (*Ni ban shi wo fang xin*) written by Mao for Hua in April 1976

Yao Wen-yuan — Shanghai journalist, born 1931, part of the Gang of Four

Year of the Dragon — 1976 in the Chinese lunar calendar

Year of the Snake — 1977 in the Chinese lunar calendar

Yeh Chien-ying — Senior remaining military hero (together with Liu Po-ch'eng) of the Chinese Revolution; born in 1898. Yeh, who is of the Hakka minority, now ranks second in the regime.

Acknowledgments

My thanks to Cornelis Schepel of the University of Leiden for facilitating the publication of the poems in Appendix 8a; to *Foreign Affairs* for permission to reprint material I wrote that appeared in the January, 1977 issue (Copyright 1977 by Council on Foreign Relations, Inc.); to *The New Republic* for permission to reprint some paragraphs by me from the issues of November 1, 1975 and September 25, 1976; to Andrew Nathan of Columbia University who made wise suggestions on the whole book; and to Roxane Witke for the photograph on page 111.

Contents

1
China
in
☙ Our Time ☙

It was for good reason that events in a land of 900 million people held the world's attention during 1976 and 1977: deaths, purges, earthquakes, the coming of new leadership. China, once merely exotic, has become part of everyone's future.

Not so many decades ago China existed in the consciousness of Western man only as a blur of diverting novelties: green jade, chop suey, laundrymen, pagan souls, firecrackers at New Year. By the 1950s and 1960s, a militant China had lost its image as "exotic" and become an apparent "threat" to the United States. But since President Nixon went to Peking in 1972, most Americans left behind the view of China either as exotic or as a threat. China has simply joined the world for better or for worse.

I do not think China aspires to march upon the world and impose a new yellow *pax sinicus,* yet its influence on the shape of tomorrow's world will be large. Nearly one-quarter of the globe's population is Chinese. Chirpy four-tone Chinese is the native tongue of more people on earth than any

A tug of war during recreation period at a primary school in Tsinan, Shantung Province. As they pull the children cry, "More oil! More oil! (*Jia you! Jia you!*)." (*Photo by Ross Terrill*)

other language. The size and pivotal location of China gives it a frontier with twelve other nations, the one with Russia being a massive stretch of 4,300 miles.

The Chinese have a good supply of nuclear weapons, ballistic missiles, jet bombers, and radar equipment. They have a formidable 3.5 million-man army, and the world's third biggest air force. Their general military capability has surpassed that of France and Britain, and has made them part of a global strategic triangle with the United States and the U.S.S.R.

Worry about China during the 1960s led the United States to the massive and tragic military intervention in Southeast Asia that culminated in the blunt, cruel shock of Vietnam. And in the Soviet Union, a lurking fear of China has been a fundamental foreign policy concern since the mid-1960s.

In Asia, China is the major defense concern of India—since Pakistan was pruned of Bangladesh in 1971—and has repeatedly been a central issue in Japan's foreign policy. For all of the small Southeast Asian lands, race and geography make China a Middle Kingdom that will not go away. Even in Europe, China has for the first time in history become a modest influence, by virtue of its close ties to the Marxist régimes that do not toe Moscow's line (especially Yugoslavia and Rumania), and of its warm support for NATO and West European unity.

In more far-flung parts of the Third World, China is a significant alternative to Russia as a source of inspiration and aid to leftist movements. Any struggle against feudalism or imperialism in today's Africa, Asia, or Latin America occurs in the long shadow cast by the Chinese Revolution.

Although the life of its own people is economically modest, China is the world's third biggest giver of nonmilitary aid to the Third World, with an annual average outlay of some U.S.

$500 million over recent years. And since being seated in the UN in 1971, Peking has become chief Security Council spokesman for Third World interests on trade, investment, law of the sea, and such matters.

Even economically China has begun to count. It has the sixth biggest economy in the world. Its aggregate energy capacity is equal to that of all of western Europe. It produces 20 percent of the world's coal.

Not least, the new way of life within China has begun to intrigue non-Chinese. Some things seem shocking: the cult around Mao Tse-tung that has outlived the man himself; the uniformity of thought; the use of culture for a political purpose. On the other hand a realization dawns that there are things to be learned from the Chinese: a public health system that serves all of the people; a system of education that combines theory and practice; and economic growth that does not ravage the environment.

China has joined the world, and no reshaping of tomorrow's world will occur without China playing a big part. In the first era of contact between the West and China, following the Opium War of 1839–42, the direction of influence between the two sides was mostly one-way. The West confidently worked its purposes in China. Western ideas—Christianity, democracy, the rule of law—were offered to an Eastern nation too weak to make an authentic choice between them and its own traditional ways. China took upon its stunned body politic a steady battering of influences from the West.

But when the Communist Party of China (CCP), led by Mao, won control in 1949, this foreign influence ceased. China went its own lofty way, as the United States drew back in horror from a nation it had "lost" to socialism. And when the sounds of Ping-Pong heralded new links between China and America in the 1970s, Old China's passive role in the world had gone forever. The direction of influence had ceased to be one-way.

The Chinese have not returned to the world merely to occupy a niche defined and allotted to them by others. They have stepped up to equality with the major global powers. No longer the helpless object of the purposes of other nations, the Chinese are helping to set the agenda—and will soon start to call some of the shots—for the international relations of the 1980s and 1990s.

In the days of British gunboats and German missionaries and American traders on the China coast, there used to be an upbeat saying among foreign businessmen about "oil for the lamps of China." Oil companies saw the chance of an immense market in a Cathay heaving itself from darkness yet lacking petroleum.

By 1963 China was self-sufficient in oil. By 1978 it was one of the ten or twelve main oil-producing nations. Selling oil to China is as much a thing of the past as the paraffin lamp.

I see oil as a symbol of China's new stance. The world has started to buy Chinese oil; and the world is becoming interlocked, for better or worse, with the Chinese and what they make of their amazing society of 900 million. The upheavals that have recently occurred under the orange tiles of Peking's palaces not only intrigue us but matter to us.

How different will China be without Mao Tse-tung and Chou En-lai? Will China soon be a world power to equal Russia and America, or will there be stagnation—even a breakup—with the Russian bear nosing around among the fragments? Are the young people of China sturdy pines of so-

Children in the coal-mining town of Pingtingshan, in Honan Province (*New China News Agency Photo*)

cialism, or are they becoming materialistic as they achieve a better standard of living? Will Peking reach out for Taiwan and will this mean a flare-up of war in Asia yet again?

This book takes a first look at the events of 1976–77. We see a China bent upon rapid economic development and settling down after a series of blows that were potentially grave. The CCP is mapping a future in which the ordinary people will be making fresh demands and seeking a larger say in decisions that affect their lives. Peking is maneuvering in a friendly embrace with America that has had its satisfactions but needs a little more passion from both partners. It is struggling to join a world in which China is increasingly influential yet still not quite at home. We see a new leadership of men (few women) who honor Mao yet must turn aside from him. We see the Chinese entering a less heroic age and yet a more rewarding one.

2

The Dragon Takes China ঙ by the Throat ঙ

Throughout the Year of the Dragon—1976—China experienced one shock after another. Death carried off half the top leadership, beginning with Chou En-lai in January and ending with Mao Tse-tung himself in September. Purge removed another large slice of the Politburo of the CCP, first with a swathe to the right, in April, then with an even wider swathe to the left just after Mao died.

To these biological and political earthquakes was added, in July 1976, a grotesque real earthquake, which uprooted the city of Tangshan and killed 650,000 people. Rural Chinese used to believe that nature's signs foreshadowed political events; severe earthquakes, it was held, meant the coming end of a dynasty and of its mandate to rule. Some peasants must still reason this way, for the official press found it necessary to criticize the "theory of the mandate of heaven" as a feudal concoction designed to "confuse the masses with evil rumors."

By the time the Year of the Snake—1977—slithered in, a more pragmatic government headed by the modest Hua Kuo-feng had begun to put a new stamp on China's affairs. A new team was in charge. Of the twenty-two persons elected to the Politburo at the Party Congress in 1973, five had been purged, five more were dead, and one was gravely ill. These eleven casualties included no less than nine of the eleven-member inner core Standing Committee of the Politburo. The Age of Heroes in China was over. Politics in Peking would no longer be the domain of one demigod, but a more sober realm of give-and-take among modern-day administrators. At the Eleventh CCP Congress in August 1977 the rearranged leadership structure strongly confirmed the pragmatic and economically minded trend of Chinese politics.

Style was changing. Politicians were speaking a bit more frankly. A lively "Letters to the Editor" section returned to *People's Daily* after years of absence, plus a humor column on this official paper's back page. In a break from the old habit of only reporting tasks safely completed, Hua announced in advance upcoming policy initiatives such as a new volume of Mao's writings, local elections, and conferences on industry and science.

And the government explained its goals in terms that came nearer than the People's Republic of China (PRC) has ever done before to acknowledging that the purpose of the state is the happiness of the people. It vowed "to create a political atmosphere in which both centralism and democracy will reign, discipline and freedom, unity of purpose, a universal feeling of satisfaction and high spirits." With this, Peking has at least defined the good society in refreshing terms. But what about the action needed to bring it to pass? Has a new era really begun, and if so will Hua Kuo-feng head it for long? A closer look at the Year of the Dragon will give us some of the answers.

During 1976, the ghost of the Cultural Revolution was exorcised. This orgiastic upheaval, begun in 1966, seemed to subside by 1969 in a backlash of disappointment. Yet years later its currents still flowed through China's body politic as an electric force which would give no one respite. When the far-leftist "Gang of Four"—Mao's widow together with three Shanghai leaders linked with her—were snuffed out in the tense darkness of one dramatic October night in 1976, the ten-year nightmare of Mao's Cultural Revolution was belatedly snuffed out with them.

The Dragon had further surprises in store. In early April a riot of 100,000 people broke out at the Square of the Gate of Heavenly Peace, in the heart of Peking. Its like had never been seen before in twenty-seven years of the PRC. Beyond the political meaning—it began as a tribute to Chou En-lai— the riot crystalized a deeper trend in Chinese politics.

Ordinary people, for several years docile toward major issues of national politics, were beginning to have their say at rallies and in vivid and biting posters. Public opinion was born in 1976 as a fact of life—which no government of China can from now on disregard.

Within a general wave of newly asserted opinion, the sharp edge of a small but influential group became visible. China's domestic and international progress has created an experienced élite which Mao might not have found to his taste. The new élite includes technicians, journalists, culture workers, communications specialists, trade and diplomatic personnel, and indeed most of the 35 million (too many for a smoke-filled room!) who belong to the Party and receive its flow of sophisticated information. It is a middle class, which has quietly stepped out from among the teeming masses. Its members are well informed, aware of science, internationalist by Chinese standards, and unready to mouth slogans if it does not see the point of them.

* * *

In the testing year of 1976 China successfully pulled through one of history's toughest succession crises. (Even Stalin, whose loss stunned Russia in 1953, headed bolshevism for only a quarter century, whereas Mao led Chinese communism for nearly a half century.) Warlords did not reappear to parcel up the country. Throughout the shocks of that year public order hardly wavered from New China's very high level. Production was affected only slightly. Four nuclear devices were tested and two earth satellites launched during the year. Moscow did not dare "do a Czechoslovakia" and reach into China to try to scrape together a pro-Soviet puppet régime. China's foreign policy went ahead without a break in either line or execution. China faced terrible danger and passed safely through it.

Even the earthquake at Tangshan, and the lesser tremors elsewhere, brought out a quiet strength in Chinese society. Technically, the Chinese lack fine instruments (e.g., for laser geodacy) which might have forecast the Tangshan disaster more precisely. In that respect China paid a price for its isolation from international science, for the United States and Japan both possess better instruments.

Yet New China's social organization showed up to great advantage, both before and after the 1976 quakes. Tiny tots had been taught about earthquakes, as about nuclear attack, wicked imperialists, and other topics not thought suitable for children in the West. They knew to watch chickens for signs of strange behavior, and this helped to forecast some lesser quakes. They proved they had been thoroughly taught to keep calm, spurn the superstitions of some of their elders, and trust in the Party and Chairman Mao. Most important, assiduous public health work averted plague or any severe epidemics after the quake.

The aftermath bore witness to some admirable traits of Chinese society: the use of simple tools rather than huge and vulnerable technology; networks of neighborhood teams working with tremendous spirit; "barefoot doctors" (paramedics) used to working outdoors with makeshift equipment; a populace whose government does not tell it much but that gets on with the job regardless. The Chinese proved stoic, skillful at making do with very little, and not inclined to take advantage of catastrophe for looting or rebellion.

In a more intangible way, though, the Dragon threw down a challenge which China failed to surmount. A challenge to the virginity of the Chinese Revolution.

The end of the Age of Heroes may not be a bad thing for the Chinese people. Hua, cozy and straightforward, enjoys a surge of goodwill from most corners of the nation. Yet China has lost its moral sheen.

For twenty-five years the high motives of China's revolution and the heroism that made it successful made China a beacon to many non-Chinese. The Year of the Dragon changed this. It is not just that Mao has gone and Hua lacks his aura. It is the way Peking did things in 1976. Cynicism arose among the Chinese people over the attacks on Teng Hsiao-p'ing, and cynicism is not easy to dispel. Nor can the dirty linen washed over the heads of the Gang of Four leave anyone under the illusion that Chinese politics is a high-minded debate over principle.

There is a growing realization that China is no longer weak and exploited but a world power which, like every other world power, gets its fingers into the sticky morass of compromise. Mao embodied in his own life the transformation of the old China into the new. But nothing about Hua smacks of struggle or the bold gambles of a rebel up against high odds. There is doubt that China can still be considered morally special.

The leadership in Peking has found that foreign policy is more complex than one more tussle between good "revolutionaries" and bad "imperialists." When China must choose between Morocco and Algeria in the Spanish Sahara, for example, the lines of black and white ebb swiftly into shades of gray.

Not long ago it was feared in the West that as China grew stronger, it would light fires of revolution on every continent. It has not turned out that way. China *has* grown stronger and become a headache for some of its small neighbors, but Peking seldom impinges as a firebrand of revolution. It is by the shadow and pressure of conventional power politics that the Chinese increasingly get their way. The moral stature of China shrinks as the actual influence of China expands.

During the Year of the Snake (1977) Peking began to bury Mao even as it went on singing his praises. Mao was a brilliant leader but in a sense he became an albatross around China's neck at the end. Even when past his prime he stood high over everyone else and monopolized the mental space of the Chinese nation. He left a gap, yet his long shadow made it impossible for anyone else to fill it.

Hua Kuo-feng faces the exquisite problem of a dead Mao. He is Mao's man in an era of de-Maoization. An awkward spot to be in; even amiable Hua, who has specialized in not making enemies, might find his left leg and his right leg torn asunder.

The agenda before the Hua government for the late 1970s is both tough and exciting. Hua must first try to acquire stature in the eyes of the nation—a hard task for any successor to Mao Tse-tung, let alone for one with all the charisma of an insurance clerk.

An ideological crisis looms. The government's explanation for the events of the Year of the Dragon was tossed to the people across a credibility gap that makes Richard Nixon seem candid by comparison. Ms. Mao (Chiang Ch'ing) and the rest of the Gang of Four were officially labeled "right-ists" when everyone could see that their policies were far-leftist. Teng was styled a "capitalist roader," but a capitalist road does not seem to exist in a nation with virtually no pri-vate ownership of the means of production. If black is called white with such abandon for long enough, the Chinese peo-ple may cease to believe in the importance of the difference between the two.

Behind the fiddling with labels lies a deep root to the crisis. For nearly thirty years in China every value judgment has been made on the basis of class analysis. Anything evil was put down to the account of capitalism—or more recently to "revisionism" (Russia's betrayal of socialism). Commit adul-tery and you must be a capitalist. Lag behind your production quota at the factory bench and you have revealed yourself to be under the influence of the latter-day czars in the Kremlin. All this begins to wear very thin.

It is true that the entire drama of the Chinese Revolution centered on class struggle, plus the twin theme of struggle against foreign exploitation. But a banquet in the evening becomes a pile of trash by next morning. Landlord and im-perialist no longer afflict China; they cannot be blamed for things that go wrong in the late 1970s.

New China's striking success has changed the priorities. As weakness and chaos recede into the past, so does the class struggle that weakness and chaos brought to fever pitch. Class has certainly faded in China—this is a real achieve-ment of the CCP. But one result is an undermining of the political ideas that were born in the midst of class struggle. Teng Hsiao-p'ing, 1976's "Villain of the Year," said as much, and he is already being proved correct.

The task ahead is enormous: how to find new ways of dealing with conflict—and of conceptualizing it—for a post-class situation. Since the fall of the extremist Gang of Four, a certain depoliticizing of literature and the theater has begun, allowing for moral nuance in characterization instead of the mere hammer blows of class warfare. But the problem is far broader than culture. The entire political system, as well as the modes of political discourse, must change gears. Relations between the government and the people have to be recast in terms more subtle than the easy certainties of a tussle between "bourgeoisie" and "proletariat."

A third item on Hua's agenda is how to deal with the People's Liberation Army (PLA). China's military is unusual. Its prestige is great because the Chinese Revolution was an armed fight, spearheaded by the PLA's peasant troops. Ties between soldiers and people are close and smooth. In few other countries do you see soldiers working amicably beside workers in a factory.

Yet the PLA has never ruled the PRC. "The Party controls the gun" is a sacred edict of Mao; just as important, Mao had the authority to enforce it. And most of the PLA declined to join the first national post-1949 challenge to Mao posed by the former defense minister P'eng Te-huai in 1959.

To be sure, there was one period when the PLA as an institution took on some of the Party's functions, during the former defense minister Lin Piao's revolt against Mao in 1969–71. But Lin lost. And after he botched a coup attempt and died in hasty flight over Mongolia, civilian authority reasserted itself. From 1972 until 1976 the PLA tried no political tricks.

But the military are in 1978 back near the top of the Chinese government. The trend began in the summer of 1976. Hard-nosed PLA officers had wearied of the empty ritual of attacks during the spring on Teng as a "capitalist roader"; at that point, PLA quiescence reached its peak. Then in July, when the earthquake sliced up Tangshan, the army was needed, relished the chance to step in, and won credit for concrete deeds in a year when hot words had tended to lose touch with cold actuality.*

If the earthquake was a hors d'oeuvre at the PLA's banquet of reemergence, the solid meat was the arrest of the Gang of Four in October. The end of Ms. Mao's career was the start of a political career for many an army man.

By mid-1977 the political prominence of the PLA had become reminiscent of the Lin period. Soldiers were in the thick of every debate and behind every good deed. As an ultimate accolade, their assistance was credited with the speedy erection—from plans to polish in eight months—of the Mao Mausoleum near the Gate of Heavenly Peace.

The danger is clear to the Chinese people, who vividly recall the Cultural Revolution and the Lin crisis. Can Hua control the gun? His problem is that he needed the PLA's support in order to move against the Gang of Four, yet the Gang's fall made the PLA far more influential than before. A trial of strength may be just around the corner, in which either Hua masters the PLA or the PLA masters him.

A fourth item on Hua's agenda is how fast and by what means to exploit China's massive mineral resources. China is one of the great storehouses of the world. Already it exports large amounts of tin, oil, antimony, coal, mercury, tungsten, and bismuth. But production is feeble compared with what it

---

* A clue to the opportunism of the extremist Gang of Four in the matter of earthquake relief came in the photo coverage of the event. One Gang member, in charge of the press at that time, killed a picture which showed Hua and a military group at the site of the quake in Tangshan. He substituted—in a show of Picture Power—photos of people from the stricken area meeting Chinese leaders in Peking. Prominent among the leaders were the Gang of Four who had *not* gone to Tangshan.

could be if the nation had better mining equipment and transportation. Large quantities of zinc, manganese, molybdenum, and fluorspar have as yet hardly been tapped at all.

The problem is a dual one of investment and of Mao's tenet of self-reliance. The mines in the southwest, like the offshore oil in the northeast, cry out for the use of high technology. A mere torrent of highly motivated manpower (the cornerstone of Maoist economics) is not enough.

The choice is fairly clear. Without foreign know-how, if not foreign investment, China's riches will remain essentially beyond the reach of this generation. With them, China could have a fantastic mineral boom before the year 2000. If Hua feels it necessary to follow Mao's principles to the letter, there will be no boom.

But a formidable man whose shadow falls on Hua, Teng Hsiao-p'ing, may be less inclined to be faithful to Mao's ideas. The irrepressible Teng was twice purged by Mao but is now back in office as one of the two top colleagues of Hua—who helped Mao effect Teng's second purge! Teng has pronounced views of his own on how China should modernize, as we shall see. If Teng gets his way—or if Tengism prevails even without Teng—the mineral boom may just occur.

The issue of natural resources will bear on yet another challenge facing the new government. A wave of rising expectation has appeared in China. In part it is a product of sheer generational change. Fewer people remember the bitter past; more people judge the government by its performance here and now. In part it is because the standard of living has been rising, and this whets the appetite for more. And in part it is a consequence of the government's own rhetoric during 1977.

The Gang of Four have been lambasted for "sitting on the toilet but not managing a shit." That is, they were splendid at ideology, but did not achieve concrete results. So the Hua régime is committed to delivering the goods. For ordinary people this means more cottons, more cooking oil, an end to rationing, more sweet foods, a chance to buy a TV. They want higher wages to buy more, and more things in the stores to choose from.

In moral terms, the issue is an old one—nearly a century old—for the Chinese. When the West forced its way into China, one response was to resist the West and all its works in the name of preserving the Chinese Way. A different response favored taking goods and ideas selectively from the West, in the name of the concrete welfare of the Chinese people.

Behind the first response was a conviction that Chinese civilization was a pure moral entity that could not and should not be tampered with. Behind the more relaxed response was a non-holistic view of China as a collection of people with jostling, and changing, interests and opinions.

Now the same issue stalks the land in new dress. The Chinese Way owes more to Mao than to Confucius, but the notion of a pure Chinese essence is still at its core. Those who are determined to improve the standard of living of the Chinese people are less concerned with pure moral forms, at least if these appear to stand in the way of concrete progress.

Sixty years ago, the iconoclast Ch'en Tu-hsiu, a founder of Chinese communism, tossed out Confucius in order "to save the nation." Today, curiously enough, the pragmatist Teng Hsiao-p'ing is his spiritual heir. To make China a strong and modern power, he is willing to pick and choose among theories and even settle for none. Hua may have to choose between Purity and Progress.

A sixth item is the need to level with China's 400 million youth. The government (in China as in the United States) has to reckon with youth's idealism and also with its career needs. Despite some dreadful aspects, the Cultural Revolution was a springtime of hope for young people. The lid was off, new ideas bubbled, and all things seemed possible.

The aftermath brought disillusion in part because the Red Guards themselves lost their way in a fog of factionalism, and in part because Mao had second thoughts and put the lid back on by sending in the PLA to quell Red Guard factionalism. But the yearning for a more perfect society does not die at the point of a bayonet.

Nor did the purge of the Gang of Four in 1976 remove the shadow of utopian dissent. The Gang had its followers. Moreover certain leftist ideas will remain in the air, by their own logic, regardless of any link to the Gang's activities. Indeed some idealists will see the *way* the Gang was purged as further fuel for the fire of their discontent.

Meanwhile the needs of China's young people change and grow, and if unmet will lead to a new wave of radicalism. Two needs stand out: good training, and the chance to participate in decisions that affect their lives.

After the Cultural Revolution more than 10 million high-school graduates were sent "up to the hills and down to the villages." In other words they became farmers with no expectation of return to the city or a crack at college. This program has been unpopular and is one main reason why thousands of young people leave for Hong Kong each year. Hua has to decide whether he can afford to ease up on such relentless rustication.

Another policy pushed by the Gang but costly to youth was the downgrading of expertise in education. To be "red" was all that counted, in the zealous eyes of the Gang, and to be "expert" was almost suspect. That was fine for the sake of an abstract political model, but young people cannot get interesting work (and they know it) if their training consists of little more than juggling slogans. This is especially true now that technology is becoming the rage in China.

Hua has loosened the ideological shackles that gripped China's sulking campuses, but there is a lot of ground to make up. And the numbers involved are huge; about 13 million new students knock on the doors of China's middle schools each year. Hua must enable these millions to make use of their skills after graduation.

A deep hunger arises among the young, especially, to participate in public affairs with more than a good pair of lungs. Zigzags in Party line have confused them, and arbitrary decisions have disheartened them. Handwritten wall posters put up clandestinely by private citizens have urged what we in the West know as "the rule of law"—starting with adherence to China's disregarded Constitution—within which each person may know his (or her) rights and have a say (see Appendixes 6 and 9c). Hua cannot afford to ignore this hunger.

A final concern for the new administration is the relationship between the center at Peking and the regions and far-flung cities of China.

The city of Peking enjoys tremendous prestige. Yet there is arrogance in the capital, and the powerful leaders of China's twenty-nine provinces (five of which contain more than 40 million people each) sometimes chafe at it. An optical illusion besets those looking at China from the outside. The Chinese press available to us is filled with ringing norms. These are laid down in Peking, but the provinces do not always snap to them.

In fact Peking has been losing some of its authority. The Cultural Revolution spurred this. Among Mao's bouts of hostility toward the bureaucracy, the Cultural Revolution was the supreme one. He wanted more decentralization (except in ideology), and his assault on Liu Shao-ch'i and other bureaucrats ensured that he got it. During my second visit to China in 1971 I noted that the provinces seemed to have more authority than a decade before.

The death of Mao tips the scales further toward the periphery. Hua simply wields less authority than Mao. He cannot toss out breathtaking edicts as the father of Chinese communism did. In 1977 the signs of local power multiplied. Regional dialects were given a reprieve. Open resistance to Peking's orders to criticize Teng had occurred in some provinces in 1976; and a different set of provinces dragged its feet in the rush to heap abuse on the Gang of Four in 1977. Tussles were visible between various regions and major cities for allocation of resources.

Hua's government has vowed to ease up on the endless political campaigns and to offer instead some bread and circuses. Yet total control by the center is the lynchpin of China's Communist system. The "liberal" goal of giving people a better standard of living may require the "illiberal" means of renewed centralization in order to succeed. One more problem for Hua.

In foreign policy Peking has much to be pleased about; yet here too it faces winds of change. China has made enormous strides during the 1970s, achieving ties with nearly seventy additional nations since 1971, a seat in the UN, and the new link with the United States. Never has Communist China been more secure, better prepared for any eventuality, or more influential on the world stage. In economic terms, also, the PRC became during the 1970s a major participant in the community of nations.

The moment of Mao's death captured, as in a snapshot, China's new image around the globe. Mao's name had become a household word on every continent. Some of his *Quotations* were quite widely known in all societies. No other

Chinese figure, not even Confucius, had ever entered the consciousness of non-Chinese peoples to this extent. China seemed to be part of the world in a new way.

Yet the actual process of joining the outside world is a complex one for the Chinese. Culturally they have a tradition of being a world unto themselves. A Marxist government compounds the suspicions in China about dealing with Western "imperialists" (or even Soviet "social imperialists"). Moreover the agricultural nature of China sets limits on its need and capacity for foreign trade.

The PRC's very success brings it to the brink of ambiguity. Ten years ago the Chinese were so isolated that they could influence few issues. In a way this set them free to make fiery general statements and do nothing. But today China has friends everywhere and must try to please them all from time to time. More links have brought more dilemmas.

Hua has to balance power and principle. Along with the United States and Soviet Russia, China has now become part of a global strategic triangle. Yet China also insists that it is part of the Third World. Mao could get away with it. Receive and praise Richard Nixon as he did, no one could doubt Mao's credentials as a revolutionary. Hua is a politician of more ordinary proportions, who will have to tackle the tension in a clear-cut way.

Within the politics of the triangle itself, Hua may have a big choice to make during 1978 or 1979. So far he has continued Mao's tilt toward America and away from the U.S.S.R. But doubts have arisen in Peking about the logic and the costs to China of an endless absolute hostility toward Moscow. The PLA in particular seems to have other ideas. Hua may not be able to keep the door open to the United States much longer unless the Sino-American relationship bears more fruit soon.

No period in the PRC's life will be more fascinating than these next years of Peking's efforts to give new direction to a revolution that has come of age. If Hua and Teng and their colleagues should fail, what would that mean for the 900 million Chinese people? If they succeed, what will it mean for the rest of us?

3
Chou En-lai
❦ Leaves a Gap ❦

The death of Chou En-lai—the first of the trio of deaths that was to shake China in 1976—came as a shock all over the nation and beyond. Chou's ability and length of service had made him the anchor of Chinese politics.

The announcement came in the freezing cold of January 8, 1976, as a grim prelude to the Year of the Dragon. Dead of cancer at seventy-eight. From the hospital where he had died, Chou's body was taken to the gilded splendor of the former Imperial Palace. A weeping crowd in overcoats watched the cortège with its hearse draped in rosettes of black and yellow.

The next forty-eight hours brought out, as if the gods were in charge of symbols, the three big reasons why Chou En-lai was a great politician. (Even in China new events cannot be hidden to the point of obliterating the outward shape of inner workings.)

In the first place, the very size of the crowd bore witness to the Chinese people's affection for their premier. The rows of common folk numbered close to one million. No death in

China for decades, whether Communist or pre-Communist, nor the deaths of the other two red titans, evoked visible mass feeling on such a scale.

At one point during the procession, according to an eyewitness, a large group of Chinese moved onto the road to try to prevent the vehicle bearing the coffin from going forward. They suspected that the plan to cremate the body was a wish, not of Chou himself, but of Chiang Ch'ing and her friends. Only when the widow, Teng Ying-ch'ao, stepped forward to explain to the group that cremation was Chou's own wish did the concerned citizens let the vehicle pass.

The Chinese masses believed in Chou. He never had a credibility problem and even Mao, in the last years, was a less vivid figure to people in the street than this man of steely will who also had a personal touch. Ms. Teng's direct and effective communication with the funeral crowd seemed a symbol of Chou's credibility. The outlook was a shade bleaker for almost everyone in China—there were some striking exceptions—without Chou En-lai.

Then too, unexpectedly, the somber funeral room beneath the orange tiles of the Imperial Palace was thrown open to foreigners. Not many non-Chinese reside in Peking, but almost all of them—ambassadors, newsmen, students, brothers in the faith who work for the Chinese government—came to view the jar of Chou's ashes and the boyish portrait behind it. This was an unusual intrusion of foreigners into the sealed courtyard of Chinese grief, but fitting too, for Chou was the international face of the Chinese Revolution.

And thirdly, it was announced at the ceremony in the Great Hall of the People a few days later that Chou had asked for his ashes to be "scattered upon the rivers and soil of our motherland." No gaudy mausoleum to freeze history into granite for this forthright man without airs. It was a typical gesture. The *way* Chou did things was always as important as what he did.

So Chou towered over most other figures of the Chinese Revolution in that he evoked affection from ordinary people; he was China's bridge to the international community; and he was a selfless man whose quality of character made him able to get fractious people to compromise with each other.

"Each person has but one death," wrote the famous scholar Ssu Ma-ch'ien, two thousand years ago, "but it can be light as a feather or heavy as Mount T'ai." Much depends on what a man did and how ably. The impact of a leader's death is also measured by its timing. Chou died at a moment which made his death a blow as heavy as Mount T'ai for China.

He went before Mao. This was a bit unexpected—until 1975 Chou seemed less clouded by ill-health than Mao—and the consequences were indeed as awesome as the great mountain in Shantung. The stage manager of the Chinese Revolution was not there to manage the last great challenge thrown down by the revolution's director, Mao—how to cope with his death.

Had Mao died before Chou, Chinese politics would not be what they are today. The feud between Teng Hsiao-p'ing and the left-wing extremists later baptized as the Gang of Four would not have polarized China as it did in 1976. Teng would not have risen so high and been in a position to provoke the Gang had Chou not sunk with cancer during 1974 and 1975. The Gang, in turn, would have lost most of its power to mold events once Mao was dead. Chou at the helm would have kept the ship of state from veering too far either to left or right.

So four of the Year of the Dragon's momentous events would not have occurred:

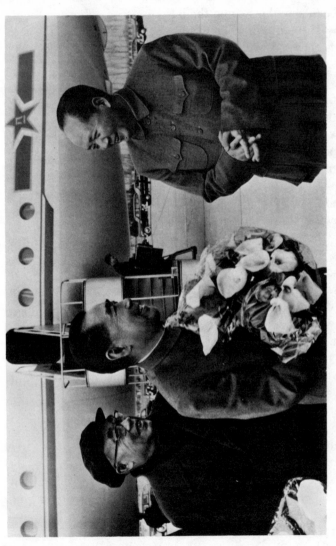

Chou En-lai in his prime, 1964, being welcomed home at Peking Airport by Mao Tse-tung, and Chu Te, after a turbulent visit to Moscow. (*New China Agency News Photo*)

- Teng, being out of the firing line, would not have been shot down from the left.
- The Gang of Four would not have surged to the fore as they did in the spring of 1976—nor in all probability would they be in custody today.
- The Chinese people would not have suffered a loss of faith in the rectitude of their government, brought on by the tragicomedy of purge and counterpurge.
- Hua Kuo-feng would still be an obscure second-rank politician and the world outside China would not know him from a bar of soap.

Chou also died at a bad moment for the U.S.-China tie. Following Kissinger's initial secret trip to Peking in July 1971, the new Sino-American bond grew in strength for two years. But 1974 and 1975 brought no fresh progress—Watergate overcame Nixon.

First it tied his hands for any gesture to China that might thin the dwindling ranks of those conservatives in Congress who would stand with him against the drumbeat of impeachment. Then by the fall of 1975, this champion of the link with China had been forced out of office.

An American President visited China for the second time in December 1975. But the Nixon-Chou handshake had given way to the limp wrist of uncertainty. Nixon had been put out to pasture; Chou lay gravely ill. The Ford-Teng encounter just before Christmas had all the excitement of a tree meeting a tractor.

On the Chinese side, there was grumbling that the new link had cost China more than it had yielded. Kissinger himself had soured on the Chinese, in part because he found blunt Teng ("that nasty little man") a comedown after urbane Chou. Chou's absence was the final guarantee—added

to Ford's immobilism in the face of his oncoming first presidential race—that Sino-American relations would remain be-
calmed until the U.S. election was over.

It was Chou who had pushed through the Politburo a concession that marked the high point of the relationship in
1973. He agreed with Kissinger to set up quasi-embassies
(the fig-leaf label is "Liaison Office") in the two capitals, even
though Chiang Kai-shek's envoy was still officially the "Chinese ambassador" in Washington. This was a step the Chinese had sworn they would never take.

But three years later the Politburo felt little warmth toward
America. Indeed it dumbfounded the White House—when
Chou was dying—by luring Nixon from seclusion in San
Clemente to make a triumphal return to Peking just weeks
after Ford had bored the manes off the bronze lions in the
Forbidden City. What Chou knew or thought of this second
Nixon visit we do not know.*

Chou's death also left a dangerous gap in China's domestic
power-political lineup. The premier had been striving for an
end to feuding, and for a push ahead with economic plans.
That was the point of his last great organizational effort—the
fourth session of the National People's Congress in January
1975. But he met resistance.

In particular the Cultural Revolution extremists had their
claws out to try to pull culture and education even further to
the left. Two months before the premier succumbed, they
began yet one more burst of chatter about "class struggle"—
as if it were a magic password that could by its mere enunci-
ation reduce any situation to stark simplicity.

---

* Nixon's February 1976 visit may have been a mere slice of nostalgia, or it may have
been an attempt by Mao—but a clumsy one—to revivify the link with America by putting pressure on Ford (see page 185).

In mid-January 1976 the mourning for Chou abruptly ended. The black armbands disappeared as if laundry day had arrived; stories of tribute in the press ended as suddenly as they had begun. Public discourse was shot through with themes which seemed contrary to Chou's policies. In fact with the death of Chou the marbles of power rolled to the left in a rush. He had died too soon to prevent the Gang of Four from making one last bid to keep China in the throes of ever-lasting "revolution."

To be sure, Chou's comrade-in-arms Teng Hsiao-p'ing remained. But Teng lacked Chou's political skills. China waited to see whether he could head off the extremists, and hold the line for socialist common sense, or whether there would be a confrontation.

My mind goes back to 1971 when I met Chou En-lai. It was a fluid and important year: in relations with Australia (which brought me into contact with him); in China's relations with the United States; on the Lin Piao question; and because Chou was beginning to feel "old and tired," as he put it.

The conservative Australian government had been following a very anti-China policy. Suddenly in the spring of 1971, China canceled a big wheat order. The opposition Labor Party, which had long proposed recognizing Peking as the sole government of China and breaking all official ties with Taiwan, took advantage of the political situation and sought to send a delegation to forge closer ties with China.

Gough Whitlam, the Labor Party's leader, phoned to ask me to urge the Chinese to hold talks with the Australian Labor Party. I contacted Chinese friends in Canada and Hong Kong, and I wrote to the French ambassador in Peking, the well-connected Étienne Manac'h.

Before long the Chinese People's Institute for Foreign Affairs invited Whitlam to visit China. At the same time the Chinese Embassy in Canada phoned to say that I was welcome to visit China also, and asked me to arrive several weeks before the period of Whitlam's visit.

Ma Yu-chen of the foreign ministry introduced me to Premier Chou in a sideroom of the Great Hall of the People. Chou was a small man, yet he seemed to dominate any roomful of people. One arm did not quite move freely as a result of a fall from horseback in 1939. His eyes were steely but sometimes they lit up with laughter. The mouth was set low in the face and the lips pushed forward in a taut way. The black hair was by now half-silver. On his gray tunic was a badge that said: "Serve the People." His manner was that of a firm and disciplined man, yet he could bend and joke and explore a new thought in a completely natural way.

Chou thanked me for my help on the Australian question. He called me "a vanguard officer" who came early to China on behalf of the Australian Labor Party. He also thanked me for helping the Chinese government better understand current conditions in the United States. "I have not been to America," he said, "but you have lived there and you gave us insights we did not have before."

It was a sign of Chou's amazingly frank and direct way of working that he should rely on a private citizen, and publicly thank that person for his help. It was a method of government very different from that which relies on images and public relations.

Chou urged me to study carefully the *People's Daily* editorial on the occasion of the fiftieth anniversary of the CCP. Only the next year did I realize the full significance of this recommendation—after Lin Piao's flight and death. Chou probably had in mind the passage about the need for the

Party to control the army. He and Mao were at that time in
the midst of a struggle against Lin Piao.

Later I attended a meeting between Whitlam and Chou
in the East Room of the Great Hall. Foreign Minister Chi
P'eng-fei and Foreign Trade Minister Pai Hsiang-kuo were
also present. These two men had talked in previous days
with the Labor Party leader.

The Australian side found that all the important points
from these talks with Ministers Pai and Chi were gathered up
and summarized by Chou, though he had no notes in front of
him. He proceeded always from the facts, never merely stating an opinion without giving evidence. He also raised broad
historical issues, the sort that busy politicians seldom raise.
He answered every question put to him by Whitlam.

Chou did not try to hide conflicts—sometimes bursting into
English to say: "No, no, no"—but he did not let small areas of
disagreement eclipse larger areas of agreement. He was
blunt at times, as when he said toward the end of the evening: "We look forward to you getting into power and carrying out your promises. It is vital for a politician and a political
party to implement its promises."

In December 1972 Mr. Whitlam did become prime minister of Australia. China and Australia immediately established
full diplomatic relations. Every promise Chou had made
about China-Australia ties was kept (including that to go on
supporting philosophically the Maoists in Australia). The for-
mulas concerning recognition, Taiwan, and other issues
agreed on in July 1971 were followed without a hitch in
December 1972 and after.

The Aussies learned several things about Chou from this
experience. That he kept his word. That he did not say what
he did not mean. And that he commanded—it was clear from
our contacts with his staff—the enormous respect of officials
who worked in the State Council and the Foreign Ministry.

* * *

The career of Chou En-lai at the center of Chinese communism was even longer than Mao's. For twenty-seven years premier, for half a century a leader of the Chinese Communist Party, Chou En-lai had engaged in leftist politics in Europe back in Lenin's time, yet lived on to welcome Richard Nixon in 1972.

Chou was a superb politician but not a philosopher of the Chinese Revolution. After 1935 he did not put forward a line of his own that he was prepared to pit against Mao's. From then on, Mao was the architect, Chou the stage manager. If this meant that Chou always remained a secondary figure, never a likely number one, it also made him a loyal, almost indispensable part of China's top team at any given moment.

By 1927, when Mao was out of favor within the CCP, Chou had become one of the Party's core leaders. From that year until his death he was a member of its Central Committee.

He was sure-footed. He sometimes switched his views as the wind changed. Thus he was a key supporter of Li Li-san, a leader of the CCP in the 1920s, and later became an equally key detractor when Li fell out of favor. But Chou was never expelled from Party office, as Mao was three times, much less ritually purged, as Liu Shao-ch'i and Teng Hsiao-p'ing both were.

Chou was a loose-limbed willow of a man, and in the storms of Chinese domestic politics he bent like a willow but kept his roots in firm soil. This was the secret of his survival for fifty years as a CCP leader. He even came through the Cultural Revolution unscathed—though for a while in 1967 Red Guards took him prisoner—when hardly anyone else did. Clearly he was a master conciliator.

Chou was a Communist of almost theatrical charm. As a student and political organizer in France just after World War I he cut a dashing figure. One of his first acts on reaching Paris in 1920 was to put on his best jacket, have a photo taken, then order a set of postcards on which his photo was reproduced to give a personalized touch. A year later he set up a Paris branch of the CCP.

He had a keen curiosity about other countries, and his mind could dart into every corner of world politics. During the 1940s and 1950s he became known as a badge of cosmopolitanism on the homespun garment of China's peasant revolution. In the 1960s and 1970s he was the great international figure of the PRC—one of its few—and this is a serious loss for China as it faces the 1980s.

Alone among the top dozen leaders of the Chinese Communist Party, Chou had seen a good part of the world. He studied in Europe and Japan, represented China on some twenty tours of Africa and Asia, was a major figure at the international conferences in Geneva in 1954 and Bandung in 1955. On Mao's behalf Chou also handled much of the fight with Russia. He visited Moscow six times in the PRC's first nine years, and handled nearly all the dealings with the United States in the 1970s.

Chou was acquainted with many Americans and liked his late-night conversations with them. He asked me where I had learned Chinese, and when told "in America," smiled broadly and said: "That is a fine thing—to learn Chinese in America." Chou said that he was deeply impressed by the creativity of American people and the courage of American youths in opposing the Vietnam War. Even from his hospital bed as he sank toward death during 1975 he vigorously beat off Chinese critics of the link with the United States.

One American whom Chou did not like was John Foster Dulles. The former Secretary of State during the 1950s was passionately opposed to recognition of the Peking government. One afternoon at the Geneva Conference on Indochina in 1954, Chou found himself for a moment in a room with Dulles. They had never met face to face. Chou stretched out his hand. Dulles thrust both his own hands behind his back and turned aside. To an aide he murmured: "I cannot."

Dulles predicted in the 1950s that the CCP government would soon "pass away." Chou, in 1971, thought Dulles an "amusing fellow." For twenty years after the Dulles prediction—through five U.S. Presidents—Chou remained premier of the régime that refused to pass away. By then, as I learned, he believed that such Dulles-type arrogance was prevalent mainly in the Soviet Union. "Dulles's successors sit in Moscow," he said, with a sharp edge to his voice.

It is odd that in all Chou's twenty-seven years as Chinese premier, Washington never was able to bring itself to accept the end of the Chinese civil war and recognize Peking as the sole government of China. Time ran out on the Mao-Chou era—and left Washington still holding the hand of the Kuomintang on Taiwan.

Chou gave a talk at a tense gathering of foreign experts in Peking during 1974. He thanked these somewhat anxious personnel for their work. He apologized for mistakes made toward foreigners during the Cultural Revolution, and reaffirmed the view that socialism is an international goal.

Difficulties over foreign residents in China had lingered on into the 1970s. Some foreign children had been artificially segregated from Chinese children in school classes, and cases of racial intermarriage had caused a terrible fuss. Chou spoke with passion about international brotherhood. He said that in his opinion people of different nations should stand shoulder-to-shoulder, and that it was as wrong to reject interracial marriage as to reject international friendship.

At times he intervened personally to enable a Chinese and

a non-Chinese who were in love to get married, over the opposition of certain of his colleagues. Unlike many in the Politburo, Chou was both Communist and cosmopolitan.

The Year of the Dragon marked a decline in altruism in the
top levels of the CCP. This brought into relief the remarkable
purity of motive (for a politician) of Chou En-lai.

He came from an upper-class family of intellectual attain-
ment and joined the revolution as his own choice among
competing values. He never lived by politics, as careerists do;
he lived *for* politics, as people with firm values do.

So he was unselfish about image and privileges alike.
There was no trace of nepotism in his career—he had no
children of his own—as there has been in the careers of some
other CCP leaders. It seemed that everything he did was
done for China and the CCP. He was faithful to his wife and
co-worker of fifty years, Teng Ying-ch'ao, among a leadership
group not as far removed from loose ways as is sometimes
thought.

As for vanity, Chou's shining lack of it puts him in a better
light than Mao. An illustration is the attitude of the two men
toward publicity about their early lives. Chou nipped in the
bud repeated plans to preserve as a shrine the house in the
province of Kiangsu where he was born; in fact he made the
house's whereabouts a secret. Mao never intervened to stop
Shaoshan, the village of his birth, from being made into a
costly and beautiful memorial.

Purity of motive made Chou unafraid. He faced physical
danger often in the early years. He met criticisms. He felt the
cold tug of despondency, especially during the Long March
and amidst the mess of the Cultural Revolution. But he never
spoke of these things, even to fairly close friends. Setbacks

did not breed self-pity within him (as Chiang Ch'ing's grievances did within her).

Unselfish motives also kept Chou from any overriding ambition. After Liberation he watched Liu Shao-ch'i move ahead
of him and become heir-apparent to Mao, but it seems he
made no move to try to forestall Liu's rise. Similarly in the
mid-1960s he accepted Lin Piao's surprising assumption of
second place with amazing good grace. He yielded, as Chinese gentlemen do.

At 10:00 P.M. on the last night of his life, Chou En-lai
opened his eyes slightly and recognized the medical personnel around his bed. "Nothing to do here," he is supposed to
have whispered. "Go look after other sick comrades. They
need you more." These last words were not untypical of the
man.

Chou had to balance various groups and viewpoints in
Chinese politics during some desperate moments. But he
generally succeeded in maintaining an equilibrium between
the two great forces that pulled at Mao-Chou policies—the
left and the military.

He devoted whole nights of persuasion to problems that
some leaders would have sought to solve by bureaucratic fiat.
A land as vast as China cannot be well led without such a talent for conciliation, and without the trust it evokes among
the people. The policies that emanated from the PRC over
twenty-seven years were usually Mao's; but it was often
Chou who made them work.

Chou's skill at handling people and conflicts went back
many years (indeed, to his own boyhood in a large extended
family household). In Chungking during World War II the
Russian Embassy gave a reception to celebrate the October

Revolution. Chou of course was there. So were Chinese of Chiang Kai-shek's Nationalist Party and representatives of various middle groups as well (wartime brought a fluidity of contacts and even of guarded alliances).

Halfway through the evening both the Russian envoy and Chou suddenly stiffened with alarm. For there in front of them a high aide of Chiang's was pulling out leaflets from his briefcase and handing one to each guest. Recovering himself in an instant, Chou stepped forward beaming and said: "Mr. Wang, I see you are selling some books—let me help you."

As he spoke he took some of the leaflets and in a casual way skimmed one copy. To his relief it was not anti-Soviet or anti-CCP but merely anti-Japanese in a general way. Resuming his wide smile Chou went around with Mr. Wang, helping to pass out the leaflets and murmuring with a co-host's insouciance: "I'm selling books for Mr. Wang." The Russian was saved embarrassment. Mr. Wang's dignity was preserved. The reception flowed on.

In the garden city of Hangchow in 1973 I was told of a Cultural Revolution struggle at the Temple of the Retreat of the Soul. Two Red Guard groups confronted each other in the courtyard of this ancient Buddhist holy place on the hills above West Lake. Everyone agreed on the slogan: "Smash the Old World." But while a university student group said the struggle should be political, a high-school student group wanted to smash the temple physically. The only thing both sides could agree on was to telegraph Premier Chou and accept his adjudication.

Chou telegraphed back to say that the temple should not be knocked down. As interesting as Chou's reply was the fact that the two Red Guard groups agreed to put the question to him. It is well known that Chou enjoyed the admiration alike of intellectuals, of officials in the state bureaucracy, and of economic planners. Evidently the militant Red Guards also trusted his fair judgment.

In 1974 a disagreement arose between the Chinese and Australian governments over the arrangements for a visit to Peking by the deputy prime minister of Australia. The Australian Defense Ministry insisted that the crew of the Australian plane should wear their military uniforms, both on the flight from Hong Kong to Peking and while in the Chinese capital. The Chinese foreign ministry said that would be contrary to Chinese law. The visit was almost canceled.

Then Chou heard about it. He said it was a small matter and why not compromise? The crew should wear their military uniforms during the flight from Hong Kong but take them off on arrival at Peking. So the deputy prime minister set out almost on time for his trip. In any situation that called for dealing with people at variance with each other Chou was a brilliant problem-solver.

I mentioned earlier Chou's blend of discipline and charm. He was firm, yet he could bend. This was his secret. Chou taught many a Chinese cadre the meaning of principled conciliatoriness. That Chou was cosmopolitan does not mean he substituted style for substance. That he was a master conciliator does not mean he lacked a basic viewpoint. From Chairman Mao, from Marxism, from experience, Chou had derived principles which he followed doggedly although he did not discourse about them.

A leader who had principles and cultural confidence, who was personally unafraid, and thus able and free to be a cosmopolitan within a national revolution, a conciliator within a Communist Party, a gay knight on the grim long trek. That was Chou En-lai.

On the issue of Taiwan, he made concessions to America over questions of timing and method, but never on the principle that Taiwan was part of China. (It was carefully noted in Peking that on the eve of his funeral, Chou's ashes, at his widow's request, were placed for the night in the Taiwan Province Room of the Great Hall of the People.)

Chou changed his view about which source of imperialism was the most dangerous—believing first that it was the United States and later the U.S.S.R.—but never about the principle that imperialism is the cause of world troubles and that the independence of the small and medium-sized countries must be supported.

For these reasons, Chou, widely considered one of the twentieth century's leading statesmen, is also thought of within China as a tough and uncompromising revolutionary. No wonder there was a "Chou revival" in China during early 1977, after the fall of the Gang of Four. Then the man for whom mourning had been abruptly cut short by the Gang, one year before, was at last praised in the press with the superlatives that he deserved. It was a clue to the emerging policies of the Hua government.

4

Crisis over
ॐ Teng Hsiao-p'ing ॐ

Both China and the United States during 1976 looked to their own body politic, and not much at broad world vistas. Yet they began from different starting points. America focused on who would be the next President, and Ford or Carter became the clear-cut choice. But the election issues were, during the campaign itself, as hard to sight as corks on a choppy sea.

In China it was, and is, the personnel stakes that are elusive. The policy issues that have recently been debated within Peking's palaces are, on the other hand, clearer than usual. Thus the official explanations given for the ouster of Teng Hsiao-p'ing in April 1976 were certainly more frank and detailed than those given by Washington for the ouster of Defense Secretary Schlesinger in the previous year. And the "what" may be as momentous for China's future as the "who."

To start with, six separate episodes reflect the recent controversies in China:

1. I am on a visit to a primary school in a northern city. The place is abuzz with sport, science, and language activities of a high standard. But Party administrators harangue me about the evil influence on the school of "class enemy" Lin Piao, the former defense chief and heir to Mao. It all seems on a par with blaming the President of the U.S.A. for bad weather.

I find a chance to ask one pupil directly (in Chinese): "Is there class struggle in your school?" The headmistress hisses "Yes" across a heavy silence to the poor boy. But he remains awestruck. At length he squeezes out a reply that the sweating headmistress must find hard to grade: "It's difficult to say there is class struggle in our school, but it's also difficult to say there is not."

2. During a chat about China's international economic relationships with a Peking official who was purged in the Cultural Revolution but is now back in favor, I mention the criticism made by Shanghai leftists of "cadres who think the moon is rounder abroad." The phrase refers to those economic officials who give a relaxed interpretation to China's sacred principle of self-reliance and wish to import more rather than less high-technology capital equipment from Japan and the West.

The Peking official does not reject the Shanghai slogan but he gently undermines it with two remarks: "Premier Chou's speech on the modernization of China's economy [at the National People's Congress of January 1975] inspired us all." After a pause he comes back to the Shanghai slogan: "True, the moon is not rounder abroad. But equally true, the moon is not rounder in China."

3. All over China the memory of the Cultural Revolution and its fallout is a divisive issue. Official Peking would still no more condemn this crisis-turned-tradition than would Wash-

ington snipe at the Constitution. But some policy-makers shudder at the thought of certain "excesses" during the storm years of 1966–69.

An economist in Hunan Province complains that Cultural Revolution "confusion" led the birth rate to rise above the desirable 15 per 1,000. Teng Hsiao-p'ing said of Chiang Ch'ing's militant post-Cultural Revolution plays: "You just see a bunch of people running to and fro on the stage. Not a trace of art. Foreigners clap them only out of courtesy." And halfway through a Chiang Ch'ing movie entitled *Spring Sprouts* he strode out muttering "ultra-leftist."

4. In the lovely old Shantung town of Tsinan, I visit a the-ater troupe. Its boss is a military man not well versed in drama (the actors sit beside him with glazed eyes as he briefs the foreign visitors). He was brought in to stamp out "the black line in art and literature of Liu Shao-ch'i," head of state for seven years until labeled "China's Khrushchev" by Mao in 1966.

It is 1975, before the fall of the Gang of Four. In four hours of railing against Liu, however, this army troubleshooter never once mentions the name of the illustrious sponsor of the *correct* artistic line: Chiang Ch'ing, Politburo member, for nearly forty years the wife of Mao Tse-tung.

That same day the vice president of the Shantung Wo-men's Federation talks about the role of women in China. Asked for examples of females in leading jobs, she speaks of pilots and sea captains, but not of Mao's wife, though Chiang Ch'ing was then still riding high.

Many people in China resent the way Chiang Ch'ing climbed up on Mao's back after the Cultural Revolution to become one of China's dozen top leaders. They disliked her barbs against twice-purged Teng Hsiao-p'ing, some army of-ficers, and the memory of Chou En-lai. They could not reconcile her luxurious style of living with her talk about the importance of "staying close to the masses."

5. During the fall of 1975 a drive was mounted against the cherished old historical novel *Story of the Marshes* * because it praises "capitulationism." Mao was less concerned about the peasant character, Sung Chiang, having surrendered to the emperor nine hundred years ago than about some of his colleagues who would like to reduce tensions with ("capitulate to") the U.S.S.R. A high official remarked evenly to me in Peking during September of that year: "There are different opinions in China about this novel."

That same month Teng told some New Zealand visitors that the *Story of the Marshes* campaign had no one as its particular target. But in the next breath he blew the stuffing out of this argument by declaring that the Cultural Revolution—which he deflated by calling it merely "China's most extensive mass movement"—was also just a criticism of wrong points of view and not a struggle "between this man and that."

Well, the Cultural Revolution *was* among other things a struggle between individuals. So in part was the modest *Story of the Marshes* affair, and Teng was its big target. As the drive ebbed a little in December 1975, an unprecedented step was taken in China's policy toward Moscow. A three-man Russian helicopter crew, captured in Sinkiang Province twenty-one months before and many times described as spies, were suddenly released, fêted at dinner by the Chinese Foreign Ministry, and sent home to the accompaniment of a stunning announcement that they were not spies after all. The helicopter with all equipment and documents aboard was also returned to Moscow.

---

* Also translated as *Water Margin* and *All Men Are Brothers*.

The PRC has never in twenty-eight years reversed itself in this way on a spy case and declared intruders, arrested by Peking, to be innocent. Were there two views on the matter at the heart of the Chinese government?

During January and February of 1976, while Teng was in eclipse following his last big appearance as eulogist at Chou's funeral, a rash of stories appeared in China's press about Russian spies all over the world. In the eyes of *People's Daily* and *Peking Review* every last *Tass* writer, Aeroflot clerk, and Soviet cultural attaché was a spy in the service of the global designs of "social imperialism." Yet the Chinese people and the outside world were asked to believe that Russian airmen in sensitive Sinkiang (it has nuclear weapons and minority peoples related to those beyond the nearby Soviet border) were *not* spies.

It was no surprise when the *Story of the Marshes* campaign was revived in April 1976 as Teng was stripped of all his high posts. Nor that Teng was accused of being ready to "give up China's independence." The issue of *People's Daily* which reported the April 5 mêlée in the Square of the Gate of Heavenly Peace also declared Teng a "capitulationist" in the *Story of the Marshes* mold.

Teng was said to be "furious" with the drive against the novel. He scoffed at its proponents: "They hear the wind and think it's raining" (*Ting dao feng jiu shi yu*). Down-to-earth Teng evidently thought that Mao was jumping to conclusions in drawing lessons out of a Sung Dynasty novel for China's policies in the 1970s.

6. The subject of Laos came up in a talk with one of a half-dozen top government leaders who handle policy toward the United States. It was late in 1975 and the coalition régime of Souvanna Phouma still existed. The Foreign Ministry man said he did not like the trend of things in Vientiane

because "social imperialism" (meaning Russia) was eyeing Laos with a hungry leer. "China would like to see a stable government in Laos." I took this to mean continuance of the coalition as against a shift to a pure Pathet Lao régime (which has now occurred and brought increased Hanoi and Moscow influence).

Then I asked whether "stability" was a reasonable aim for other Southeast Asian governments. The dour official lit up like a candle: "Certainly. In the era of superpower contention these governments need to pursue stability." I walked out of the Foreign Ministry recalling that I had never before heard a Chinese leader praise stability as an aim for Asia. But I did hear John Foster Dulles do so in the 1950s.

These six diverse episodes sum up, I believe, the chief issues that have characterized the momentous year of Mao's death: whether life in China is still shot through with class struggle; the degree to which self-reliance remains a viable principle; varying verdicts on the Cultural Revolution; the passions aroused by Mao's third and last wife, Chiang Ch'ing; the issue of how to deal with Russia; and the wisdom or otherwise of the pursuit of stability in foreign policy.

From some of these issues was woven the political rope that hung Teng in the spring of 1976. The strident debate over them put a surprise man—the modest regional figure with good reason to be modest, Hua Kuo-feng—into the shoes of former Premier Chou. They give us some clues as to what lies ahead for Chinese politics and the future role of China in the world.

The Emergence of Teng.

Teng Hsiao-p'ing is one of the grand old men of the Chinese Revolution. He was born in 1904 when the Manchu Dy-

Teng Hsiao-p'ing, after having done a "double Lazarus," speaking at the Eleventh Congress of the CCP in August 1977. (*New China News Agency Photo*)

nasty still clung to power. He went to France after World War I in a work-study group from his home province of Szechwan. Already a demon organizer, he acquired from his friends in France the label "Ph.D. in mimeographing" for his brisk technical work in putting out the leftist magazine *Youth.*

He joined the CCP in 1924 and played a role in the great events of the climb to power. He won distinction as a PLA officer, made the Long March of 1934–35, and exercised great

authority in southwest China. He was one of a handful of
China's leading rulers from 1955, when he entered the Politburo, until 1967, when he was purged as the "number two
man in power taking the capitalist road."*

Short and squat, Teng lacks stylistic finesse. He spits and
curses with gusto. Red Guards discovered to their horror that
he loves a game of bridge. In sleek Shanghai, chunky self-
made Teng has been referred to as a man "without a neck,"
who "wears his pants at half-mast." But no one, from Mao
down, has doubted his brain and his vigor as an organizer.

Mao liked Teng. Yet Teng was a terrier who often snapped
at Mao's heels. After Teng's first purge Mao observed: "Teng
is deaf. At each meeting, he used to sit far away from me."
And again: "Teng believes himself to be a genius. He thinks
he can take charge of everything himself." In a way Teng became Mao's nemesis.

Among the public at large, if Teng had never become a folk
hero, neither had he been actively disliked. He was never so
popular in China as when the Gang of Four hunted him
down for the second time in 1976. Before being twice purged
he was respected, but outside his home turf of the southwest
he was probably a fairly gray figure.

One night soon after Teng reemerged in 1973 I was in a
Hangchow cinema watching some newsreels. Suddenly
Teng's chiseled face flashed onto the screen, welcoming a
delegation at Peking airport. The cinema was alive with

* Teng's history of ins-and-outs is as follows: by the mid-1960s he was one of the top
leaders of China; between 1967 and 1973 he was in disgrace, though never arrested or
imprisoned; from 1973 until 1975 he again occupied high office; in January 1976 he
disappeared from public view and in April 1976 he was stripped of all posts—though as
before he was never arrested or tried for crimes; in July 1977 he was restored to all
his high posts in Party and state and as of early 1978 he seemed almost a co-equal of
Hua.

"oohs" and "ahs." People must have read that Teng was making a timid comeback. But they probably had not seen his face in the cinema or on TV for six years. It was a shock.

The Hangchow audience did not cheer Teng. Yet it did not fall silent with embarrassment, nor show any displeasure at seeing the cocky leader again. The reaction was a bit like that to the sudden appearance in a movie of a favorite villain. A character known to have been in trouble with "them," whose faults can hardly be denied, but who is thought to be not all bad.

By 1975 Teng had become the effective number two man—and number two men did not fare well in Mao's China. Chou was still premier but already had cancer. As a vice premier, Teng began to flex the muscles of his regained power. Like Liu and Lin before him—for complex reasons, including his own lack of ambition, Chou had never been an heir-apparent—Teng reached the treacherous ultimate threshold of Mao's own supreme authority.

He became, within two years of his reappearance, Chief of the General Staff of the PLA and deputy chairman of the CCP, as well as vice premier. Then Mao once more saw the fingers of a second in command itching for the crown, and he chopped them off. *People's Daily* noted drily in the spring of 1976 that Teng had "got above himself in the past year."

A related problem for Teng was that he had made enemies. He has the strong will and abrasive ways often found among Szechwanese. His peremptory, bureaucratic methods have brought mixed reactions, and he uses administrative fiat to smash problems that Chou would tackle through patient persuasion. If Chou was a supple willow, Teng is a solid oak.

More important even than his style, Teng had irritated the

Cultural Revolution left by rising like Lazarus from the political grave in which they laid him in 1967. Chiang Ch'ing felt this way. So did the Red Guards who were thrust after 1969 from the center-stage of politics to the dust and drudgery of farms, while "revisionists" crept back to power in the army, the state center, and the provinces.

Teng, who has a sharp tongue, had quipped that the Cultural Revolution leftists had "risen up by helicopter" while the correct way to get to a high job was "step by step." He talked of "educating the young" but seldom of promoting them to high positions.

Moreover Teng had never liked the policies of the Cultural Revolution. Mao himself by 1968 had pulled back from extreme ideas like re-melting the big cities into "Paris Communes," and cutting out private plots on which peasants grow vegetables for their own use or sale. After his resurrection in 1973, Teng spurred the retreat from the typical policies of the Cultural Revolution. He proceeded to flesh out in state policy the bare bones of his brisk maxim which had so shocked the Red Guards: "Black cat or white cat—it's a good cat if it catches mice." And he even uttered the last word in blasphemy by observing: "In real life, not everything is class struggle."

So Teng went full throttle for modernization. He dared to question whether China's paramedical "barefoot doctors" should not eventually get more solid medical training. He complained that if the Shanghai left kept on sniping at the "theory of productive forces"—a bread and butter view of socialism as dependent on material progress—then Chinese planners would wake up one morning to find that "nobody dares any more to grasp production."

The Peking newspaper *Brilliant Daily* summed up the danger which afficionados of the Cultural Revolution saw in

Teng's stress on economic progress: "The satellite goes up to heaven and the red flag falls down to earth."

The final reason why Teng had become by mid-1976 a Chinese version of Nixon—idly reading in the papers what a monster he had been in the days when the papers used to praise him—is that he had come to doubt Mao's view of Russia. The question is whether the U.S.S.R. has really taken America's place as chief enemy of China and world socialism alike.

Equally involved are the socialist priorities according to which China is being modernized. Moscow is the great negative example of the satellite going up and the red flag coming down. But is Russia so hopelessly wrong—Mao called it "Fascist"—that China must do the opposite of anything Moscow does?

At this point the issues of Russia and of the Cultural Revolution became intimately linked. Those who disagreed with Mao on the one tended to do so also on the other. It is highly significant that all the Cultural Revolution themes appear in embryo in the letters written by Peking at the height of the Sino-Soviet ideological debate during 1963–64.

Not that Teng has been pro-Russian. But as the number two man, who no doubt glanced ahead to a day when he might become number one, Teng had to think during 1975 about China's post-Mao policy toward the Soviet Union. He apparently wanted to keep a door open to Moscow for various reasons. The hostility against the U.S.S.R. has cost China friends in Africa, Indochina, and other parts of the Third World. And by tilting so far away from Russia, the Chinese have lost leverage with the United States on Taiwan and other issues. The Soviet helicopter crew, one notes, were released just after Ford's unproductive trip to Peking in December 1975.

Parts of the army would prefer a more even-handed policy toward the two superpowers. Lin apparently once queried Mao: "If you can ask Nixon to China, why can't I ask Brezhnev?" During 1975 many pro-Soviet officers came back to high posts in the PLA. These included men who had served under Teng in earlier years, and men who had been purged for speaking up for military cooperation with the U.S.S.R. in the mid-1960s.*

To contain Soviet influence all over the world, moreover, is to crib resources from China's internal development needs. Steelworkers in Wuhan (China's Chicago) put up a poster which asked why their steel was being sent to build the Tanzam railroad when underdeveloped China needs more railroads itself.

Why is China active in Africa? The answer is mainly because Russia is. Detente with Moscow would probably suit the Chinese economic planners, who want more than anything else in the world to fulfill Chou En-lai's great call for the modernization of China before the end of the century.

Teng's preference for butter over guns was expressed in a scoffing remark made to some American visitors about India's nuclear bomb: "What good is it if you don't have food?" Talking to some New Zealand visitors, Teng made even clearer his lack of appetite for global confrontations: "China has no intention of competing with the superpowers. There is no way it could compete, unless the Chinese people were willing to have nothing to eat, nothing to wear, and nowhere to sleep."

If Teng got out of step with Mao on Russia (and released that helicopter crew in December 1975) he is only the latest

---

* Among them: Su Chen-hua, Li Ta, Yang Yung, Ch'in Chi-wei, Liu Chih-chien, and Kuo Lin-hsiang. Almost all achieved very high office during 1977.

in a long and distinguished line. In almost all of the eleven "official" Party struggles, dating as far back as the 1920s, the issue of Russia was involved. Mao beat back one colleague after another whom he judged pro-Soviet.

The eighth culprit was P'eng Te-huai, who went behind Mao's back to share his doubts about the Great Leap Forward with Russian leaders. The ninth was Liu, "China's Khrushchev," who wanted "joint action" with Moscow to help Vietnam (Mao confessed to Kosygin in 1965, during the last meeting he had with a Soviet leader, that some of his colleagues disagreed with his opposition to "joint action"). The tenth was Lin, who died when fleeing to Russia.*

Someone once asked Mao when the polemics with Moscow would cease. He replied: "The sky won't fall, trees will grow, women will have children, fish will swim, even if they [the polemics] go on forever." It is not surprising that Chinese leaders less bold and stubborn than Mao have had doubts about his breathtaking view of Russia. The Cold War with Russia cannot go on forever, Teng may have thought, any more than old Mao could go on forever.

The Fall of Teng.

In April 1976 a rope from these various strands tightened around the short neck of Teng Hsiao-p'ing.

The balance of forces had tipped back and forth three times since January 1975. The watershed National People's Congress and Party meetings of that month struck a note of

---

* Even the eleventh struggle against the Gang of Four, although it mainly concerned domestic issues and style of conduct, touched on the Russian issue via the Albanian connection; the Gang's closeness to Albania probably carried implications of agreement with Lin Piao's even-handed policy toward the superpowers, as against Mao's policy of using America to counter Russia (see page 221).

order and stressed economic tasks. Chou was making his last big appearance. Teng emerged with a Party vice chairmanship to add to his high posts in state and army. Moscow's chief negotiator in the China-Russia border talks returned to Peking for a fresh effort in the wake of the meetings.

But Mao did not bless the January meetings with his presence. Illness cannot have been the reason, for at the time he received visitors from both Germany and Malta. And in fact no sooner were the January meetings over than a strong breeze began to blow from the left.

Yao Wen-yuan, a Shanghai leftist who belonged to the Gang of Four, signaled the mood by manipulating the photo coverage of the NPC meeting in the media which he controlled. *People's Daily* planned a four-page spread of thirty pictures of the meeting; Yao stepped in and cut it down to two pictures. One was merely of the Congress Hall. The second depicted the entire presidium of the NPC—a way of downgrading Chou En-lai and Chu Te who were the leading figures at the meeting.

Scribes of the Shanghai Cultural Revolution left wrote restless articles about "bourgeois rights" that still exist, even in a socialist society, and ought to be whittled down. Wages are still very unequal in industry, they stressed. Money itself is a capitalist hangover that must eventually go. The danger exists that new class enemies will emerge to use these remnants as levers for turning the Chinese social machine back to capitalism.

In the summer of 1975 I heard these themes set forth at the Shanghai Diesel Engine Factory. It was a pet plant of the former Shanghai radical leader Wang Hung-wen, now vilified as part of the Gang of Four. His photo was everywhere and a bulletin posted near the front door reported on a recent visit by him to the factory: "We all said, after he had gone: 'Vice Chairman Wang's warm-hearted visit shows that the

Center does really regard us as precious—not like before
when we were scorned as mere grass.' "

The politically with-it cadres at Shanghai Diesel Engine
Factory viewed bonuses in any guise roughly as Methodists
view whiskey. The factory chairman struck a note of pride
and challenge as I left: "We know not all factories in China
are like us."

They are certainly not, and most of Chinese industry
turned a blind eye to the "bourgeois rights" campaign so far
as the real world of policy went. By late summer the left
breeze had dropped. The chief of all the purged pro-Soviet
military officers, Lo Jui-ch'ing, returned to power in August.
October saw a rash of reinstatements of senior victims of the
Cultural Revolution. Big national conferences on agriculture
and coal suggested that Teng was giving priority to the economy. Indeed a Teng slogan—"Stability, unity, development of
the national economy"—soared to prominence during the
fall.

By contrast the "new-born Socialist things" were little
touted. The fruits of the Cultural Revolution were hardly
mentioned. The emphasis on "new-born Socialist things"—
political doctrinaires taking the place of qualified teachers
at colleges, model operas that sound like an editorial from
People's Daily set to Tchaikovsky—was minimal.

True, Chiang Ch'ing did make a speech at the agriculture
conference in Tachai, but *People's Daily* published only the
speeches of Teng and Hua—not a line of Chiang Ch'ing's
was made public.* The pen of Ch'u Lan, pseudonym for a
writer who expressed the ideas of Chiang Ch'ing, remained

---

* It was Mao himself who blocked the publication of his wife's speech. Hua showed it to
him, and Mao found that it was about *Story of the Marshes*, as much as about agriculture, and that it drew strained comparisons between villains in the novel and villains in
China in 1975. He wrote on the speech: "Shit! Barking up the wrong tree! Don't
publish the talk."

unusually idle. And the crown jewel of radical doctrine, the principle of "going against the tide," was even criticized in Hunan.

But the reprinting of a well-known Mao poem mocking "goulash communism"* at the New Year of 1977 was the first shot of a fresh militant campaign against pragmatism. Typically it arose in education circles. Typically it complained that "modernization" was being used "as a big club to kill the new-born Socialist things." Typically it quibbled with statements made at the coal and agriculture parleys. That same month *People's Daily* made a fresh charge of "capitulationism" against Lin: "The anti-Party crowd of Lin Piao openly announced they intended to enter into secret talks with the Soviet revisionists." Meanwhile the press indulged in fire-and-brimstone language reminiscent of the Cultural Revolution.

The climax of the Teng crisis in April was indeed stunning. It produced sights one had come not to expect in Peking. The circumstance was innocent enough. At Spring Festival, when the dead are remembered, wreaths in honor of Chou En-lai were brought by admirers to the Square of the Gate of Heavenly Peace and piled around the Monument to the People's Heroes.

Yet within a few days all hell had broken loose. The wreaths were suddenly removed by the Peking authorities—and a crowd of 100,000 turned a calm memorial into a mêlée. Vehicles were burned and police roughed up. One hundred people were injured and several died.

Throughout the day of April 5, crowds milled around in

---

* The reference was to a speech Khrushchev had made years before, in Budapest, in which he declared that a good test of a socialist government was whether or not it provided the populace with a good plate of goulash.

unaccustomed anarchy. Poems were displayed and onlookers copied them down. Impromptu speeches were given and listeners gave voice to varying reactions. One man seemed to express an anxiety that transcended the issues obliquely addressed in the poems and inscriptions. "What is the greatest problem at present?" he cried from the steps of the Great Hall of the People. "Where is China going?—that is the biggest problem."*

Many of the inscriptions had been carefully, even cunningly prepared. Praising Chou, some of them also swiped at Mao. They alluded to him as the Emperor Ch'in Shih Huang, a dictator who unified China 2100 years ago, but who used ruthless methods and had his work undone by others who came after him.

Other inscriptions made unflattering allusions to the Gang of Four. Slogans referred to *yao mo*—monsters—in a play on Yao Wen-yuan's name. Anti-Chiang Ch'ing inscriptions dotted the square like mushrooms after spring rain. One poster used a clever pun on Chiang Ch'ing's name— "Chiang" means "river"—to honor Chou. "Don't let the river waters (*chiang shui*) wash away the memory of Chou," ran the swipe at Ms. River.**

---

* The paradox of these sentiments being condemned as "reactionary" is shown by comparing them with Mao's own poem written to Chou En-lai during 1975. Mao felt a similar anxiety about the future:

> *Loyal parents who sacrificed so much for the nation*
> *   never feared the ultimate fate.*
> *Now that the country has become Red,*
> *   who will be its guardian?*
> *Our mission, unfinished, may take a thousand years.*
> *The struggle tires us, and our hair is gray.*
> *You and I, old friend, can we just watch our efforts*
> *   being washed away?*

** The full reference is probably to *huo shui*, an old Chinese term for a woman who causes trouble. Thus in "river waters," *chiang shui*, *chiang* would stand for Chiang Ch'ing and *shui* would be a short form of *huo shui*.

The government, to its great credit, was not heavy-handed.
The demonstration had gone on for some fourteen hours.
Police and militia used argument as much as force to end it.
At nightfall Mayor Wu Te made a law-and-order speech over
a loudspeaker. But the government did not—could not—hide
the fact that politics had spilled out into the streets and onto
the holy place of the PRC's capital. It reported the events
quite fully. And it allowed its hand to be forced into two dramatic decisions hastily announced: Teng was denounced by
name and fired from all office; and Hua Kuo-feng was elevated to the full office of premier and made "First Vice Chairman" of the CCP. (Text of report and decisions in Appendix
1.)

So Peking experienced its first full-blooded demonstration.
There had been nothing so unstaged and so open-ended as
this during the Cultural Revolution. The most basic reason
why a Spring Festival remembrance turned into a massive
political demonstration was Teng Hsiao-p'ing himself. It is
not that Teng organized the event. Nor, despite claims in
People's Daily, did those who gathered in the square openly
praise Teng.

It was never said who gave the order to remove the
wreaths from the Monument to the People's Heroes. But
since the whole event was turned into a weapon to attack
Teng, one concludes that the Gang of Four had the wreaths
removed. They had the power to do so, given their association
with the mayor of Peking, Wu Te. They had the motive,
since, in the atmosphere of the moment, pro-Chou sentiments seemed like pro-Teng sentiments. Thus was Teng
undermined by his enemies.

Sad weeks for China followed the riot. "Victory" rallies—to
celebrate the twin triumphs of Teng's fall and Hua's elevation to the premiership—unrolled with all the spontaneity of

an army band performing before its commander-in-chief. The tone of *People's Daily* rose from a cry to a screech.

One long-time British friend of the PRC was profoundly disturbed to watch the sullen rallies. He saw a column of several hundred marchers ebbing through the Square of the Gate of Heavenly Peace. A crew from China TV arrived to film them. For this purpose the TV producer asked the column to shout in unison the slogan: "Ten Thousand Years to Chairman Mao!" The Briton was shocked to see that, in response, the marchers scarcely moved their lips, and emitted nothing more than a murmur.

Teng was out. The Politburo had been frightened by the riot; it was possible that more demonstrations would break out in other cities. They decided that the trial balloon of denouncing Teng had floated long enough. Back in February the leftists had achieved a majority for the policy: "Give Teng a hard shove in the back, and watch the results." It could now be claimed that the results were in.

The Politburo Resolution that was issued on April 7 read: "Having discussed the counter-revolutionary incident which took place at the Square of the Gate of Heavenly Peace, and Teng Hsiao-p'ing's latest behavior, the Political Bureau of the Central Committee of the Communist Party of China holds that the nature of the Teng Hsiao-p'ing problem has turned into one of antagonistic contradiction." It was a surprisingly frank, brief, and prompt resolution.

Only one sentiment was added, and it turned out to be an intriguing one in the light of later events: "The Political Bureau allows him [Teng] to keep his Party membership so as to see how he will behave in the future."

At the age of seventy-two, Teng had become a victim of the succession bugbear; of his own peremptory ways; of the perfectionist fantasies of the Gang of Four; of being a pragmatist out of season; and of thinking that détente with Russia might not be a bad idea. In the words of a Shanghai wall poster that soon appeared, he was "China's second new Khrushchev."

It must have been a bitter fate for an old warrior. A few months later Chu Te—the military genius and second greatest hero of the Chinese Revolution—died at the age of eighty-nine. Even at Chu's funeral there was no letup in the denunciation of Teng. In his eulogy, Hua found it appropriate to ask the nation to "criticize Teng's counterrevolutionary revisionist line."

Teng had said at the height of the battle that he was "not afraid" of being purged a second time. He had looked the Gang in the face and despised them. It seems he had settled with the god of fate; but he had certainly not given up the fight.

The Implications of the Teng Crisis.

The way in which the Politburo handled the fall of Teng revealed some key trends. In the first place it was clear that Mao was in charge. Only the top man can kick down an aspiring second man in today's China. In the months after December 1975 Mao made many appearances. New quotes from him—always a sign that he was up to something—popped up in the press during the spring. Thus an axiom appeared in February 1976 that was a devastating shot at Teng's efforts to cancel out the effects of the Cultural Revolution: "Reversing verdicts will not win the support of the people," declared Mao. Teng's fall and Hua's rise were conspicuously said to have been effected "on the proposal" of Mao.

The importance of this for the future is that without Mao, Teng would not have been re-purged, and without Mao, Hua would not have reached the top rung. Hua owes everything to Mao; Teng owes less than nothing.

The various reversals since January 1975 suggested either that Mao's role was intermittent or that he flashed signals so oblique as to seem green from one angle and red from another. Between May 1976 and his death in September, the chairman pulled back and apparently more or less retired.

This underlined just how serious the Year of the Dragon crisis at the top of Chinese politics was. No matter how messy or risky the lurches in Peking since 1949, Mao's authority had always been there to set a limit on struggle and ambition. But that day had ended. During Mao's last years, few of his colleagues had been sure what the old man was thinking, what new animal he would unleash next. With his death that source of unpredictability was gone.

A tone of caution and a lack of enthusiasm marked the campaign against Teng. *People's Daily* admitted on February 17, 1976, that the Central Committee of the Party was "split"—and that was the point. The campaign was not given a label that stuck. Everyone was strictly forbidden to go outside his own organization to form "fighting groups."

Teng was not expelled from the Party as "counterrevolutionaries" have always been before. Curiously, the struggle against him was not admitted into the ranks of the great struggles—the one against Lin was known officially as Number 10; this would have been Number 11—in the history of the CCP. Parts of China, such as Shanghai and Liaoning Province, lambasted Teng with glee. But little was said in other parts, such as the south, where Teng was strong and Russian revisionism does not seem the most pressing menace under the sun.

Remarkable was the amount of quotation from the "bad guys" that crept into the press. An entire eloquent poem written by the Peking demonstrators was reproduced in *People's Daily*. Their likening of Mao to the old emperor Ch'in Shih Huang whose day is done was noted, as was their cry for "genuine Marxism-Leninism" (a favorite Moscow phrase for hitting at Mao's alleged descent to nationalism). Either people of influence were sympathetic to these quotations, or the Chinese public was just too disquieted to be kept safely in the dark.

And here we reach a third trait of long-term significance: public opinion is on the rise as a force in Chinese politics. With the fall of Teng, it may in fact have come of age. The eloquent, if black, poem at the square put it well: "China is no longer the China of yore,/And the people are no longer wrapped in sheer ignorance."

The mêlée by the Gate of Heavenly Peace was not purely spontaneous, yet many of the crowd of 100,000 were spurred by genuine affection for Chou and by agreement with his policies. *People's Daily* conceded as much in a remarkable May 5 article with the odd title: "Use Revolutionary Public Opinion to Smash Counterrevolutionary Public Opinion." "Smash" does not seem a fit term for dealing with public opinion, however reactionary that opinion may be. In the future there will probably be more expression of opinion and less smashing.

Teng was said to have begun his drive to turn back the left by "creating a counterrevolutionary public opinion." Very different from Lin Piao, who began with a secret blueprint for an armed coup.

In an extraordinarily revealing talk to his colleagues in May 1966 Lin had said: "Seizure of political power depends upon gun barrels and inkwells." Teng stuck to inkwells, and was proud of this difference. "Lin was able to carry along with him only two people," Teng remarked derisively to New Zealand visitors; "his son and his wife."

Ordinary folk wrote letters to the Central Committee urging Teng as the new premier. Teng himself tried to start a new magazine to air his views. "Bad elements" were accused of dealing in rumors about a will Chou may have left that expressed Teng-like views. Such cut and thrust of opinion was unusual in Chinese politics.

From its side, the official media did not keep silent about Teng's fall, as it had done for months about Liu's and for nearly two years about Lin's. On April 8, 1976, for the first time ever, readers of *People's Daily* saw a prompt, detailed official report of a political quarrel that they could compare with the reality they had just observed (the text appears in Appendix 1a).

It is no coincidence that Teng's fall is the first such Chinese affair that resembles a purge in the West. Mao "leaked" his lack of confidence in his vice premier—much as Ford did in the case of James Schlesinger, his Defense Secretary, and of Nelson Rockefeller as his future running mate in 1975—and dismissed him only after a brief but damning period of public doubt-casting.

Public opinion as a political force grew especially fast because the succession was a universal issue that was accessible to all. Everyone thought about it; official ideology had no answer to it. Mortality itself—not a class enemy—had brought on the crisis. The person in the street understood this and could chat about it.

One poem written in a school notebook at the demonstration in the square voiced the shared dilemma of the Chinese people: "A generation of heroes created this world. A million people worry—who will succeed them?" The events of 1977 suggest that public opinion, aroused by the Teng case above all, continues to rise as a force in China.

A further significant feature of Teng's fall in 1976 was that the PLA did not play a big role. It was not the army, but the leftist militia, with Shanghai as its model, that put down the April mêlée. It lasted fourteen hours; the PLA could have squashed it in one. Amazingly, *People's Daily* wrote of rioters who "sported a crew cut"—pejorative slang in China for soldiers. If PLA officers found that provocative, they resisted temptation and kept a low profile throughout the spring crisis.

The army kept its fingers out of politics partly because it had burned them doing the opposite during Lin's era. But some of the PLA were also dubious about the case against Teng. Many "rightist" officers had come back since the Cultural Revolution ended and Lin fell. Some had been accused of leaning to the Soviet Union, like the former Chief of the General Staff, Lo Jui-ch'ing; others had suppressed Red Guards in the name of order, like the former commander at Wuhan, Ch'en Tsai-tao. They were apparently forgiven.

The PLA seemed a bit divided on the Teng affair, as it was on the Cultural Revolution. Some officers, mainly in the navy and air force, supported the left, as some did at the climax of the Cultural Revolution, and as a similar lineup backed Lin's coup. But these were a minority. Most PLA leaders had nothing against Teng's policies, whether toward Russia or on "private plots" (land which peasants till aside from their duties to the commune). Some old marshals said so forthrightly.

One of these was Liu Po-ch'eng, one of the two most respected military men alive in China. Liu's feelings about Teng surfaced while the eighty-two-year-old marshal was ailing in hospital soon after the fall of the Gang of Four. According to a document obtained by the Chinese-language newspaper in Hong Kong, *Brilliant Daily,* Teng was visiting Liu's sickroom when suddenly Hua arrived.

Teng announced to the blind marshal: "Chairman Hua is here to see you." Then Teng humbly got ready to depart. But Hua restrained him with the words: "Do you think I can push you away?" A chat ensued among the three men. (How important age is in Chinese politics! Teng respects Liu, ten years his senior. But Hua cannot forget that Teng, in turn, is more than fifteen years his senior.) Liu took advantage of Hua's presence to make a significant request: in front of Teng, he asked Hua to allow Teng to preside over his funeral, since he and Teng were old confreres who had worked together for more than fifty years. The old marshal could not have made clearer his pro-Teng inclination.

Teng was not involved in the witch-hunt against Lin sympathizers within the PLA during 1972 and 1973 (he was in eclipse at the time). The soldiers who resented this purge for purely professional reasons blamed some pragmatists, but not Teng. Chiang Ch'ing and her Shanghai friends tried to coax the People's Liberation Army leftward, but with little success. Soldiers were, and mostly are, on the side of order at home and peace abroad.

There is one more interesting trait of the Teng crisis: *Principle lost ground to prejudice in the Politburo.* Mao always said that struggle should be based on line and not on personality. In this respect PRC practice, too, marks an immense advance over the warlord era after World War I, and Chiang Kai-shek's rule from 1928 to 1949. Yet since the Cultural Revolution, Chinese politics have been colored by personality far more than from 1949 to 1966.

Back in January 1967, Chou En-lai strode to the microphone to address a Cultural Revolution rally. The Red Guard crowd was flushed with excitement, *Little Red Book*s in hand, and sporting armbands that gave an impression of self-importance. The cry was heard: "Down with Liu! Down with Teng!" Chou turned his back on the audience. He agreed to begin his speech only after the Red Guards had adjusted the slogan to: "Down with the reactionary line of Liu and Teng!"

The issues between Teng and the left merited debate. But a few scribes in cultural circles dipped their pens in the ink of innuendo. Trivia stinking of personal rivalry was tossed about. Teng was supposed to have said that "tickets are never even sold out" for Chiang Ch'ing's model plays and operas. At a high level it was joked that Teng—whose wife's family had a pre-Liberation interest in a pork factory in the southwest—"can always go back to Kunming and run his ham shop." He was ridiculed as a "three-headed monster."

People's Daily found it relevant to mention that a "bad element" in the mêlée was "wearing spectacles"—a cheap crack at intellectuals. (The paper never once mentioned that the original act at the square, placing wreaths to Chou En-lai at the Monument to the People's Heroes on the occasion of Spring Festival, was in itself a valid one.) Maybe Chiang Ch'ing did not draw the distinction between personality and principle drawn by Chou in 1967. For this reason, over and above policy views, the selfless and self-assured Chou was being grievously missed in Peking's over-personalized politics; so too was the straight-from-the-hip old warrior, Chu Te, who exclaimed in 1959 when fights began to break out at the top of the Party: "And to think that we once all ate out of the same dish!"

The issues of Chinese politics were caught up, like cotton thread bunched at the eye of a needle, in the 1976 crisis over Teng Hsiao-p'ing. Throughout 1977 he continued to be the *cause célèbre* of the Peking scene. Of course he welcomed the fall of the Gang of Four; behind the scenes he may have

even had a hand in it. Much of what he had stood for suddenly became the conventional wisdom again. The case that
had been made against him in 1976 was dismantled, brick by
brick, in the first half of 1977.

In July 1977, belatedly, Teng was officially rehabilitated.
He was restored to "all his posts" (see Appendix 10) which
made him third man behind Hua and Defense Minister Yeh.
He immediately made himself at home in the cockpit of
power. At the Eleventh Party Congress he spoke as bluntly as
ever: "There must be less empty talk and more hard work."

His followers flocked back to office like workers returning
to a building after the checking out of a bomb scare. The new
Central Committee elected at the congress contains more
people from Szechwan—Teng's home province—than from
any other single province. The new list of government ministers bristles with men who have long been associated with
Teng.*

Gently but unmistakably the blame for Teng's second
purge was shifted onto the bent backs of the Gang of Four.
An awkward fact is that Mao himself sponsored the removal
of Teng from office in April 1976. Will it one day have to be
explained—with all the risks involved—that the ailing Mao
became a puppet of the Gang for the last nine months of his
life?

A second awkward fact about Teng's having risen again
like Lazarus is that Hua, too, vociferously denounced Teng
during the spring of 1976. The two men are as different as
chalk and cheese. Tensions could easily develop between
Mao's chosen comrade-in-arms, Hua, and Mao's twice-
chosen villain, Teng. It is time to take a closer look at this
man Hua.

---

* Notably the Minister of Public Security (Chao Ts'ang-pi), the Minister of Railways
(Tuan Chün-i), and the Minister of Public Health (Ch'ien Hsin-chung).

5
Who
ৡ Is Hua? ৡ

Who was this Hua, casually revealed by *People's Daily* in February 1976 as "Acting Premier,"* made Chou's full successor as premier in the wake of the riot in April, and put into Mao's shoes as chairman of the CCP after a climactic showdown with the Gang of Four in October of the same year?

Hua had been in national politics only seven years. At the time of Chou's death he ranked sixth among the twelve deputy premiers. He was a novice at foreign affairs, never having traveled abroad. He had taken part in few of the great historical events of the Chinese Revolution.

One can only say he had a fitting name for high and perilous office: "Spearhead of the Brilliant Kingdom" is a translation of its three characters.

On a television show at the time I was asked how on earth an obscure figure like Hua Kuo-feng could suddenly become

---

* The appointment was not announced as such. *People's Daily* merely mentioned, in a small box on page one, that the new ambassador of Venezuela had been received by "Acting Premier Hua Kuo-feng." That week the Communist paper in Hong Kong, *Ta Kung Pao*, did not even list Hua's appointment in its summary of important news for the week.

China's leader. Remember, I said, Hua has been the governor of a rich and rising province (Hunan). Later a Peking official complained to me that American politics is truly inscrutable when an obscure figure like Jimmy Carter can step from his Southern farm to the White House. "But recall that Carter has been the governor of a rich and rising province," I sparred.

Well, Hua's career in Hunan did prove important to him. And if the new chairman is not all that obscure, a degree of obscurity did work in his favor—at first.

The reasons for the rise of amiable Hua are the mirror image of the reasons for the fall of high-powered Teng. Teng has enemies and spectacular black marks on his record; Hua's career is too slim for him to have much of either.

Few past battles scar Hua. He was not a major national target of Cultural Revolution attacks, like Teng and many others who came back to office in the early 1970s. Yet he is not as young as such leftist "helicopters" as the Shanghai boy-wonder Wang Hung-wen, who abruptly rose to displace moderate officials during the Cultural Revolution—and so made enemies of them.

Hua survived the Cultural Revolution from the middle of the pack. It turned out an advantage not to have been a front-line partisan in that maelstrom of the mid-1960s.

It was only in Mao's home province of Hunan that I had heard of Hua when visiting China in 1971, 1973, and 1975. His name is a big one around Changsha, the furnace-hot capital of Hunan. He has links, through smoothly done irrigation work, with Mao's home village of Shaoshan and nearby areas. He also supervised the building of a Mao Memorial at Shaoshan, and it cannot have hurt him one bit that Mao's foe of the 1960s, Liu Shao-ch'i, criticized him for the amount of money spent on it.

Hua's name also cropped up during the national ironing out of the Lin Piao affair. On the eve of the Tenth Party Congress in 1973, I heard in Peking that Hua had been entrusted with a delicate investigation into the crimes of Lin, later laid before the Congress.

Back in Changsha, moreover, Hua had stood up against Lin's local military followers in the late 1960s. All in all, he did good service for Mao on the painful matter of Lin. So Mao judged him to be trustworthy in the murky succession atmosphere of 1976, when trust was in very short supply. Maybe no one who was *not* obscure was really trusted by a Mao sinking toward pessimism and death.

Hua's Background.

A cottage industry has sprung up in China to weave an impressive past for Hua Kuo-feng. But in fact the new chairman's past is an ordinary one. He has been a solid apprentice in the more humdrum stages of the Chinese Revolution—not a shooting star who achieved feats beyond the reach of others around him. What I had heard about Hua, when in Hunan, is the key to all there is to know. But the details are worth telling.

He is a son of the soil and that is a good thing in a Chinese leader. The Huas were a peasant family from barren Shansi Province in northwest China. Kuo-feng was born in 1921 and no one outside his village noticed him for twenty years.

By the 1940s he was playing a worthy grass-roots role in the mixture of political and military activity that formed the CCP's guerilla resistance to the marauding Japanese in the north.

During the land reform that followed Japan's surrender, Hua began to express his own views. They were not leftist.

Indeed he opposed a left slogan—"The poor peasants and farm laborers conquer the country and should rule the country"—on the ground that it wasn't fair to middle peasants (the CCP had classified peasants into rich, middle, and poor).

When Liberation came, Hua (then nine years a Party member) was sent to Hunan and there his career took form. He married a Hunan girl—she is apparently dead now—and there have been four children.

In the early 1950s he became Party chief of Mao's home county of Hsiang T'an. The associations built up there were to help him when hot winds of challenge hit him later. China has 2100 counties. Had Hua become head of almost any other but Hsiang T'an, he would not have met Mao as early as he did, maybe not at all.

Especially timely was a return visit by Mao to his home county and village in 1959. Hua was the chairman's local host. He even joined Mao at an intimate reunion with a surviving brother of Yang K'ai-hui (Mao's adored young wife of the 1920s) and a close girlfriend of the martyred Ms. Yang.

Not long after this pilgrimage of Mao's to Hunan, Hua became, on Mao's personal nomination, a Party secretary of the province. He also burst into print around this time with writings in praise of Mao's controversial Great Leap Forward.

By then among the five or six most prominent voices in this lush province, Hua had become a figure to watch in the regional politics of China. Trade and finance had often been his special topics. But by 1960 his speeches and activities made it plain that he had become a farming specialist. This was a vital step toward a national role.

During the early 1960s Hua had the eye of Mao, and he in turn pushed Mao's causes in Hunan. A model agricultural district called Mao T'ien had been developed under Hua's guidance. In 1963 Mao visited Hunan and wrote a note praising Mao T'ien as an example to all. In the Socialist Education Campaign—a drive to raise the political temperature in rural China—Mao gained support from Hunan; Hunanese reports and models were brandished to browbeat lagging provinces.

During the Cultural Revolution Hua's fortunes rose steadily, if not with "helicopter" abruptness. He was among the pro-Mao forces of Hunan. His rivals tended to side with Liu Shao-ch'i, the organization man and head of state whom Mao put down in 1966 as "China's Khrushchev."

It was one of these rivals, Wang Yen-ch'un, with whom Liu made common cause in trying to downgrade Hua's gaudy projects for Shaoshan. Liu and Wang felt that part of the Mao Exhibition Hall would be better used for low-income housing. They urged that a huge parking lot for visiting buses be cut up into private plots for needy peasants.

During the Cultural Revolution Hua was criticized from the left, like nearly everyone else. But this was merely the nibbling of Red Guard extremists. Moreover his domain was still Hunan Province, so he was not really exposed to the furies of the national struggle.

When the time came to restore order and regroup, in 1967, Hua was assigned to spearhead the creation of a new province organization, the Hunan Province Revolutionary Committee. In this way he remained one of the top three or four leaders in Changsha after the storm, just as he had been before it.

In fact he quietly became first secretary of the Hunan Party—and so chief politician of the province—in December 1970. The basic surge of the Cultural Revolution had carried him forward; its choppy side currents of extremism had washed harmlessly off his broad back.

The key to Hua's success during the Cultural Revolution was probably his direct link with Mao. Being one of Mao's men, he could switch and turn as Mao himself did. It was the safest way to sail the stormy seas of the Cultural Revolution.

Hua's Emergence.

It was only after 1969 that Hua mounted the national stage. In that year he was elected to the Central Committee of the CCP. From now on the pace of his progress quickened. His role in mopping up the Lin Piao mess, after 1971, was of particular help to his career.

In the Lin crisis—as during the Cultural Revolution—the luck of the national struggle dovetailed nicely with Hua's interests in Hunan. Hua's two top colleagues in Changsha (the military leaders Li Yuan and Lung Shu-chin) were both close to Lin. When Lin fell, Hua was supreme in Hunan. He served Mao well at the national level during the Lin affair; the Lin affair served *him* well at the province level.

Meanwhile Hua did not neglect Mao's home village. He had it linked by rail to Changsha—a rather lucky break for tiny Shaoshan—and he set up in its tranquil valley a color TV plant that provided pleasant employ for many of the Mao clan.

By 1972 Hua was spending most of his time in Peking. He still had his Hunan posts, but he was also working for Chou En-lai as secretary (director of the General Office) of the State Council. And he had entered the power vortex of police work (the euphemism is "public security") at the center.

China's apparatus of public security was shattered by the authorized rebellion of the Cultural Revolution. Then, amidst the tensions of its aftermath, the public security chief, Hsieh Fu-chih, was murdered by someone on his own staff in 1972. Hua was given control over public security work within the

Party. He was now in the midst of Peking politics in its purest—or most impure—sense.

At the Tenth Congress of the CCP, in 1973, Hua was named to the Politburo. In the Central Committee he had been among the top three hundred leaders of China; now he moved into the top two dozen.

His was a fresh generation in the Politburo. Most of its members were old and had made the Long March (such as the PLA men Ch'en Hsi-lien and Hsu Shih-yu). A few were even older and had been CCP leaders in the 1920s (like Mao and Chou). Still others were young "helicopters," who had risen during the Cultural Revolution (Wang Hung-wen was the leading case). At fifty-two Hua was one of the few standard bearers of "middle age" in our Western meaning of the term.

Eighteen months after the Tenth Congress, Hua received posts in the state to match those he held in the Party. At a 1975 meeting of the National People's Congress, China's intermittent Parliament, he was made a vice premier. He also became Minister of Public Security, and thus stepped fully into the cold shoes of the hapless Hsieh Fu-chih.

The public security job was an especially important one. The new State Constitution of 1975 had given public security officials a bolstered authority, by fusing the procuratorial organs with the public security structure. The policeman became, in effect, both prosecutor and judge. Hua possessed more power than Hsieh or any previous Minister of Public Security.

K'ang Sheng, for years the senior supervisor of all kinds of security work, died in December 1975. This put Hua in line for even greater responsibilities in security work than he had acquired as formal head of the Ministry of Public Security. A year later K'ang Sheng's absence helped Hua in a cruder fashion. This tough old warrior, close to Mao since Yenan days, had leaned toward the Cultural Revolution left. He was especially a protector of Chiang Ch'ing, whose marriage to Mao he persuaded skeptical colleagues to accept in 1939. When the Gang of Four truly needed him, K'ang was no longer there to help. The élite Peking security unit No. 8341, long controlled by K'ang, accepted Hua's orders and put the Gang of Four under arrest.* Death's timing had again helped Hua.

At the National Conference on Learning from Tachai, in October 1975, Hua gave an organization man's speech which took a middle line whenever it was possible to do so. The conference was designed to bring about a great spurt in agriculture, based on emulation of the once-poor but now-heroic Tachai Brigade, which had raised its income elevenfold between 1955 and 1974.

What Hua did, a bit unexpectedly, was to invoke the spirit of Tachai for fulfillment of Chou En-lai's vow to make China a front-rank modernized power before the year 2000.

Hua in his summing up offered something for everyone. He stressed the mechanization of agriculture, a favorite theme of Mao's. He insisted that strong local county organization, not mere spirit, would be needed for the task ahead— which is not the way the Gang of Four used to put things. He called for more research—which pleased the modernizers in Teng's camp. But in the next breath he said that communes and other low-level bodies should organize the research— which seemed like a bone tossed to the left. He took a middle

---

* Unit No. 8341 was now controlled by a rising star named Wang Tung-hsing, K'ang's successor in security work. Wang had long been Mao's aide and bodyguard. He had always been part of the left, but in the crucial weeks following Mao's death he threw in his lot with Hua. His reward was not long in coming. In 1977 he became very prominent in many spheres of policy and at the Eleventh Party Congress he was catapulted to fifth place in the regime. Much more is likely to be heard of Wang.

line on the heated issue of wage inequalities; they were re-
grettable but could not be done away with in a flash.

In a word, Hua took the balanced position between "spontaneity" and "regulation" which Mao then held against fire-
brands on the left and bureaucrats on the right. He showed
signs of the traits for which he had become known in
Hunan: a talent for problem-solving; an instinct for listening
to all sides of a question; a bent for organization; a plain
manner without a slogan on his lips all the time; and a certain opportunism which has kept him in touch with all the
right people.

By the end of 1975 Hua had a finger in many pies. He
seemed to be handling agricultural policy, but like all senior
figures in Peking he had diverse responsibilities. He headed
the delegation from Peking that descended on Lhasa to celebrate the tenth anniversary of Tibet's baptism as an Autonomous Region of the PRC. He was gaining clout in the
Politburo as he grew in the office of police chief. He seemed
to have made no large mistakes.

But he was not yet Spearhead of the Brilliant Kingdom. To
be worthy and rising is one thing; to be chief is another.
When Chou En-lai died in early 1976 very few people indeed,
inside China or outside, expected the burly Hunanese to take
his place. Yet 1976 became Hua's year of glory.

By October he had even succeeded Mao as chairman of the
CCP. Being named also head of the Military Affairs Commission, he became simultaneously head of army, Party, and
government. Mao himself had never held all three posts. No
figure in the CCP's history has ever come so far in a single
year as Hua did during 1976.

Hua's advantages had been mostly bland ones. Very few
shadows of past battles fell on him. The Cultural Revolution
had borne him up without putting him in the vulnerable

front line. He came out safely from the Lin Piao crisis. Mao found him loyal and trusted him.

Circumstances beyond his own role and merit also contributed to Hua's rise. Teng had too many enemies and overplayed his hand during 1975. The Gang of Four lost support—especially from political security and public security circles—and were also too unpopular among the masses to form a post-Mao government.

As the dust settled in late 1976, Hua enjoyed the goodwill of the overwhelming majority of the populace for having chopped down the Gang of Four. He was benefiting from the longing at high levels and low to keep things steady for a while. And he had a piece of paper with six characters in Mao's handwriting: "With you in charge I have no worries."

The authenticity of this document is not in doubt, though what it actually refers to is far from clear. Did Mao mean with Hua "in charge" of China's future, or merely of some particular current project? Mao scratched out those six characters on April 30, 1976, almost five months before he died, in the aftermath of Teng's second disgrace. Perhaps we may after all have a case—to paraphrase Pirandello—of "Six Characters in Search of a Meaning."

At any rate those characters have become six sturdy pillars for Hua's hoped-for legitimacy. By May Day 1977, visitors to China's parks came upon replicas of a giant new oil painting entitled *With You in Charge I Have No Worries*. It showed Mao and Hua sitting close together in heart-to-heart talk about affairs of state.

Hua's recent policies make sense in the light of his situation at the time he assumed office. His scrap of paper is a fragile mandate. Mao chose him; the CCP did not—let alone the Chinese people through their National People's Congress.

All this is out of line with both state and Party constitutions.

No wonder, then, that Hua has been cultivating his legitimacy. He has immodestly praised Mao's wisdom in "arranging personnel matters" before he died. So insistently is it stressed that Mao chose Hua that one cannot but ask: Are there people who doubt it? Hua has alleged (with little evidence) that the Gang of Four were bent on a *coup d'état*. Of course this enables him to present himself as China's savior from the Gang's clutches. But such justification would seem unnecessary if Hua felt truly secure.

On the other hand no sign of massive opposition to Hua exists. The year 1977 saw an anti-Hua poster here, a skeptical handbill there, but hardly a groundswell. The new chairman has taken care to please everyone some of the time and displease no one all of the time.

He has ushered the PLA to a central position at all events and in all policy areas. Old Marshal Yeh Chien-ying, the defense minister,* was given billing second only to Hua through 1976–77, until Teng came back in July 1977 to a prominence that made him seem Yeh's equal, although he was officially third in the regime.

The military were lavishly praised for their role in smashing the Gang of Four, and their discipline was pointed to as a model for the spirit and organization of industry. A call went out to the troubled railroads, for instance, "to build the ranks of the railwaymen into a semi-military army." This was an unusual touch for China, with its low-profile PLA.

With a certain peasant shrewdness—a trait that could possibly lift Hua above his troubles—the new chairman appeared at the rally in October 1976 celebrating the fall of the Gang of Four in the green fatigues and red star of the army. It was the first time in his career as a leader that Hua had

---

* In March 1978 Yeh gave up the defense ministry to Hsu Hsiang-ch'ien.

worn a PLA uniform—but far from the last.

The PLA, in turn, was handsome in its reciprocation. No sooner were the Gang in custody than the Peking Garrison swore allegiance to the new leader. In an extremely rare step, Peking widely publicized two editorials from the PLA newspaper in October and November of 1976. *Liberation Army Daily* is not available to foreigners; my efforts in China to buy a copy have always failed. But the New China News Agency distributed to the world the two editorials extolling Hua.

"Great revolutionary struggles produce great leaders," the paper declared in a tone more flat and blunt than we are used to from *People's Daily*. Hua is "loyal to the Party and selfless, open and straightforward, modest and prudent."

Liberation Army Daily went on to offer an astounding theory of leadership. "The masses are divided into classes," it declared in no-nonsense style; "classes are usually led by political parties. Political parties, as a rule, are directed by more or less stable groups composed of the most authoritative, influential and experienced members, who are elected to the most important positions and are called leaders."

It is like coming upon a page from an engineering manual in the middle of a romantic novel. So much for "To rebel is justified." So much for the Cultural Revolution. So much for youth and turmoil and revolutionary initiative.

In its frank concern for good old-fashioned authority, *Liberation Army Daily* went even further. "Love for our Party, our state, our army and our people finds concentrated expression in love for our leader," it declared. The words are well worth noting. If China were not so different from Germany, one might take them as the first rustle of Fuhrerism.

At any rate by November a love affair between Hua and the PLA was in full swing. The two sides had come to terms back in mid-1976. This had sealed the fate of the Gang of Four. It was indeed wise and necessary for Hua to make a deal with the military, who offered all the things that he himself lacked. The Gang of Four lost out because they did not—or could not—make a similar deal.

For the PLA, praising Hua to the skies was a very practical way of making sure that their civilian man-at-the-top possesses enough authority to deliver what goods they want from him. The PLA has also moved into a supervisory role in the provinces—such as Fukien, just opposite Taiwan—where cleaning up the debris of the Gang proved especially difficult. A very practical way, this, to guard against any new outbreak of that "anarchism" which the military so hates.

It is possible that the PLA leadership is at least as powerful as Hua, now that it is free of the scourge of the Gang. In her indiscreet interviews with the American scholar Roxane Witke, Chiang Ch'ing made a pregnant reference to the former Chief of the General Staff, Lo Jui-ch'ing (purged at the start of the Cultural Revolution). Lo had been a bête noire of the extreme left. Chiang Ch'ing recalls that when she discovered that Lo was opposing her Cultural Revolution activities, she telephoned him to object. She found his attitude to be: "Anything the army did was fine." She hurled back at him a question: "Is the PLA living in a vacuum?" Both quotes are full of meaning for China's future—and the extreme left is no longer there to fire potshots at the military.

Hua has also offered balm for the multiple wounds of the veteran cadres. "Patriots above suspicion," the French writer Alain Jacob has aptly called these Party elders, "but who have inevitably 'settled down' in a régime they consider an end in itself." They are the old Communists who really made the Chinese Revolution, but their path has been strewn with rocks for much of the time since the outbreak of the Cultural Revolution. They were made giddy by Mao's abrupt changes of course; intimidated by the Gang of Four's blood-curdling shouts. They feel wronged. Some of them have almost decided that timidity is the best policy.

Hua's first big gesture to these veterans was the campaign to glorify Chou En-lai in the spring of 1977. The press erupted with articles belatedly lauding the dead premier. During the spring of 1977 Hua referred to Chou's 1975 blueprint for the modernization of China as "that magnificent plan." He gave important tasks to Chou's widow, Teng Ying-ch'ao, including jazzy trips to Burma and Sri Lanka, although Ms. Teng is only vice chairman of the fairly toothless parliament.

In May 1977, Hua answered point by point most (but not quite all) of the criticisms that the Gang of Four had made of the veteran cadres. Are they relics of the "soft" period of New Democracy, before the real man's work of socialist construction began? Hua said—and the point justified also his own late arrival in the ranks of the Party—that no matter what era cadres date from, "they are valuable." Did the veteran cadres make errors in the Cultural Revolution? Yes, many of them did. But Hua added: "Facts show that this body of Party cadres is indestructible and that they have proved to be an insurmountable barrier for the Gang of Four."

At the same time Hua made gestures to the left. It was not clear at the end of 1977 whether followers of the Gang of Four were still a force to be reckoned with. The PLA seemed to think so. It urged—with incredible overkill in its choice of terms—an "all-out people's war" against the remaining sympathizers of the Gang.

Yet on balance it seems that the remnants of the left are few and weak. Before the Eleventh Party Congress in August 1977 this was probably not true, but at that meeting a sharply new Central Committee was elected to lead the CCP.

No fewer than 46 percent of its members were fresh faces; those whom they replaced were in many cases sympathizers with the Gang of Four.

Meanwhile, those top leaders who were associated with the Gang—Wu Te, mayor of Peking, and Li Te-sheng, the military commander in Shenyang, among others—have apparently accepted realities and dropped their earlier leftist positions.

At the same time the *ideas* of the left have a life of their own which is not to be despised. Nor should Hua's own past sympathy for leftist positions be entirely forgotten. True, Hua has trimmed his sails before the winds of pragmatism. But he was pro-left in the Great Leap Forward and the Cultural Revolution. He continues to salute the Cultural Revolution, long after some of his top colleagues have lost the appetite for doing so. He has declared that it is over but he still praises it fulsomely. Anything good he calls a fruit of the Cultural Revolution.

Indeed he declared in mid-1977: "The smashing of the Gang of Four by our Party is . . . another great victory in the Great Proletarian Cultural Revolution." If the fall of Chiang Ch'ing is a fruit of the Cultural Revolution, are not the air and the clouds so too? Still, it is a significant part of Hua's balancing act that he has refrained from attacking the Cultural Revolution.

Hua has made a point of courting out-of-power foreign Communist parties and liberation organizations. He has met far more of these fiery pilgrims than Mao or Chou ever did, and top billing is given to such occasions, even above Hua's meetings with foreign government leaders. So Hua's talk with E. F. Hill, leader of an Australian pro-Chinese group whose entire membership could fit comfortably onto a tennis court, was reported more prominently than his talk, the same

week in December 1976, with a Tanzanian delegation led by
Vice President Jumbe and including the foreign minister and
three other ministers. Numerous are such cases of Hua's
predilection for foreign "300-per centers." It is all part of his
balancing act.

Hua's chances of being a strong chairman into the 1980s
rest on three main challenges. His attempts to meet them
will carry the solid Hunanese into new areas, where his relative obscurity will no longer be an asset.

First, Hua must *build up a constituency*. The military and
the veteran cadres are basic entities, as we have seen, and so
are the leading regions. In addition there is apparently a remnant of the Cultural Revolution left which Hua wants to keep
on board rather than toss to the sharks of history. He may
have to make some tough choices among these constitu-
encies.

Second, Hua must also *negotiate his legitimacy problem*.
This is worth dwelling upon. Hua's policy so far has simply
been to present himself as Mao's chosen man. All over China
today, two portraits hang side by side whenever a nod to the
state is called for: Mao's and Hua's.

But this means that Hua is tied to the future fate of Mao's
image. If Mao comes under criticism, however marginal, it
could include criticism of his choice of Hua. Especially so
because, in choosing Hua, Mao did not work through regular
constitutional channels.

Hua has also tried to shore up his legitimacy by raking up
a doctrine of his own. In this he carries on a tradition as old
as Chinese history. A new emperor needed a "word" if he was
to be successful. Both Liu Shao-ch'i and Lin Piao built up a
body of writings. Yet, if the "word" of Liu and Lin was puny
by comparison with Mao's, Hua's is puny even by comparison

with Liu's and Lin's. Hua has been a man of organization rather than of theory or poetry.

In Hunan, Hua was a self-effacing fellow; he often did not publish, or even sign, the pedestrian articles he wrote. Still, pieces he wrote on rural topics in Hunan have now been dug up and touched up.

When Volume V of Mao's *Selected Works* came out in April 1977, Hua wrote an essay of commentary on the book. This 14,000-word piece is a classic of fence-sitting, and it is rather dull. But it is Hua's own. A quotation from the essay appeared in a box in *People's Daily,* just as Mao's quotes did and do—except that Mao's are always at the top of page 1 while Hua's was on page 2.*

Soon there will be enough copy for a Hua volume. There are risks in the supreme leader committing himself to paper in this way, since it forces him to take a position on tangled issues that are still unfolding; but it is an absolute necessity in China that he do so.

Legitimacy is a question, too, of meritorious deeds. Here the fifty-seven-year-old Hua has a headache. He has few meritorious deeds—and none of the dimension to capture the imagination of the man and woman in the street. The Long March? The birth of New China's style and fellowship in Yenan? Hua was a farmboy through it all.

In April 1976 a poster written by a veteran and signed by the "United Action Committee" went up without authorization in Peking. This underground committee was clearly disgruntled about a number of matters. One riposte in particular packed a certain punch: "Hua Kuo-feng! When I was fight-

---

* By late 1977 Hua's quotes were regularly appearing in a box at the top of page one of *People's Daily,* but in early 1978 the trend was to fill the box with an array of material, including Hua's quotes, Mao's quotes, quotes of other leaders (including Teng), and news items.

ing in the south and the north, you were still playing and your nose was running." Nor did Hua take part in the tit-for-tat struggle against Moscow in the 1960s. He was still in Hunan during those argumentative years.

If Hua cannot be called a hero, he can be portrayed as cozy and upright. This is what his staff aimed at during the Year of the Snake. A picture was found of him in the fields of Hunan, clad in a huge farmer's hat, caring for rice seedlings (photo on page 86). A story described him going off dutifully—not in a car but on foot—to a parents' meeting at his daughter's primary school. A man without guile and without airs.

By mid-1977 an appropriate word had been found for the new supreme leader. The choice raised him above every other living leader, but kept him modestly a niche below the dead giants. He was to be invariably called "wise." To keep a proper perspective, Mao was styled "great," and Chou "beloved." But it seemed reassuring—and it did not exclude future brilliant development—that the Forbidden City was now headed by "wise" Hua Kuo-feng.

Chinese politics has an all-or-nothing tendency. "When the lead rope is raised," an old saying goes, "the fish net opens wide." The lead rope can be an idea. In early 1976 it was "class struggle" and the slogan was: "Take class struggle as the key link." Everything else followed from that. The net did indeed open wide; it caught just about anyone the Gang of Four wanted to catch.

The lead rope can also be a person. In the Year of the Snake it was Hua. All of China became a mirror for this one man's will. Hua was built up beyond life size. The political line boiled down to a simple call to obedience: Hua is a good leader, he must be followed. And the slogan was frank: "Bring about great order across the land."

A man of the soil? Hua Kuo-feng helps farmers transplant rice seedlings in Hunan Province in 1970. (*New China News Agency Photo*)

Back in 1966 Mao pointed out the brittleness in such a system. "A tall thing is easy to break," he wrote (quoting a statesman of the Han Dynasty) in a letter to his wife Chiang Ch'ing; "a white thing is easy to stain. The white snow in spring can hardly find its match; a high reputation is difficult to live up to." Much easier to break the tall thing, too, if its loftiness is an artificial construction rather than a grown organism.

In a word, Hua cannot replace Mao. If he really tries to do so—and the cult around him suggests the possibility of an attempt—he will find that Mao's warning applied to him far more than it did to the great Mao himself. He will break easier; he will be easier to stain.

Hua's third challenge is *to harvest fairly quick policy results*.

It would be a feather in his cap if he could resolve the issue of Taiwan (dealt with in Chapter 10), but he will find it difficult. This is an intractable problem in itself, and Hua does not have either the experience in foreign affairs, or the authority within his own land, that are needed for bold international initiatives.

Two other policy tests will be decisive. The Chinese people want and deserve a hike in their standard of living. Industrial trouble in Chekiang and other provinces during 1975 warned that the elevation of "revolution" over "production" does not please the people. Yet Hua has little choice but to please them. It is clear from 1977's big drive on economic tasks that he knows economic results must be offered soon. No fewer than forty national conferences on economic topics were held in the year following the fall of the Gang of Four. It is not yet clear whether he can deliver the goods before the grumbling turns into disaffection.

Hua will also have to satisfy the desire in China for the rule of law. Here he is in a tricky spot because his own occupancy of the CCP chairmanship came about by *disregard* of law. Yet the very irony of his position may make Hua sensitive to the issue. At any rate the desire for legitimacy is mounting.

Caustic unofficial wall posters in many provinces reveal it: "Abide No Dictatorship Exercised Over the People," and: "No Excuse Can Be Given for Strangling Democracy."

During 1977 two senior officials also quietly raised the issue of the rule of law within Party meetings. A document out of Canton—almost certainly authentic—found the city's two top men, General Hsu Shih-yu and Party chief Wei Kuo-ch'ing, airing disquiet at the irregular way in which Hua was promoted.

Their low-key words carry devastating overtones: "Comrade Hua Kuo-feng assumed the posts of Party Chairman and Chairman of the Military Council without a convening of the National People's Congress," they apparently wrote in a letter to Peking, "without even a convening of a plenary meeting of the Party Central Committee. That was only an expedient." That Hua was later ratified as leader by the Eleventh Party Congress does not remove the discomfort of the points made by the Canton pair.

Hua shows some sensitivity to the existence of a rising public opinion. But he has taken no institutional steps to make the views of the people an ongoing input into policy-making. It is one thing to give more duties and visibility to the National People's Congress, as he has done, and to include the long-slighted Supreme Court judges in occasions of state, as he has also done. It is quite another to give sway to public opinion. The CCP is used to leading the people—less used to listening to the people. It will be very difficult, even for Hua's generation, to think of the people as individuals with expressed desires, rather than as masses whose assumed needs are crystal clear to the all-knowing cadres. Maybe it will be impossible. Yet I think Peking will have to move in the direction of democracy of some kind (certainly it will not be the Western kind).

Some signs are not promising. In November 1976, travelers saw an official notice in the city of Changsha which announced the execution of a man for defacing a wall poster that had proclaimed Hua's appointment as chairman of the CCP. Does Hua really feel so insecure?

Hua's arrival at the top mirrors certain traits of China in the late 1970s. If he is dull and cozy, that signifies the end of the Age of Heroes. No one will or should replace Mao. Now that the revolution has been made, another bold maker would be as out of place as a sculptor on an assembly line.

If Hua's first big act was to deal with the Gang of Four, that is a reminder that the Cultural Revolution is finally over, that it did not win most of its goals, and probably could not have done so.

And finally, if Hua seems engaged in a balancing act, this is a true reflection of the new sophistication in Chinese politics. Ideology gives way a little to sociology. Ringing generalities mean a bit less and the pull and tug of increasingly assertive groups, regions, interests a bit more. Hua's government will need to keep its eye on the people.

At any rate Hua at least grew in confidence during the Year of the Snake. Back in September 1976, when he received James R. Schlesinger, the American group noticed something highly unusual in a conversation with a foreign leader. In his neat, square Chinese characters, Hua was taking voluminous notes! A year later he had thrown off this solid old habit; in sessions with foreigners the note-taking was now done by aides.

6

The
🦎 Legacy of Mao 🦎

During the Year of the Dragon, Mao Tse-tung was like an arrow near the end of its flight. If his role in the 1976 crisis is not a wholly admirable one, that hardly reverses the verdict that Mao was a brilliant leader who gave China a new start.

The arrow had come a long way. Mao was born under the Manchu Dynasty and his first task was to analyze the half-feudal and half-colonial world around him. He did in China what Marx had done in Europe: found the concepts to call the bluff on an obsolete social order.

He grew to adulthood amidst warlordism and his second task was to organize a new political movement that could win power and bind China's fragments into a nation. As a maker of revolution he was China's Lenin.

When victory came he was still there to face the socialist future, exchanging the gun for the mimeographing machine. He became the builder of New China as Stalin had been the builder of Soviet Russia.

Such a span gave Mao an influence on Chinese history which few emperors ever had. But being the Marx-Lenin-

Stalin rolled into one of the Chinese Revolution also posed some acute challenges, which Mao could not in every case surmount. For these the Year of the Dragon was a time of reckoning.

What Mao did achieve before he began to falter was mighty enough. He arrived at a version of Marxism adapted to the traditions and peasant reality of China, thus steering clear of the peril of echoing Moscow. He tapped patriotic feeling—in the face of European imperialist assault and especially Japanese aggression—for the cause not only of national defense but of social transformation. He led China to a new dignity in the world and this made even non-Communist Chinese feel proud.

He brought innovations to the building of a Marxist society which made the PRC seem a more hopeful place than the Soviet Union: a periodic shakeup from below for bureaucrats; as much stress on the ethics of socialism as on the administration of socialism; an agriculture which develops its own new vigorous forms and is not treated as industry's ugly sister.

Starting with the Great Leap Forward of 1958–59, Mao became a man of doubts. He wanted a quicker march toward communism; he wanted a more ardent spirit of socialist citizenship. He refused to believe that China had made a revolution only to produce a replica of Russia's gray regimentation.

By the time of the Cultural Revolution, Mao had become quizzical about the state of China's socialism to the point of eccentricity. Youth seemed to him soft and memoryless, and rules and regulations a mixed blessing. Intellectuals were hankering for the bad old past of privilege and art for art's sake. The Communist Party itself—to Mao's jaundiced eye— had ceased to be the sure citadel of Chinese revolutionary values and was full of "revisionists" and even "capitalist roaders." As for the world outside China, Mao had apparently lost his vision of socialism as an international movement.

All this led directly to the events of the Year of the Dragon.

Mao had just entered his eighty-third year as Chou En-lai died and the year of horrors began. He was ill with Parkinson's Disease and could no longer do a full day's (or rather night's) work. His speech was not clear, he looked stiff and drawn, his eyes stared into the distance with resignation.

Very few of Mao's old comrades remained. Chu Te still had six months to live. At a less intimate level there was Yeh Chien-ying. Most of the rest were either dead or had been removed from office as Mao grew dissatisfied with them. The old survivor must have felt sad at the loss of comrades—and of comradeship—along the way. For three years, too, he had been living separately from Chiang Ch'ing.

When Chou En-lai was on the point of death, Mao drove to Capital Hospital in Peking to sit at his bed side. He was the last person apart from medical workers to talk with Chou. Pathos showed through the emotion of this visit. Mao had rarely made such gestures toward colleagues. There must have been pangs of loneliness—and perhaps of remorse for past coldness—as he sat with the dying Chou.

In place of colleagues Mao had courtiers. Access to him and obtaining his apparent approval were still crucial, even though the basis for his judgments became ever flimsier. Inevitably, contenders for the succession pushed their own groups of courtiers into Mao's entourage whenever possible. As so often with the oncoming of death of a political titan, affairs of the great man's family became entwined with affairs of state. Mao's wife, nephew, and niece all swirled in and out of the revolving door that was the Mao court during 1976.

Peking did not try to hide Mao's decline from China or from the world. This was wise, even though it could not take away the strain of the situation. He met half a dozen foreign leaders between January and May. Chinese TV reported these frail, brief appearances, and no one could fail to conclude that Mao would soon die.

The last three foreign visitors to go to his book-lined study were the prime ministers of New Zealand, Singapore, and Pakistan. They found him barely able to conduct a quarter hour of conversation. In mid-June it was announced that the chairman would receive no more foreigners.

Yet Mao was still arbiter of the affairs of 900 million people, and his presence dominated the Year of the Dragon. He struck down Teng; he chose Hua from the pack; and he retained some kind of veto against any action to get rid of the Gang of Four.

All this kept a left-wing breeze alive. It gave a provisional look to everything that was decided. The fact that Mao was dying also served to make the Tangshan earthquake even more depressing than it would anyway have been.

An enfeebled Mao outliving Chou made the vacuum of power colossal. Everything would have been different had the deaths of Mao and Chou been reversed. Teng would not have been purged. It would not have fallen to Mao single-handedly to choose Chou's successor as premier. And Hua might have remained obscure to this day.

Indeed the whole polarization between Teng and the Gang of Four might not have taken place. The Gang would never have been able to aim so high; nor would they—or the better half of them—have fallen so low.

Mao's mere presence, then, was crucial. His conscious aims are less easy to fathom. Was the crisis of the Year of the

Dragon Mao's last great drive for something important to China's future? And was the Year of the Snake kind or harsh toward Mao's legacy?

In some ways Mao himself contributed to the troubles of 1976. The first we can hardly blame him for: the Great Helmsman could not let go of power except by dying, since the system does not lend itself to either resignation or retirement.

But there was a major problem—far more than with, say, Winston Churchill or Franklin Roosevelt—of capacity shrinking before power did. Mao remained at the helm during a year of intrinsic difficulties after he had lost the strength to be helmsman. Hovering between life and death, he was a mixed blessing for China. Courtiers and family members were elevated above their proper roles. The succession issue turned into a matter of biology, rather than of ordered political decision. The whole nation lived under a cloud of uncertainty that could be lifted only by an act of God. Too many realms of policy were left in confusion, because Mao's shadow, but not his controlling hand, still touched them.

A second major problem was that Mao's notion of revolution was by 1976 out of kilter with the times. True, Mao's ideas on the subject of "continuing the revolution" had enriched Marxism. Under him China had avoided complacency and kept bureaucracy at bay by periodic self-examination. But history does not stop still while yesterday's vision struggles to realize itself. *The people had changed.*

Mao was like a preacher addressing an audience that has moved to another hall. The vision was out of date—in part because it had already brought forth its children, and they had their own fresh visions. He talked of the need to curtail "bourgeois rights," but for many Chinese this merely meant a denial of rewards for skilled or extra work. He spoke of tracking down "capitalist roaders" within the CCP, but it is doubtful that any exist.

A strongly subjectivist streak ran through Mao's Marxism. He assigned a central role to the conscious will of man. He never believed—as perhaps Liu Shao-ch'i did—that socialism would come by an even and inevitable historical process. And Mao liked to operate in direct contact with the masses. He said that of all his roles the one he enjoyed best was that of teacher. It is true that he was a brilliant organizer as a young man. But the older Mao had little patience with the labyrinth of organizations which, of necessity in a nation of 900 million people, stood between himself and the masses.

Mao's subjectivism—based on his stress upon will and his impatience with structures—did not diminish as he grew old. During the mid-1960s his pessimism about the future of the Chinese Revolution may not have been justified; certainly it was not shared by most of his top colleagues. He launched the Cultural Revolution over the opposition of some, and in the face of the incomprehension of most of them.

Mao wanted renewal through heroic acts. He wanted a deeper moral community. Although the Cultural Revolution did not achieve these aims, Mao never repudiated it. It remained the touchstone of political rectitude in China until his death. Even since, as we have seen, Hua has paid lip service to the idea that the Cultural Revolution was the watershed between darkness and light.

Teng sabotaged the shimmering myth of the Cultural Revolution. It was not only that he did not like the Cultural Revolution or most of its policy fruits. His very presence in the leadership seemed an affront to the aims of a crusade that had a decade earlier named Teng its second most important target. His efforts to press ahead with urgent tasks of devel-

opment in 1975 brought him up against the young but hallowed traditions of the Cultural Revolution.

Teng was Mao's nemesis because he did not forsake his
convictions when brought back from the pit in 1973. He had
not reformed himself. His deviant past excused by Mao, one
might have expected him to become bound more loyally than
ever to Mao's service. But to fall out of line *again* was very
damaging to the system.

It seemed both to call into question Mao's judgment and to
make a mockery of "reforming oneself." For the first time in
a long and magnificent career, Mao looked absurd. His subjectivism had reached a new height of eccentricity. Was
Teng, after all, a Marxist or was he a capitalist? The Chinese
people surely had a right to know this of one of their top
leaders.

The trouble was that Mao was stretching class analysis
beyond its limits. This was his crowning contribution to the
1976 crisis, and it was linked with the others. He was still the
demigod who held sway over his realm. He was committed to
"continuing the revolution"—the hallmark of his difference
from the despised Soviets. But he interpreted as "class
struggle" any conflict that frustrated him, which was as inapt
as using a sledgehammer on a flea.

More tragic, it went against Mao's own theory of contradictions. He seemed to forget his own famous distinction between non-antagonistic contradictions (those among the co-
workers for revolution) and "antagonistic contradictions"
(those between class enemies). He suddenly declared that the
"Teng problem" was of the latter kind. This may have been
the biggest blunder of Mao's life. With shocking indulgence
he reached back to the pristine past for a black-and-white
concept that was garish amid the gray shades of the present.
What had once been a first-hand social analysis was now
mere political invective.

To explain this we must recall Mao's early life. Class was not a deeply emotional issue for young Mao. He had few personal confrontations with landlords, and he did not straightaway latch on to the peasantry as the base for China's revolution. He turned first to the urban workers, as Marxist ideology suggested he should, and even to urban merchants. Only much later, when these bases had proved inadequate, did he gravitate back to the peasants as the revolutionary class.

The point is that Mao made a practical search for an effective class basis for his future political-military struggle. For him the issue of class was an *instrumental* rather than a gut issue. It was this that made it possible for him to manipulate class analysis late in his life—to wrench it from its moorings in actual economic facts and to toss it around as mere polemic.

If Mao contributed to the crisis of the Year of the Dragon, there were also ways in which his legacy helped to modify it. His sheer prestige was (and is) the focal point of the PRC's unity. As few monarchs have ever done, Mao held his people together in pride at what had been achieved under him as leader. Moreover, it was less "Mao" than "Mao's Thought" that was made the fount of truth. This reduced the danger and loss of his death; the Thought, however elastic, gave continuity.

The Chinese public were used to political conflict, because Mao had taught them to regard struggle as healthy, and as a continuing feature of the road to communism. There was no panic. People did not mistake conflict for a breakdown of the system.

Mao's insistence on remolding the wrongdoer had its advantages. Mistaken as the reasons for the re-purge of Teng were, Maoist doctrine allows for any number of purges and reentries. Teng could come back; he was alive, after all, if in disgrace (in Stalin's Russia he would have been dead as well as purged). The resolution dismissing him from office had contained the Maoist rider that he could remain a Party member "so as to see how he will behave in the future." And who knows whether two purges may not have purified and streamlined the man?

At best, however, the Mao legacy complicated the tasks before Hua, Yeh, and Teng as the Year of the Snake wore on. In the early 1960s Mao had revived talk of a struggle against the bourgeoisie; this laid the groundwork for the Cultural Revolution. He spoke of the Cultural Revolution as nothing less than a second revolution. The enemy was no less real, he insisted, than before Liberation; the stakes no less high. Thus Mao made a tremendous ideological investment in the validity and success of the Cultural Revolution. The result was a buffeting for his ideological credibility.

One bad investment led to a second. The twists and turns of the Cultural Revolution had to be explained in retrospect. It happened that not all the evils that sprang out of the woodwork were due to the machinations of capitalists. There were at least two other kinds. One was factionalism pure and simple. Another was the "ultra-leftism" of those who wanted to achieve full communism overnight.

From 1967 onward, ultra-leftism had lost out badly. For several years it was the key target of ideological criticism in China. I found this to be true on a visit during the summer of 1971, and the tension came to a peak when Lin Piao made his bid for power later that year. But two years later, in an explanation of the Lin crisis, a magic wand was passed over ultra-leftism and it now was reborn as "ultra-rightism." This was a second big step toward the ideological crisis of 1976.*

---

* See the dissident puzzlement over quick policy changes in Appendix 6.

In 1976 Mao fiddled once too often with ideological labels. The nature of his grievance against Teng we cannot be sure of. Maybe he did think that Teng had made a philosophic switch back to the right. Maybe a single act of Teng's—perhaps releasing the Russian helicopter crew—annoyed him. Maybe it was once again Teng's style that was unacceptable. Whatever it was, to characterize Teng as a "capitalist roader" was a disaster; Mao was shooting at phantoms.

What China needs now is a drastic pruning of the scope of the term "rightism," and a clear definition of what is leftist. Organizational issues should not be painted over as class struggles. Intra-Party struggles should be handled by fixed procedures, rather than by midnight fiat followed by months of mythology. All of which must mean a degree of de-Maoization.

Mao's legacy on the question of the PLA's role in politics was a sound one, but it will not be easy for Hua to live up to. Mao was superb at controlling the military. He always put military questions within a political context (it was one big reason why he beat the glorified warlord Chiang Kai-shek).

True, on one occasion Mao gave to the PLA a larger political role than his principles appeared to permit by calling in soldiers to restore law and order when the Cultural Revolution spiraled into factionalism. Yet in the end Mao was able to restore civilian control. Lin Piao was beaten, and the soldiers went back to the barracks.

Throughout the first half of 1976 Mao kept the PLA in its place. He allowed the Gang of Four to help him do this. But the tide ran the other way during the second half of the year and Mao was too tired to resist it. Indeed his support for the Gang indirectly helped the PLA to come into its own politically. For the Gang got above themselves. Hua could only get rid of them with the PLA's aid.

The freshly built Mao Memorial
Hall in the Square of the Gate of
Heavenly Peace, Peking, May
1977. (*New China News Agency
Photo*)

In fact the opposite of what Mao probably wanted came
about. He would not have purged the Gang. He would not
have called the PLA to the summit of political power. The
Year of the Dragon ended on as un-Maoist a note as it had
begun on a Maoist one. At the same time Mao's enduring
prestige will probably veto any future overt militarization of
China's political system.

Mao's absence will be important for the future of China's
military budget. He held a striking view of defense preparedness. "Do you genuinely want atom bombs?" he asked in his
famous speech on "The Ten Great Relationships" in 1956.
"Then you must reduce military and administrative expenses
and increase expenditure for economic construction."

It is a far-seeing line of approach, and probably the correct one for China. Yet it is unlikely to be shared by all professional soldiers. Hua, Yeh, and Teng will have to fight this one out between them. Hua will seek to uphold the view of Mao; Yeh and Teng will be less inclined to do so.

In the realm of economic development, Mao sought a modernized China, but of a particular type. His vision was of a rich and strong nation—not so much of a bigger pay packet and more gadgets for Chinese individuals. He may even have suspected that a higher standard of living would lead to a slackening of revolutionary values.

In the spring of 1977 a huge Mao Memorial arose, like

some giant mushroom after a cloudburst, to dominate the southern expanse of the Square of the Gate of Heavenly Peace, and house the crystal box in which Mao lies. No effort or expense was spared. Work on the structure of semi-Chinese style went on all night and the whole job was done in a mere eight months. Machines wheeled and whirred; specialists arrived from all over the nation to ensure the best of everything. A meeting could not convene in Peking but that its delegates would, for a few hours, put down their documents and hammer in a nail or two to signify their participation in the most hallowed activity of the season.

Hardly a stone's throw from the square was a humbler scene. Here too building was going on, but without floodlights, electric drills, architects, premier materials, and VIP visits. The people of Peking were knocking together makeshift shelters in case of further earthquakes. Their earthmoving equipment consisted of shovels and buckets and their own muscle power in the hours after daily work. Few materials were available to them; they made a people's concrete of mud and trash and hoped it would hold.

The contrast was arresting. Of course Mao was a very great man; furthermore the Chinese people can endure much and they do not expect the moon. Yet China is a land where a mighty revolution came to sweep away all feudal awe, to demystify politics and make the happiness of working people the true goal of politics, and to replace China's age-old gulf between rulers and ruled with a people's government.

Whether or not the outside observer is disturbed, something is changing within China. Whether or not the Chinese people are struck by the symbolic contrast between the Mao Memorial's magnificence and their own gray frugality, the expectations of most of the people are rising. The question of standard of living is urgently in the air. People want results, after all the rhetoric and hoopla. Results that are less ethereal than the delights of struggle, that can be measured in the quality of daily life.

Confucius stood in the way of China's early twentieth-century progress. There may be Chinese who think that Mao came to stand in the way of China's late twentieth-century progress—and for the same reason. A collective moral ideology is very nice, but you cannot eat it, wear it, or repel invaders with it.

From his student days Mao was a believer in youth's crucial contribution to China's future. He always saluted youth's spirit of rebellion. Yet by the 1960s he had some pessimistic thoughts about Chinese young people. In a way he remained a rebel while new generations ceased to be so.

The youth of the PRC could hardly rebel as Mao's generation had done. Except during the Cultural Revolution, when rebellion was demanded from above, Mao's government would not have welcomed opposition to the status quo. And what youth *did* want, Mao had become indifferent to. Mao from the 1960s onward was skeptical of the value of formal higher education. Yet the young people themselves felt that good schooling was the key to a bright future.

Mao made repeated statements belittling college. "In the Ming Dynasty there were only two good emperors," he remarked to a meeting in 1964, "T'ai-tsu and Ch'eng-tsu—one of whom was illiterate and the other semiliterate. Later, in the Chia-ching reign (1522–66) intellectuals took power and the country became misgoverned." Again, he pointed to the lack of credentials of great foreigners: "Gorky was at school for only two years; he taught himself. Franklin of America was a newspaper boy. Watt, the discoverer of steam power, was a working man." All this did not boost the morale of teachers and students. Old Mao seemed to be going against the tide of youth's keenest aspirations.

Meanwhile he had developed a taste for misty speculation that did not move a secular and technically minded youth. Talking with a niece of his who was a student, Mao suddenly rebuked her for not having read the Holy Bible and the Buddhist sutras. Mao wanted his niece to have a questing mind; she seemed more interested in useful knowledge for a smooth career.

It is not surprising that Teng, rather than Mao, appealed to the tastes of ambitious youth during the 1970s. When the crunch came in the spring of 1976, Mao had misjudged public opinion. As we have seen, some of the poems, speeches, and inscriptions at the April demonstration mocked Mao as a latter-day Ch'in Shih Huang. For China's youth, Mao's passing removed a theoretical champion yet an actual dead hand.

Mao was ambivalent about the tug between Peking and the regions. He had grown up in the south, and found the north at first inhospitable. He disliked Peking as the seat of the arrogant imperial bureaucracy which had for centuries oppressed the Chinese people. Yet in the 1950s Mao became something of a "Peking man" despite himself. He liked People's Peking to be shown the awe that Imperial Peking had commanded.

By the 1960s Mao had mixed feelings. He had always hated the cold northern winters; now he sensed a cold northern socialist bureaucracy as well. He spent more and more time outside Peking. When he was ready to launch the Cultural Revolution, he found the capital a rock impossible to move. Only in Shanghai did he receive the cooperation necessary to pull the trigger and fire that battle's first shots. And the Cultural Revolution did, in fact, usher in a state of decentralization in many policy spheres.

In purging Teng, Mao felt he was getting rid of an over-centralizer. Teng wanted the economic ministries in Peking to carry out detailed planning for the whole nation; Mao objected that this quashed "initiative from below." On the other hand Mao was quick to oppose any bid for regional autonomy by military commanders. In this respect he may have been more of a centralizer than Teng.

Under Hua, Yeh, and Teng, a centralizing tendency has appeared in economic work. Yet a sharply decentralized situation exists in the relation of some military commanders to Peking. This is pretty much the opposite of what Mao favored.

In foreign affairs 1977 saw Hua faithful to Mao's vision of the world. From his teens onward, Mao felt deeply about China's sufferings at the hand of imperialists. No one in the CCP leadership would have been less likely than he to give up imperialism as the framework for analyzing the world scene.

It is fair to say that Mao's anti-imperialism was China-oriented rather than oriented to a bloc of socialist nations. He was never one for summit meetings of Marxist leaders. By the same token, China's anti-imperialism was for Mao a springboard to China's national revival.

China's current ambivalent status—as a Third World land yet also a world power—was therefore deeply rooted within Mao's own mind. He felt passionate about race discrimination wherever it occurred. He also felt pride in China's status as a nuclear power.

Mao died when Peking's foreign policy was at a crossroads (I will take up this theme again in Chapter 8). For the time being it is Hua, Yeh, and Teng who must weave their way through the current ambiguities. It hardly seems likely that any of them could be more nationalistic than Mao. Toward Russia, Hua—but maybe not the other two—is likely to maintain the rigid anti-imperialist framework. All of them will have to take economic factors more seriously in foreign policymaking than Mao tended to do. All in all Mao's foreign policy served China superbly; he left the scene just before the dilemmas of success arose.

Putting Mao into a crystal box did not dispose of him. Anyone who thought it would must have been surprised by the sequence of events in October 1976. Two days after the arrest of the Gang of Four, the pruned Politburo came out with its first post-Gang decisions. Foreign policy? Economic development? Balm for the bruised realm of culture? By no means. The first announcements were about the Mao Memorial and the preparation of the new volume of Mao's *Selected Works* (text in Appendix 4).

It is not all that surprising. Three months before his death Mao asked some of the Politburo to come to his home.* "No one in the world is immortal," Mao apparently remarked. "Few live beyond seventy and as I am more than eighty, I should have died already." In a gloomy mood the chairman went on: "Are there not some among you who hoped I would go to see Marx sooner?" Hua hastily replied: "None." Mao exclaimed: "Really, no one? I don't believe it!"

Mao in his later years had become the inescapable central issue in Chinese politics. If Mao at eighty was a liability to China, Mao for most of his life was little short of the savior of China, so the issue was far from simple. His authority was still needed after September 1976. His reputation was still sky-high, too, among many of the Chinese people. But which Mao was needed?

The volatile nature of the Mao heritage is illustrated by the

---

* According to a document obtained by the reliable *Brilliant Daily*, a Chinese-language newspaper in Hong Kong.

strange career of Volume V of the *Selected Works*. For years
the book had been in preparation; none of the essays in it
date from later than 1957. Yet publication was a hot potato
that burned every hand that touched it (the eventual publication announcement is in Appendix 4). Lin Piao and the Gang
of Four (among others) suffered for trying to have a say in
editing this Bible of the philosopher-king.

To be sure, Hua's Mao-problem is smaller than Khrushchev's Stalin-problem. It is nearer in type, despite the vast
gulf of circumstance, to Stalin's Lenin-problem.

China does not seethe with anti-Mao feeling, as Russia did
with anti-Stalin feeling by the 1950s. Mao's sin, like Lenin's,
was not evil tyranny but mere obsolescence. It is not a question of attacking him, but of easing him out of the chairman's
office and up to the higher benches of sainthood. But this is
still a tricky business. Timing and nuance are everything.

The matter has to be handled on three different levels. The
first is the problem of the *gap in the political structure* which
the death of a demigod leaves. After Mao, the Politburo
will have to start almost from scratch in pursuing democracy in the leading organs of Party and state.

One danger is timidity: that Politburo members will continue to act and talk as if the portrait of Mao on the wall is
the man's real presence. Another is that they will put Hua in
Mao's place, which would be to treat a string like a rope.

In the second place, the *intellectual gap* left by Mao must
also be negotiated. It is not that China lacks good thinkers
who could have spoken up over recent years on the large
moral and theoretical issues of socialist life. Rather, sad to
say, many brilliant nonscientific thinkers felt inhibited from
doing so by Mao's presence. Intellectual renewal is needed in
China.

China could surely produce some novels that explore psy-

chological themes of life under socialism. Also a serious
Marxist explanation of the social bases of the emergence to
prominence and power of the Gang of Four. And discourses
on social policy that distinguish—in a more detailed way
than Mao's theory of antagonistic and non-antagonistic contradictions—misbehavior that is a class hangover from the
old society from misbehavior which has nothing to do with
class background.

Do any philosophers think Confucius had some good
points? What is the actual social character of Soviet society—
leaving aside Mao's mere epithet that it is "Fascist"? Has the
superstructure taken over from the base in Chinese Marxist
theory? The list of themes to be explored is endless.

Revision of work-style is the third challenge of political life
without Mao. The emerging technique (already touched
upon) is to cut his ideology into little pieces and then make a
selection for current needs.

Yeh Chien-ying is good at this. He has explained that
Hua's style of work is to be applauded and emulated because
it "carries on Chairman Mao's traditional style of work." The
key word here is "traditional," for Yeh cites examples all of
which are from the Mao of many years ago.

Mao "used to call several national conferences annually to
consult with responsible members of provinces, municipalities, autonomous regions and departments on important
Party and state affairs." In fact in the last years Mao did not
do this, as any Chinese knows. Yeh quietly concedes it by
giving examples only from the 1950s.

The same goes for Yeh's praise of Mao for touring the
country and making on-the-spot investigations before issuing
directives. Hua has been doing this. But his trips come almost as a shock, for since the Cultural Revolution the top
leadership (Mao above all) stayed holed up in Peking and sel-

dom went among the people in far-flung spots. The technique is a deft way of revising work style without letting Mao's image be too badly tarnished.

Mao's reputation is not going to be dismantled in China as Stalin's was in Russia after 1956. He will remain a giant for the Chinese, as Lenin has remained a giant for all Communists. But in its treatment of Mao Peking may change gears well before the year 2000.

Probably his Thought will ascend to the level of a general ethic—and thus influence policy less. Possibly he will be reassessed as a very great revolutionary who nevertheless did some things better than others—thus opening the way to a departure from the line of late-Mao.

Certainly the habit of quoting proof-texts from Mao has already begun to go out of fashion. "Using a quotation from Chairman Mao," ran one *People's Daily* criticism of a Gang of Four follower, "he gave a great air to the thesis of the Gang of Four, as if saying, 'Chairman Mao said this—who will dare to say No?' "

During 1977 the official press reported attacks on Mao in Chekiang and Fukien provinces. "We must resolutely put a check on statements and actions that are detrimental to the brilliant image of Chairman Mao," said a Hangchow newspaper in April. Any significant surge of criticism of Mao would of course be fatal to Hua, clutching his piece of paper with its six characters.

7
Fall
of the
🐉 Gang of Four 🐉

On October 6, 1976, the leaders of China, bereaved for less than four weeks by Mao's death, sat down to an evening meeting which turned into high drama. It was a sign of the tension and distrust that Hua had convened the meeting not in the government compound at South and Central Lake, where such meetings are usually held, but in the home of his ally, Defense Minister Yeh Chien-ying.

The Politburo was divided on a range of issues that ran all the way back to the Cultural Revolution. This time Mao's absence made a division dangerous as never before. Yet before the night was out the CCP was rent by the biggest split in its fifty-five-year history.

On one side were Hua, military heads such as Yeh, and pragmatists who had backed Teng Hsiao-p'ing against the left's hurricane six months before. On the other side were the leftist Gang of Four. (Of course some Politburo members also sat on the fence.)

The sixty-six-year-old Ms. Chiang Ch'ing was the Gang's standard bearer; the Shanghai ex-journalist Chang Ch'un-

Chiang Ch'ing before her fall, posing in her favorite orchid garden, Canton, 1972. (*Photo by Roxane Witke*)

ch'iao, sixty-four years old, its brain. There were also two lesser lights: Wang Hung-wen (then thirty-nine), the ex-cotton mill worker whom Mao had plucked for high office; and Yao Wen-yuan (forty-five), a pamphleteer with family links to Mao and a pen that kept unfailingly to the left.

Who had a blessing from Mao? This ultimate issue brought on the shabby sight of Chiang Ch'ing waving one piece of paper (which she had probably doctored) and Hua waving another (probably genuine) with a tape recording to back it up. Hua's piece of paper bore the six vital characters scratched out by an ailing Mao: "With you in charge I have no worries."

Seeing that time was against them, now that Mao's protecting hand was gone, the Gang of Four moved at this meeting to have its members appointed to (mostly vacant) high offices. They proposed Chiang Ch'ing for the Party chairmanship, Chang Ch'un-ch'iao as premier, and young Wang Hung-wen to be head of the National People's Congress. Earlier than expected the Gang was making a do-or-die bid for the succession.

They are now accused of a coup—although they probably only fired words around a table rather than bullets in the street, and their proposal to reshuffle jobs was not in itself unconstitutional, if the selections were to be ratified later by full Party and state meetings. They were arrested at Hua's order that same night and put behind bars in southwest Peking.

Never before had so many top CCP leaders fallen at one stroke. Never had there been such a breathtakingly sudden purge—nor one in such an extreme atmosphere of crisis, when the affairs of the Chinese state hung by a thread, and the moral force of Mao's Party by less than that.

Some of the details are not yet clear. Were the Gang, while caucusing with supporters in the Western Hills, rudely interrupted by the troops of the Peking security unit No. 8341? Were three leftists—including a nephew of Mao—killed and Wang Hung-wen wounded in the fracas? Had the Gang ordered shots fired at Hua's car the night before the meeting in Yeh's house? All this we cannot yet say. From what is known, it is a fine point of definition which side mounted a "coup." A dispute over jobs does not amount to a coup. The real issue is *who broke the rules*.

Both Hua and the Gang—if they were acting as a quartet, for which we have only Hua's word—put out their hands for supreme power. Neither could succeed without removing the other. Unless new facts come to light, proving that the Gang resorted to the gun, the conclusion must be that Hua acted first and won a battle of strength. He himself undoubtedly used force, judging that he could not become chairman without ending the Gang's political career. It looks like Hua's coup.

Of course had the Gang won the struggle of October 6, the coup would have been theirs. Neither side, that night in Yeh's house, had the right finally to rearrange high office. Only the Central Committee—composed of some three hundred people—can select a new Party chairman. Only the National People's Congress can select a new premier.

It was a night for disregarding the Constitution. It was a night when force came rapping at the door. Both sides, it seems, unnerved by Mao's loss, faced with an unprecedented power vacuum, tried to grab power. All one can say for Hua is that he won.

It was probably a good thing for China that he did. His victory is no doubt less unpopular than Chiang Ch'ing's would have been. But Hua is in no position to hang the charge of "coup" around Ms. Chiang's long stately neck.

All office was stripped from Chiang, Wang, Chang, and Yao. They left their homes, lost their staff, were denied a voice in the press, and cut off from their contacts all over China—in a word, purged.

The willful former actress who had wielded a big stick over China's long-suffering cultural life left the stage of politics, which she probably should never have mounted. Guilt by association, plus shared sympathy for the drumbeat of "uninterrupted revolution," dragged the three male Shanghai leaders down with her. Some thirty additional officials close to the Gang were also arrested within days.

The link with the Teng affair was quickly made. In one of its first post-Gang directives, the new leadership of the CCP unraveled a key rope of accusation tied around Teng six months before. They declared that he was *not* a "counter-revolutionary." Mistakes he had certainly made; but the contradictions between Teng and the Party, it was now laid down, were non-antagonistic (among co-workers) and not antagonistic (between the enemy and all co-workers). It was proof, if proof was still needed, that the clash between Teng and the Gang of Four was the gut issue of Chinese politics during 1976.

Within a month the Shanghai quartet had been turned into monsters without a single redeeming feature. A giant rally on October 24 gathered the whole nation in a raucous cry of "Victory" over all the Gang had ever stood for. (Appendix 5 has the text of a celebratory editorial.) As in a festival, the cities of China throbbed with the sound of drums, horns, gongs, and cymbals. People did not blush to walk around Peking shouting: "Death to Chiang Ch'ing!" all the while holding aloft in mindless conformity a huge photo of the man who had been her husband for thirty-seven years.

A cartoon cast the Gang as the Four Pests which plague China's crops. Chang's head rose from the body of a rat, Chiang's bedecked a spider, Yao was depicted as a fly, and Wang leered from the canvas as a grotesque mosquito. China's court poet weighed in for the occasion. Kuo Mo-jo's petty verse—how easy it is to jump on the fallen—spoke of Chiang as a "devil risen from a heap of white bones," and labeled Chang "the canine-headed adviser."

There was a real enthusiasm, though, in the public rejoicing. Firecrackers—a truly people's entertainment—were hurled around as they had not been for many years. The joke in Canton was of "two empties": liquor stores were empty because the masses had been celebrating so thirstily; and hospitals were empty because malingerers who had checked in only to escape the endless campaigns mounted by the Gang of Four were now flocking back to work. A senior official told a foreign visitor that his life so far contained two overridingly happy moments. One was the victory of Chinese forces over the Japanese armies in Manchuria—he was a student in Shenyang during the 1940s—and the second was the fall of the Gang of Four.

It all seemed more colorful than it was well grounded, except for the Shanghai end of the mid-October story, which was both. Wall posters in the port city—later confirmed in part by a New China News Agency dispatch of March 8, 1977—told of a near-revolt in Shanghai just after the Gang was nabbed in Peking.

On October 7, Peking informed Shanghai that Hua was the new CCP chairman. At the same time, it summoned two big fingers of the Gang's fisthold upon Shanghai to present themselves in the capital: Ma T'ien-shui, a Party secretary, and Chou Ch'un-lin, the commander of the Shanghai Garrison.

Ma and Chou were alarmed. Especially so because try as they might they could not phone Chiang, Chang, Wang, or Yao (the quartet were of course already in custody). The pair flew off to Peking after fixing on a code for communicating with their anxious brethren back in Shanghai.

It was not easy for the leftists to phone back to Shanghai. Ma more than once was simply denied a long-distance line by the Peking operators. Eventually an aide of Ma's got through to Shanghai at dawn on October 9. He was suffering from a stomach ache, he said; this meant that the PLA and the veteran cadres had taken control. Later in the day another aide phoned a colleague in Shanghai to announce that his mother had suffered a heart attack; this meant the Gang were in deep trouble.

Bleak as the situation seemed, the Gang's chief followers in Shanghai decided to fight. The city's media received instructions to carry nothing from Peking without checking it through the Shanghai Party headquarters, which was still pro-Gang. The militia was mobilized.

Here surely was the radicals' trump card. For years the Gang had cultivated the militia as a counter-force to the PLA. These paramilitary masses were injected to fever pitch with the apocalyptic gospel of Chiang and her friends. On October 9, orders went out from the huge ex-bank on the Shanghai Bund which, as the city's Party office, remained for a night or two the Gang's nest of power: guns and ammunition were to be put into the hands of 30,000 city militia.

Meanwhile more phone calls in code from Peking brought a cascade of news about grave ailments. When two more radicals in the Shanghai leadership were asked to come to Peking—is it a tribute to the city of Peking's supra-political mystique that they went?—Shanghai resolved that if these two did not return within two days the flag of revolt was to be raised.

Meanwhile Shanghai Radio was ready with the scripts of two announcements—one addressed to the Chinese people, the other to the whole world. Both rang with resistance to the "right-wing takeover" in Peking.

It was too late. The Shanghai remnant discovered that Hua had moved with unusual haste. The left, as usual, was squabbling over fine points. Hua had already leaked word of the fall of the Gang to the foreign press. (Chinese working at the British Embassy blandly passed on the news to their bosses.) This step, rare in Chinese politics, made it far harder for Shanghai to fight back at Hua. What two days earlier could have been a dramatic warning about Hua's coup could now be only a whine of protest against a *fait accompli*.

The 30,000 militia never raised gun to shoulder. The stunning announcements of what amounted to secession lay unread on the desks of Shanghai Radio. All over China a wave of angry attacks on the Gang of Four had begun. Ma and Chou came back to Shanghai and declared that the game was up. Within a week both were out of office. Peking sent three fresh leaders to run the world's largest city, headed by Naval Commander Su Chen-hua. The cause of the Cultural Revolution, as Ma and Chou felt, lay trampled in the dust under military boots.*

The whole affair testified to the Gang of Four's unreadiness for what happened on the night of October 6/7. The Shanghai radicals did not mobilize for emergency action until *after* their four leaders were in trouble. This suggests that what occurred in Peking was Hua's coup, rather than Chiang Ch'ing's attempted coup. Hua at least had done more preparation—by lining up support in the PLA and in security circles—than the Gang appears to have done.

But there was one further reason—and a very simple one—behind Hua's success in clipping off China's political left wing. All over China, stony silence was the warmest attitude to Chiang Ch'ing that I ever met. In 1975 I went to see the memorial exhibit on Mao's life in the hot green Hunan village of Shaoshan. My eye was caught by large photos of Mao's first wife, Yang. These were new since my previous strip to Shaoshan in 1971. Whoever put them up—and Hua

---

* Ma has not been publicly heard of since, but Chou returned to a modest post in 1977.

Kuo-feng was then boss of Hunan—did not do so with
Chiang Ch'ing's blessing. Paying tribute to an earlier wife is
an old ploy in China for damning the present one.*

Old cadres resented her swipes at their work. Intellectuals
were aghast at her militant policies in art and literature. Ordinary folk disliked her barbs against Teng and Chou.

Above all, she was seen to have entered the halls of power
through the back door of marriage rather than the front door
of merit. Fairly or not, she has been suspect to many people,
and hated by not a few, ever since she apparently sat down in
the front row at a lecture by Mao in Yenan forty years ago,
and applauded vociferously so as not to fail to receive the
chairman's attention. (She did not fail, which is one reason
why some women hate her.)

Rioters at the Square of the Gate of Heavenly Peace
mocked Chiang Ch'ing as an "Empress Dowager" gone to
seed. The Empress Dowager, Tzu Hsi (1838–1908), was a
Manchu concubine of low rank who clawed her way to supreme power. Willful and narrow, sunk in despotism, she let
China drift and decline. It was not fair, because it was sexist,
to paint Chiang Ch'ing with Tzu Hsi's brush. Yet the parallel
was neat in the eyes of many Chinese. And Chiang Ch'ing
herself was defensive about it. In sixty hours of talk with the
American visitor, Roxane Witke, she contrived never once to
mention Tzu Hsi's name. Ms. Witke understandably found
the omission odd; one might even call it damning.

---

* It was piquant that Chiang should suffer from the exploitation of marital ties, for she
practiced the same ploy against others. In December 1966, when Liu Shao-ch'i was
being denounced, his own daughter Liu T'ao joined in the attacks: "I am of the opinion
that my father is really the number one person in authority taking the capitalist road."
Chiang Ch'ing thought the criticism insufficiently fierce. She arranged a meeting between Liu T'ao and her mother, Liu Shao-ch'i's former wife. (President Liu had not permitted the two of them to meet regularly.) The former wife gave T'ao such horrible details about her life with Liu that T'ao came up with a second more vigorous
denunciation of her father. This one satisfied the scheming Chiang Ch'ing.

All this was not very just, any more than is the lingering tradition in China of viewing a widow as a bird with one wing (Mao as a youth had enraged the establishment by proposing that widows should be allowed to remarry). Chiang was in part the victim of the very sexist prejudices that the Chinese Revolution was born to sweep away. One weeps at the prejudice, even if not for its every victim.

So it is fair to say that the Gang of Four, in part because of Chiang Ch'ing, were not popular with the Chinese people. To be sure, Hua broke the rules in October 1976 as the Shanghai quartet did. But the full measure of what constitutes a "coup" must take into account the degree of popular support enjoyed by the various feuding leaders. To say the least, the Gang, had they won out in 1976, would have had an even more serious legitimacy problem than Hua has.

If Hua's grab for power was a coup with substantial justification, a Chiang Ch'ing succession would have been a coup with no justification.

The deeper point about the Gang's fall is that, ten years after its birth, the ghost of the Cultural Revolution was finally exorcised. Some young people found the Cultural Revolution a thrilling chance to participate in politics, but many Chinese found it puzzling and wrong-headed. The effort by Chiang and the left to keep its memory alive through the 1970s, as a litmus test of socialist faith and love for Mao, became strained and even reactionary.

In asking for the bill at a restaurant in China you generally say *Suan zhang* ("Reckon the account"). At least you used to. The phrase is now a virtual no-no, because *Suan zhang* was the term used by radicals to declare war on Teng and assorted veteran cadres who were a target of the Cultural Revolution. "Reckon the account," on Chiang Ch'ing's lips, meant "Get even with power-holders like Teng." The Gang poisoned

a simple term out of acceptable daily usage. The Cultural
Revolution was no joke for many Chinese; its noisy, whirring
"helicopters" are no heroes.

Visiting China in 1971, 1973, and 1975, I found the tide
moving increasingly against the radicals in nearly all policy
areas. Except in Chiang Ch'ing's domain of culture and education, the left appeared to be up against the wall. This made
the purge of the Gang look like the end of a leftist influence
artificially prolonged by Ms. Chiang's privileged position as
Mao's wife, rather than the start of a new uncertainty in
Chinese politics.

Cut out private plots in the name of a quick advance to
communism? But peasants love to grow vegetables and raise
pigs around their houses and dispose of the produce as they
wish. Abolish the bonus? But the hard worker or man of
special skills expects a material reward to match his contribution. Put politics in command of the arts? But people tire
of "correct" opera-ballets that bristle with a political message.
These policy fruits of the Cultural Revolution were far from
popular.

Mao protected the left, yet he did not always approve of
flesh-and-blood leftists (he judged himself a "center-leftist").
Indeed he came to share the general dislike for his own wife.
During 1975 he revealed at least one side of his feelings
toward her with a neat phrase in classical mold about Three
Mores and One Less. "Chou should rest more, Teng should
work more, Wang should study more; Chiang Ch'ing should
talk less." Mao reportedly added that his wife ought to take a
tip from nature: "The ears are made so as to remain open but
the mouth may shut."

It is clear that Mao's personal relationship with Chiang
Ch'ing deteriorated. The couple did not live together after
1973. In 1974 Mao wrote her a note: "It's better not to see

each other." But it is not at all clear that Mao would have favored the purge of the Gang of Four. He had often changed his mind. Which was the real Mao: the one who unleashed the Cultural Revolution, or the one who curbed it from 1967? The Mao who purged Teng in 1967, or the one who brought him back in 1973? No one can say.

Chiang Ch'ing admitted that Mao grew critical of her. But she said that in his last months the chairman softened his view and tossed her a garland of praise. "You have been wronged," he wrote in a poem she said he addressed to her. "Today we are separating into two worlds. May each keep his peace." The poem, which Chiang Ch'ing claimed Mao sent her in the summer of 1976, is open-hearted at the personal level and far from opposed to the Gang at the philosophical level. "I have tried to reach the peak of revolution," it goes on, "but I was not successful. But you could reach the top."

In a line which—given that it circulated well before October 1976—contains uncanny foresight of what befell the czarina of Chinese culture, Mao added: "If you fall, you will plunge into a fathomless abyss. Your body will shatter. Your bones will break." A pity we cannot as yet authenticate this haunting poem.

The entire Gang of Four owed their careers to Mao. Three of them he plucked from obscurity; Chang he brought from the third rank to the first. With the partial exception of Ch'en Po-ta (Mao's longtime intellectual secretary), this cannot be said of any other leaders of the People's Republic of China— not Liu Shao-ch'i or Lin Piao, not P'eng Te-huai (Lin's predecessor as defense minister), or Kao Kang (boss of the northeast in the early 1950s). All these had long careers of merit in their own right. Until he was too ill to rule, Mao gave the Gang his general support. It is hard to believe they could have been purged while he still inhabited the Forbidden City.

It is also clear that a crucial change of political lineup occurred as Mao sank. What can be called the Coalition of the
Left frayed at the edges during 1976. The Gang were the core
of the left; Mao was their original sponsor. But they had
enjoyed some support in the PLA, too, and in the security port-
folios.

As Mao's health deserted him, the Gang lost some influential friends. The two key ones were Li Te-sheng, commander
of the military region centered on Shenyang, and Wang
Tung-hsing, the security chieftain and bodyguard writ large
who controlled the elite unit No. 8341. Li and Wang—and
others like them in the Politburo—decided it was wisest to
throw in their lot with Hua.

Their shift is strong circumstantial evidence that Mao was
judged to be the left's lynchpin. Due to Mao, the Gang sat in
the Politburo; without him, they would do so no longer. This
was no doubt the calculation made by Li, Wang, and other
satellites in the outer orbit of the Coalition of the Left. The
result was the acute isolation of the Gang before Mao's body
was even cold. Again, the death of Mao seemed to have
brought on the political death of the Gang of Four.

To read the Chinese press in 1977, you would think that
Chiang, Chang, Wang, and Yao had been moral pygmies and
nitwits since birth. What are we to make of the accusations
against them?

The black rope of denunciation is woven from three separate strands: accusations as to moral conduct, foreign policy
issues, and domestic issues.

To start with the question of behavior, the litany here is
hair-raising. Both Chiang and Chang are said to have murdered or tried to murder senior officials (of that more in a
moment). Chang was called a spy in the pay of Chiang Kai-
shek.

It is alleged that the handsome Wang took advantage of his position to coax pretty young girls into his bed, amass nine automobiles, and import stereophonic and TV equipment. Just four days before his purge, he had 114 photos taken of himself to enhance his image (53 in regular clothes, 16 in military uniform, 21 at his desk, and 24 outdoors).

Chiang Ch'ing lived in the lap of luxury. She drank saffron water and ate golden carp; closed a Canton shipyard because the noise kept her sleepless; had a worker stand barefoot in the freezing cold for failing to heat her bedroom properly; ordered a forest razed to the ground because it obstructed her view; watched obscene foreign films in the privacy of her silken chambers. And so on.

All four are said to have undermined Chou En-lai and twisted the words of old Mao. The 1974 "Anti-Lin and Anti-Confucius" drive was reshaped by the Gang, so a broadcast originating in the army charged in the spring of 1977, into an "unleashing of three arrows"—the third target being Chou. Yao spent $500 on a sumptuous banquet to celebrate Chou's death.

Chiang slipped quietly into the Party archives and tampered with a document in Mao's hand. But an archivist, Little Chang, saw her, and phoned Wang Tung-hsing. This led to a scene between Chiang and Hua, at which Chiang became inflamed and burst out: "Chairman Mao's body is not yet cold and you want to get rid of me. What a return for Mao's kindness to you!"

Chiang interfered with Mao himself as well as his writings. She hastened his death—I am still presenting the allegations—by having him shifted from one bed to another at the eleventh hour. And just before he died she was seen to play poker and heard to peal with carefree laughter.

Are the charges true? Most of them are clearly exaggerated, so far as they can be checked. *The Sound of Music* is not an obscene movie, no matter how often *People's Daily* tells readers (who haven't seen it) that it is. Stripped of the embroidery, the gap between the methods and lifestyles of Chang and Yao and Wang, and that of other Chinese leaders, is not one between black and white. Of course there have been outstanding men like Chou En-lai, who was modest and unmalicious in the extreme. But I doubt that three of the four were often, or drastically, out of line with the average way of working and living at the Politburo level.

Chiang Ch'ing is another cup of tea. She was a lightweight among the Chinese leadership. A woman of humble origins— few CCP leaders really sprang from poverty as she did— whose father beat his wife and daughter brutally, Ms. Chiang, once she gained power in the 1960s and 1970s, turned Chinese politics into a private theater for her own struggle to get even with anyone or anything that obstructed her ego.

She was subjective in her view of things, and psychologically driven in pursuing goals, to a degree that outstrips her senior colleagues by a geometric ratio. When in the early 1960s she was ill (and nearly mentally ill in her own morbid preoccupation with her own physical illness), one of her doctors suggested that she should see some theater to take her mind off herself. Thus was born her fatal plunge onto the neck of China's culture! One woman's hypochondria resulted in a straitjacket over the art, literature, and theater of 900 million people.

Sadly for this would-be feminist, the best image of her career is that of a mundane housewife. In her own diatribes all events and conflicts are reduced to trivial or personal terms. The Russians emerge as nasty neighbors who can't be trusted not to steal chickens from her side of the fence. Lin Piao is talked about as if he is an ex-lover from down the street who slanders her up and down the village. Chou En-lai she trivializes into a reliable valet who generally does the right thing when instructed. Teng is a deviant who undermines her good work at the local drama society.

As for the good guys, Chang Ch'un-ch'iao is like a younger brother who always understands her. Yao Wen-yuan is a smart research assistant for her bouts of investigation or denunciation. Mao is a grandfather who occasionally raps her over the knuckles if she shouts on the telephone or spends too much money. This, alas, was the world of Chiang Ch'ing.

The allegations over foreign policy issues were interesting. We can leave aside the charge that Chiang had "illicit relations with foreign countries." These were minor—stemming from one rash interview with an American scholar—and did not involve alternative foreign policy proposals, unless it turns out to be true that the Gang were conspiring behind Mao's back with ultra-left Albania.*

It is charged that the Gang sniped at China's international economic relationships with western Europe, Japan, and the United States. Wang opposed oil exports as "selling off resources." He and Chang put pressure on the plants under their influence in Shanghai and the northeast to switch from coal to petroleum as a source of fuel, in order to frustrate the oil export program. Ms. Chiang asserted, in speaking against trade with the West, that China's exports were saving Western economies from collapse!

There is some truth in this bill of goods. The Gang simply had no stomach for dealings with the capitalist world (see Chapter 12). Petty sabotage of exports occurred when the Gang rode high. Foreign importers were startled to find green buttons on a white shirt, or a rash of inkspots on a roll

---

* Albania's displeasure at the fall of the Gang is discussed on pages 220–221.

of silk. The atmosphere of trade talks was soured by Gang-inspired rigidity and lectures about the evils of capitalism.

The steel and oil trade with Japan was a clear case of the Gang damping down the level of activity. Chinese oil exports to Japan in 1976 dropped to 6 million tons as compared with about 8 million tons in 1975. The Japanese contributed to this by declining a long-term purchase agreement which Peking had first proposed. Yet the inability to move beyond that setback, to keep the oil flowing in 1976, was due to the Chinese left. Their attitude of "After all, you can't trust capitalist buyers" avidly capitalized on Japanese hesitations.

Steel is a major Japanese export to China; 2 to 3 million tons are generally sold each year. The year of Teng's ascendency, 1975, was a good one, with a total sale of 3.9 million tons. But the 1976 program ran into one difficulty after another. The 1.9 million tons contracted for the period of April through September—from the purge of Teng until the eve of the purge of the Gang of Four—shrank into an actual sale of only 0.6 million tons. Suddenly, by late October, life surged back into the trade.

A Japanese steel delegation, invited to Peking, concluded a new contract within the record time of two weeks. The agreement called for sharply increased sales—1.6 million tons for the period from November 1976 until March 1977—and this figure was achieved. Trade with other countries bears out the pattern with Japan. When the Gang was wielding a big stick, foreign trade faltered; when the Gang fell, trade sailed ahead.

The radicals called for a plague on Russia and America alike. Their absence has probably made it easier for Hua to continue Mao's tilt to the side of the United States. They sensed a loss of purity in China's recent trade and cultural links with the West and Japan; Peking's ties with the world economy and with foreign cultures are going rather more smoothly in 1977–78 without the Gang.

On the other hand the left's loss was the military's eventual gain, and there is a danger here for the West. The PLA is a peasant army. It leans to the moderate side on bread and butter domestic issues. Abroad, though, the army may hanker for détente with Russia (a theme that is taken up in Chapter 11).

Far more mixed were the charges against the Gang on domestic issues. We must draw a veil over the rhetoric. The Gang no more wanted to "restore capitalism" than Mao wanted to fly to the moon. Such talk is merely the time-honored, increasingly debased coinage of political fights in the PRC. Labels like "capitalist" are myths, just as the labels "big spender," "soft on communism," or "free marketeer" generally are in the United States today. The reality is less clear-cut, although the myths are astonishingly persistent.

Yet the Gang—or its intellectual better half—did have a standpoint on three or four basic issues. In a nutshell, they placed the highest possible priority on class struggle. It is not even clear that class struggle exists in socialist China. Teng has his doubts, as we have seen. But the Gang insisted that classes are still there, that class struggle goes on—albeit in new and furtive forms—and that this political tension outweighs all technical or organizational considerations.

Class is the key to life in China, said the Gang. The enemy still abounds, hardly less than in the years of the anti-Japanese war or of the armed battle against Chiang Kai-shek. Now and then Ms. Chiang even called for rooting out class enemies within the PLA—a stroke that did not endear her to military officers who feel that the PLA is, by its very function, the guardian of the interests of People's China. Nor did the PLA like the way the Gang elevated class struggle above serious study in the schools. "If education is such," someone in the army grumbled, "what will happen if war breaks out?"

The Shanghai quartet also took a fearsome view of the

scope of class struggle. Nothing lay outside politics, in their fundamentalist view. Not science, not sport, certainly not the theater. (The glaring exception, of course, was Chiang Ch'ing's own private life. She could order special melons flown in from Sinkiang for a dinner party without a blush of class-consciousness. Like a fervent Baptist preacher who goes to bed with his disciples, she was simply locked in, by the tightness of her very dogmatism, to an unshakable double standard.)

All the charges against the Gang in domestic policy flow from this conviction about the persistence and scope of class struggle. Chiang said she would rather have socialist trains that run late than "revisionist" trains that run on time. Chang avowed—oblivious to the strained nature of the distinction he set up—that he preferred uncultured workingmen to cultured exploiters. And so on.

Two very important disputes bubbled up. Does the bourgeoisie exist within the bosom of the Communist Party itself? The Gang said that the bourgeois class had come to root itself in the Party. Mao indeed may have agreed with them. "You are making revolution," he lashed out at pragmatists in 1976, "and yet don't know where the bourgeoisie is. It is right in the Communist Party." Hua's cooler line is that a few odd representatives of the bourgeoisie worm their way into the Party, but not the bourgeois class as a whole. While this seems arcane, it undoubtedly stirred passions.

The second dispute was about class struggle in industry. The Gang came out with a fancy slogan: "Oppose *kuan, chia, ya*" (the three words mean management, restriction, suppression). This controversy has simmered for years in China. Basically it pits the values of spontaneity against those of a settled order. Chou En-lai was always firm on the issue. He liked to call for "rational rules and regulations." This inflamed the Gang, who feared the dead hand of management, restriction, and suppression.

Yao intoned that "rules and regulations reflect the relationships among people in production and are of a clear-cut class character." This is an interesting, if extreme viewpoint. But Chang slid right over the brink of anarchism: "It is necessary to set up enterprises that have no rules and regulations."

In April 1977, a writer in the official press made clear the link between this standpoint and the issue of whether or not China, in pressing on with economic development, has anything to fear from capitalism:

> The "gang of four's" logic was: "Strict" means *"kuan, chia, ya,"* *"kuan, chia, ya"* is bourgeois, and what is bourgeois is irrational. We hold that "strict" and *"kuan, chia, ya"* cannot be indiscriminately regarded as bourgeois and, also, it is not justified to say everything capitalist is irrational. Isn't it necessary to *kuan* [control] anarchist tendencies?

This is a cunning way to dress up pragmatism in a respectable suit of theory. Thus fortified, the writer is emboldened to say that not everything about capitalism is to be rejected. A rare statement in China since the Cultural Revolution, and a sign that the Gang has truly fallen with a bang.

One further set of charges against the Gang falls between conduct and issues. From where, and how, should new leadership be recruited? Wang, still in his thirties, was the classic "helicopter." Teng disliked such sudden vertical promotions. Chiang was the classic "empress." She is alleged to have remarked: "Even under communism there can still be an empress."

Yet beyond their own careers, the Gang genuinely threw

open the gates of political life. They stood for new blood. The shakeups which they loved did throw opportunities down to young talent. They drew more ex-manual workers into positions of responsibility than Teng or Chou ever did.

Of course they are now accused of favoritism, and arbitrariness, in this recruiting process and such abuses did occur here and there. Yet important differences over the sociology of leadership existed between the Gang and the veteran cadres who most resisted them. In fact, support for "the door open to talent" was one of the Gang's redeeming features.

A criticism the Gang made of railroad management clearly reflects the entire set of issues that put the left out on a limb. "They lower their head to pull the cart," said the leftists of the railroad managers, "instead of raising their head to look at the road." The image tells us much about China's mood at the end of the 1970s.

To get on with the concrete job at hand? To renew the vision of long-term goals? Both are essential to any great political enterprise, yet the difference of emphasis can sometimes be momentous. So it has been recently in China. Teng wanted to solve problems using what light was currently within reach. The Gang—particularly its thinkers, Chang and Yao—kept raising questions about the light, warning that to do the best you can with the light you have will count for nothing if the light turns out to be darkness.

As for the tone of the criticisms of the Gang, one cartoon best sums it up. We see Chiang Ch'ing at ease with a scatter of books around her plush armchair. The titles are of two kinds. Sordid tracts of Russian "revisionism" (*Complete Collection of Soviet Political Coups, Khrushchev Remembers*). And morsels from the compost heap of Western dissipation (*Paris Fashions, Handbook of Hong Kong Beauty Salons*).

The cartoon maybe reveals more about Red China as a

whole than about Ms. Chiang. There are two points above all others that Peking is still defensive about. The first is that the West, which oppressed China, has nevertheless flourished under the capitalist system. The second is that the Soviet Union, which took the true path of socialism, later betrayed the cause.

On balance one cannot weep for Ms. Chiang or even for the rest of the Gang. They lived on a memory. They did not have roots in the solid, earthy Chinese masses. They lifted ideology from reality, spinning handsome but useless phrases from their own overheated brains and rendering Mao's Thought a totem when it should have been a guide to action.

Not least, the best of them made the fatal mistake of rallying around a woman who was a weak reed but for her husband's intermittent blessing. A woman with no sense of history, no feeling for the age she was living in, no sensitivity to the masses as people who work and suffer and laugh—she viewed them merely as a force with which she must be careful to negotiate a profitable diplomatic relationship.

At the same time the purge of the Gang of Four left a bad taste in many a mouth. It smacked of authoritarianism, of which the Chinese have had enough. House arrest is a poor substitute for debate. Many people would feel better, too, if the Politburo had moved only against Chiang Ch'ing, rather than demoting the entire radical high command. Especially if Hua had been able to salvage Chang Ch'un-ch'iao, who had been the influential leader of China's first city, Shanghai, chief commissar of China's armed forces, and a fertile man of ideas.

Like cockroaches emerging from under a shiny stone, sordid reports about the underside of Chinese politics poured

A cartoon of the Gang of Four, borne aloft by demonstrators in Canton on October 25, 1976. (*UPI Photo*)

out of Peking after the Gang's fall. They raise grave questions about China's direction.

Two of the Gang were apparently asked by Hua late in 1977 to give an account of their role in the assassinations of four Chinese politicians. Chang was questioned about the death of Chu Te, the titan of the Chinese military who died in July 1976. Ms. Chiang was under suspicion of having had a hand in the deaths of three middle-level figures, including a general who died on duty in the province of Fukien, opposite Taiwan, and a Yunnan Province leader who may have foiled an attempt on Chou En-lai's life in 1971.

Meanwhile Chiang, not long ago the empress of China's schools, art, and theater, according to a reliable source several times tried to commit suicide—once by banging her head against the wall of her cell in the prison north of Peking where she and the other three Shanghai militants were being interrogated in early 1977.

And official Peking said ominously of the Gang of Four: "When rats scurry across the street, everyone cries, 'Kill them, kill them.' "

Assassination in a land with so little crime? Suicide in a land which radiates hope? Execution in a land whose rule for dealing with those who err has been "Cure the illness and save the patient"? How to reckon with the *way* the Gang were treated?

During the fall of 1976, just when Americans were transferring a mandate from Ford to Carter by means of settled rules, China was resolving a conflict by means of an extralegal struggle that seemed morally on a par with court intrigue of the Ming Dynasty.

In Peking's politics, as in that of most capitals, there come moments when a bid for power must lead to all or nothing; the loser leaves the game. But in Peking he or she not only exits from politics, but becomes a non-person in society as well. And in China to lose power is to lose truth also, so that one is repainted in totally new and degrading terms as a "capitalist" or a "counterrevolutionary."

To fall from doctrinal grace in this way is severe—far more so, for instance, than LBJ's sudden loss of prestige after leaving office in 1969. More even than Nixon's. After all, it was still possible, if rare, for some of Nixon's achievements to be praised after his fall in 1974.

Although the Chinese purgee gets vilified, he or she is not necessarily finished. I do not expect any of the Gang to return to office, not even Chang, yet the record shows that purgees often do. Teng (just like Nixon in 1968) sprang back to the top after six years in the wilderness, from 1967 to 1973. And the cocky, pragmatic Teng (this time unlike Nixon) sprang back again in 1977 for a second time, following his tragic repurge in 1976.

In 1971 Chou En-lai urged me to study an editorial which recounted nine great struggles within the CCP. Each time someone was purged. The first had been Professor Ch'en Tu-hsiu, who was the Party's original secretary-general from 1921. The latest was "China's Khrushchev," Liu Shao-ch'i, head of state until knocked down along with Teng and other "capitalist roaders" in the 1960s.

Even as Chou spoke a tenth struggle was under way, which was probably why the premier drew attention to the previous nine. This time the defense minister Lin Piao got on the wrong side of Mao. Within two months Lin had gone. Since then the Gang of Four case has brought the official tally of great struggles to eleven (Teng's purge in 1976 is delicately omitted).

One recent "repainting" in Peking is an arresting one. *People's Daily* has likened the able theorist Chang to Trotsky, and the dying Mao to the dying Lenin. Chang, like Trotsky before him, tried to grab the mantle from the true heir. That seems to equate Hua with Stalin as the heir—which is exactly what *People's Daily* goes on to do.* One might wonder whether China after all is going the way of Russia.

In fact the pattern of purges in China does not resemble the Soviet case. None of the eleven Chinese purgees (or in some cases groups of purgees) has, it seems, ever been executed. This is in sharp contrast to Russia, where five of the six members of the Politburo at the time of Lenin's death in 1924 died at the hands of the régime,** and where, in 1937 and 1938, no less than 70 percent of the Central Committee were arrested and shot!

True, there has been much death at the grass-roots level during the Chinese Revolution. Millions of people died during land reform at the start of the régime; tens of thousands more probably died by violence in the Cultural Revolution.

Nor would Chiang Ch'ing, if she does take her own life, be the first prominent figure in post-1949 China to do so. The Cultural Revolution saw suicides of well-known people cast down by criticism, such as the writer Lao She, author of *Rickshaw Boy*. It led to attempted suicides, such as that of the army leader Lo Jui-ch'ing (now back in favor and in office), who tried to end the torment of denunciation by jumping off a high building in 1966.

And harassment hastened the death of a number of senior figures. The coal minister, Chang Lin-chih, died after forty days of interrogation by Red Guards. The life of the president

* One of the most intriguing remarks Chiang Ch'ing is alleged to have made concerned Trotsky. "Say no more about Stalin!" she snapped at someone. "For all I know, the case of Trotsky is far from settled."

** Of the six only Stalin, the executioner, was not executed.

of Wuhan University, Li Ta, was shortened by Red Guards who upbraided him with the gay certainty that ideologues seem always to possess. Even assassination has occurred more often than is generally realized. Hua's predecessor in the hot seat of police minister, Hsieh Fu-chih, was killed by someone on his own staff. And case number ten, that of Lin, ended in an airplane crash over Mongolia in 1971 which was most likely an accident, but could have been an "accidental" murder.

For all this, the lack of a single execution by the state of a top CCP leader is striking and marks the CCP off from the Communist Party of the Soviet Union during a comparable period.

Moreover even imprisonment of a purgee is rare. Before he became leader of the Party in 1935, Mao himself found out what it is like to be purged. Several times he was demoted— the minimum sense of purge—and in 1934 he was put under virtual house arrest by Party bosses who thought him rightist and guerilla-minded. Both before and after Liberation, the Party has imprisoned a few middle-level officials whose errors were crass—like Hsiao Ching-kuang, who got five years in 1934 for, among other things, living indulgently in a time of austerity with two horses set apart to carry his personal effects. But imprisonment of a senior leader was almost unknown until the Gang of Four were led away to house confinement.

Far more common has been the milder fate of Liu and Teng in the 1960s. Both lost all office. For a while they had terrible ordeals at meetings where they were styled "monsters" and made to confess to bad ways almost from childhood. Yet they lived on for many months in their own homes. No doubt they lounged in armchairs and read in *People's Daily* the record of their hair-raising misdeeds.

Later each was sent to a village. Liu's health declined and in 1973 he died of cancer. But the case of Teng, who did odd jobs as a member of a commune on the plains of Inner Mongolia, suggests that the rustication was not punitive in its effects. He seemed almost as fit and cocky in 1973 as he was a decade earlier.

Even the Gang of Four have not exactly been treated like ordinary political prisoners. Chiang and Chang apparently asked Hua for a meeting to explain their case. Hardly less striking than Hua's questioning them about the four possible murders is the fact that the chairman of the CCP should have agreed to sit down with these two "rats" and "criminals." To say the least, there is a gap between rhetoric and reality in China, and the reality is less awful than the words.

The purges have grown more frequent over time. For twenty years before the tragic Great Leap Forward of 1958–59 only one big struggle followed by a purge occurred. The villain (Kao Kang, an apparent suicide) was a separatist in Manchuria who had dealings with Russia that bypassed Peking. Yet thereafter a string of crises came without long intervals of unity. The years of the Cultural Revolution and its long aftermath were especially rich in casualties.

This trend may well have been due to Mao growing old. We cannot be sure how much the great man cared about the shabby image of his purges. At a superficial level he certainly did so. When Red Guards gave a tough time to Ch'en Yi, the plump bon viveur who was foreign minister from 1958 through the Cultural Revolution, Mao rebuked them with the remark: "He's lost twenty-seven pounds in weight. I cannot show him to foreigners in this condition."

Yet at a deeper level there was a massive openness, and nothing of Stalin's furtiveness, in Mao's criticisms of others. He seemed to have no self-doubts and to genuinely want the purgee to see the error of his ways and come back to work. He did not, like Stalin, get rid of colleagues as one might dispose of furniture that has outlived its function.

At the same time Mao's growing pessimism made him perceive more and more flaws in people during the 1960s and 1970s. The question is whether the purges will slacken off now that Mao is dead. Probably they will. One could have predicted that after Mao died, Chiang Ch'ing and her militant friends would lose out.* But the Gang were embers from the fire of Mao's Cultural Revolution. Hua is most unlikely to trigger off anything a fraction so bold as that storm of the 1960s. Nor to make the shifts in policy—he lacks the authority—which Mao pulled off while spewing out purgees like chaff from a thresher.

Will the fate of the purgees change? Probably not. Mao himself was against execution of top people; "once a head is chopped off," he said in a reference to the danger of error, "it can't grow again as chives do after being cut." But Chinese cultural ways are against it too. To remold is regarded as a victory; to kill is an admission of defeat.

Hua will likely be Maoist enough not to execute the Gang, yet un-Maoist enough never to march them around with dunce caps in a theater of political morality (one wonders how many Chinese still believe in political morality). In this respect Hua's China will be less comparable to Stalin's Russia than to Russia under Khrushchev and Brezhnev, where dramatic purge has given way to quiet demotion.

If Chiang is done to death, it will probably not be by act of the Chinese state but by a bullet in anger from an unofficial (but not entirely private) source, just as Lin Piao's daughter

---

* I did so in *The New Republic* for September 25, 1976.

was apparently killed in the green hills north of Canton in 1973. "Bean-bean," as the girl was called, had betrayed her father by tipping off Chou En-lai to his movements. Some military entity in the south which admired Lin evidently thought "Bean-bean" did not deserve to live on. There may be men in the army who think the same of Chiang Ch'ing.

Mao would not savor these things, yet he was in part responsible for bringing them about.

In America we may be tempted to feel superior to all this sordidness. Power was transferred from Ford to Carter by means of settled rules, and Ford has certainly not lost any of his human rights. Yet the comparison can be misleading—and not only because CCP rule sprang out of a recent civil war, whereas we have not known such a situation for a century.

Morals and politics relate to each other differently in the two countries. In America the entity of moral significance is the individual; unity at the political level is constructed, not organic. Often it is an expedient which everyone privately accepts as such: the proposed Reagan-Schweiker ticket in 1976, the oil-and-water mix of Northern liberalism and Southern conservatism in the Democratic Party.

But in China the entity of moral significance is the entire revolution. Unity is a moral end, compared to which the views of any particular individual are a bagatelle. In America, the human rights issue is the procedure by which the individual is dealt with; in China, the goals of the whole society form the human rights issue.

This is why the past record of an individual—be it Lin Piao, Chang Ch'un-ch'iao, or Chiang Ch'ing—can be rewritten. The overarching moral concern which justifies it is today's unity. In China we have the politics of symbolism; what matters is the whole. In the United States we have the politics of logic; what matters is the individual with his own life and reason.

8
The Shape
of the
☞ Post-Mao Era ☜

As they struggle toward a shape for the post-Mao era, Hua, Yeh, Teng, and the other Chinese leaders can observe with satisfaction that the PRC is less threatened from outside than ever before in its twenty-nine years. Until the mid-1960s China felt a grave threat from the United States. For a period of several years, highlighted by the Cultural Revolution and crystalized at the Ninth Congress of the CCP in 1969, the Peking leadership felt danger alike from the U.S.A. and the U.S.S.R. (and decided to defy both simultaneously).

From 1969 to 1972 the American threat was felt to be much diminished, but the Russian threat seemed acute. Now, for the past five or six years China has experienced a reduced danger from the north and a negligible danger from across the Pacific. Its formal military budget shrank in the mid-1970s.

In economic affairs the Politburo may observe a mixed but not bleak picture. The good part is that the Chinese can look after themselves and are not threatened by most of the elements of world economic uncertainty. China, though backward, remains unruffled by a post-1973 world of monetary mess, energy maldistribution, price fluctuation, and general economic uncertainty.

We used to fear Peking because it seemed the sponsor of an "unstable" world; yet in the heavy seas of late-1970s international economic relations China often seems like an island of stability. The Chinese feed their own 900 million people, produce more oil than Algeria and export sharply rising amounts of it, have no apparent inflation, enjoy rich reserves of natural resources, and keep under strict restraint the consumer aspirations of their populace.

The darker part of the economic picture is that the Chinese people's expectations are rising fast, and some hard political decisions will have to be taken to meet them. Chinese young people think of their country as a major world power striding toward a modern industrial future. Yet the per capita income is unlikely to be more than U.S. $600–700 by the year 2000. A country so grand—and yet so austere. The Chinese will have to live with that tension for a long time to come.

Then, too, the aging nature of the Chinese Revolution raises ideological and political problems, the most important of which concern the credibility of ideological appeals for people who have been through many ideological fluctuations, and the difficulty of achieving political change without a crisis that goes beyond politics. Where the United States is strong in that its political system allows for change within settled rules, China is weak.

Two Overarching Priorities.

The Chinese government and people are united on two supreme priorities: modernization and anti-imperialism.

China's revolution has been a military, political, even spiritual struggle; yet its main goal is economic. It was a goal frankly stated by Mao—and repeated with force by Chou at the National People's Congress in January 1975—as the modernization of China.

China will remain a primarily agricultural nation for the foreseeable future; to import much of its food would be impossible for such a large population. Yet agriculture now accounts for only 30 percent of China's GNP, and China is set on a path that will soon make it a major industrial power.

Although there is a strong moral tone to Chinese socialism, no group in Peking questions that industrialization is the shape of the Communist future. The growth of industry has sometimes been slowed by the demand placed upon it to serve agriculture, yet industrial growth generally has reached a fairly fast 10 percent a year, with agriculture a steady 4 percent. This balanced pattern can be expected to continue.

Again, although its rhetoric tempts one to believe otherwise, China is a self-contained and rather self-concerned nation, whose pressing cause is not world revolution or spiritual athleticism but pulling China out of its backwardness. Its foreign policy is designed to give the time and peace needed for the task; the moralizing of *People's Daily* is for the purpose of affecting how such development should proceed.

Even the debate about "how" subsided quite a bit during 1977. Since the fall of the Gang of Four, China's development policy has been fairly set. The struggles of tomorrow will be less about the philosophy of development than about cutting up the resulting pie. Guns or butter? Extra investment into machines for agriculture or into the advanced industrial sector? Special consideration to be given to the far west, the minority areas, or the south? Such are the emerging issues.

The second overarching priority in Peking is the fight

against imperialism. This has been China's twentieth-century political religion. The present foreign policy of opposing the superpowers and championing independence is at once consistent with the experience of the Chinese Revolution and a means of turning China's weakness into an intangible strength on the international stage.

Saying that the troubles of the world are due to one form or another of imperialism has proved successful for China. It may continue for some time to be the framework for Peking's analysis of the international scene. Yet there are pressures against such a world-view. Some stem from changes in the world at large; others from China's changing relation to other nations.

First, who are the imperialists these days? Mao in his later years made a dramatic new analysis: Russia had become imperialist. Indeed, by 1972 Russia was said to be the most dangerous imperialist power in the world. The new view bristles with implications.

Was Mao still using the term "imperialism" in its Leninist sense ("the highest stage of capitalism") or had he switched to a purely political analysis? If Mao really meant imperialism as Lenin's "highest stage of capitalism," would not the United States be chief imperialist?

Lenin found imperialism to be the salient feature of international relations in the lead-up to World War I. After World War II, imperialism was still such a force that dozens of nations in Asia and Africa and Central America had to struggle against it in order to win independence. Yet into the 1980s imperialism is unlikely to remain the salient feature of the world scene.

If we mean by "imperialists" what Peking means—the old-style European colonialist countries plus the U.S.S.R. and the U.S.A.—then imperialism hardly rules the roost in 1978.

These nations are often rebuffed in the UN. The two superpowers are unable to exert their will in the Middle East. Small allies of the United States often get away with murder, to the extent that it sometimes becomes unclear who is dominating who.

Perhaps the rich are the imperialists. But there are many exceptions: some Third World oil producers are wealthier than some colonial powers; per capita GNP in one or two European countries is likely, by the year 1985, to be lower than that in many "neo-colonial" Asian countries.

Foreign bases have decreased sharply in number and importance. The nuclear arsenals of the superpowers seem unusable—for any purpose that would not incinerate them along with any intended victim. And America and Russia are unable to stop the smaller wars that punctuate our era. Power is in a state of flux.

It is not only that few colonies remain. The pattern of wealth and poverty changes; so does the relation of power to capacity to kill people. And the moral force of imperialism is spent (thanks, in part, to China's sustained and convincing testimony against it). The world of 120 sovereign states is not Lenin's world; the chances of another "Suez 1956," "Czechoslovakia 1968," or "U.S. in Vietnam" seem remote.

The proof is that the Third World is losing its cohesion. As imperialism sags, its victims fall away from their past half-unity. Most new international crises arise between Third World nations. The imperialists lurk in the shadows, to be sure, but the conflicts would occur without them: Ethiopia and Somalia; Pakistan and India; Algeria and Morocco; Vietnam and Cambodia; the list is a long one.

Economically, the Third World lands have lost some common interests since 1973. Those rich in scarce natural resources—such as Saudi Arabia, Nigeria, Kuwait, and Malaysia—do not stand in the same position as those which are not—for example, Bangladesh, India, and several states of West Africa.

All this raises doubts as to China's future foreign policy course. Peking declares that China is part of the Third World. But as that entity unravels, the meaning of the declaration loses its edge. Being a spokesman for the Third World, as China has been, becomes a taxing job. Certain issues are clear-cut: support for a 13-mile territorial waters limit and a 200-mile economic zone; for commodity agreements that give secure prices for primary products; for total disarmament measures; for action against racism of every kind.

On others any spokesman for the Third World has a dilemma. With whom to side in the intra-Third World wars listed above? Should the Third World take a Marxist view of the world (actually many of its member countries are rather capitalist)? Does the Third World want the West to disappear from Africa, or does it want the West's help in toppling the white minority régimes of southern Africa? How much of the oil in the South and East China seas belongs to Korea, to Japan, to the Philippines, to Vietnam—and how much to China?

Moreover China is not a typical Third World country, the less so as time goes on. Many features of the Chinese experience are not found, and could not be duplicated, in most countries of Africa, Asia, and Latin America. For an enormous land like China, autarky is an option, as it cannot be for a tiny country like Cuba or Sri Lanka. China is far from being a new nation. Certainly it has no inferiority complex about the West.

One may doubt that China can go on for much longer being a member of the Third World. Consider the traits that seem to set it outside: possession of nuclear weapons; permanent membership, with a veto power, in the UN Security Council; an economy that is the sixth biggest in the world; and an aid program that is the third largest in the world.

Then, too, many of China's policies diverge from those typical of the Third World: refusal to oppose nuclear testing and support nonproliferation schemes; enthusiasm for a NATO bloc armed to the teeth and studded with foreign bases; coldness toward Angola, Cuba, India, and other up-front Third World nations, on the ground of their cozy ties to Moscow.

China has in fact been facing an accelerating series of exquisite dilemmas. If it supports each oil price rise made by OPEC, Western Europe suffers—hence defense against China's enemy, Russia, is weakened. If it asserts that the gravest problem in Africa is not white neo-colonialism but Soviet meddling, then Tanzania and other staunch friends of China in Africa are not pleased. If it praises ASEAN (Association of Southeast Asian Nations) as a model of regional organization, it is reminded that some ASEAN members are hosts to U.S. bases from which Vietnam, the hero of the Third World during the 1960s, was bombed to rubble. It is a complex world for a nation with a big tongue.

In sum, "Imperialism versus the Third World" may not be a sufficient framework for Peking's foreign policy into the 1980s and beyond.

At the conceptual level a foreign policy change is likely before the 1990s. The younger Chinese leaders may not continue to see imperialism as the overriding world trait. Certainly they cannot go on forever viewing their own formidable land as the victim, as valiant David pitted against the Goliath of the two superpowers, as the authentic voice of the dispossessed.

I do not say that China will join the establishment (which

may anyway be a mirage seen only by those far off). To say that China is not really part of the Third World is not to say that it belongs to the club of the superpowers. There are possible positions in between.

A China concentrating on development at home may well become more selective in its foreign policy concerns. Steel needed at home, for instance, may not be spared for railroads in Africa. In Asia, certainly, China expects to be the major influence, and will be; in other regions, it may not necessarily sustain a generalized, high-pressure commitment, if the cross-currents become too complex to fit in with Chinese values and experience.

Peking stands now at a crossroads. China's past, forced isolation was galling, but it was pristine. Its new influence in the world is satisfying but requires unaccustomed choices among varying shades of gray.

The West should be cautious about any future changes in China's foreign policy. A change of gears, from "imperialism" and "Third World" to less ideological concepts, would not necessarily mean a future policy that would seem moderate to non-Chinese. The main reason is that Chinese power *is* growing, and China can be expected to cause more problems for Asia in the future than in the past. It will impinge more. It is getting beyond the stage of an essentially reactive foreign policy.

To say this is to be reminded that the term "moderate" can be used in different ways. Lack of moderation is no worry if the government in question lacks the power to back up rhetoric with action. Can the Soviet leadership today be called "moderate"? On the spectrum between militancy and revisionism among Communist élites the U.S.S.R. may indeed be moderate. But in terms of its control over its own people and the boldness of its interference with other peoples, it is not.

A less militant China in all probability would *not* mean a China that concerned its neighbors less, or a China to which the West could with impunity pay less regard.

.

Raising the Standard of Living.

Hua has promised his people a better standard of living. The promise will face a triple test. In the first place, economic targets can only be met if morale is high. The signs here were good during the Year of the Snake. The fall of the Gang of Four seemed to bring a shot in the arm to industry in particular. "In large and medium-sized cities," the official press observed in June 1977, "a festive atmosphere prevails in industrial enterprises."

Yet this mood of public happiness is a coin with two sides. Better morale has already spurred production; output for the whole economy rose sharply in 1977 as compared with 1976. But with a loosening up there also came assertive demands for wage increases and more participation in decisionmaking. Hua must trade time against space. Depending how the transaction goes, the new spirit in China could either solidify his chairmanship or unravel it.

The future standard of living will hinge in the second place on Hua's choice of development policies. Here the signs are good. At first sight it seems disturbing that in 1977 the rhetoric of economic policy should have been drawn from the work of the 1950s. Has wisdom been absent since the first Five Year Plan? Is Volume V of Mao's *Selected Works* the last word on the subject?

But it happens that China's economy did well during the

Partial view of Great Celebration
(Ta Ch'ing) Oilfield in northeast
China, 1977. (*New China News
Agency Photo*)

1950s. Mao is Mao and it can never be wrong to quote him.
Yet also involved is a wise decision of development policy: to
opt for the careful planning of the 1950s rather than the spiritual athletics of the mid-1960s.

Hua expressed the realistic philosophy clearly. "We must
encourage people to work . . . in a down-to-earth way, rather
than making a lot of fanfare or working recklessly," he wrote
in 1963 (when China was still recovering from the utopian-

ism of the Great Leap). His article was resurrected with a flourish in May 1977.

We see, too, that the policies of the 1950s are not being embraced mechanically, or without regard to changes of circumstance since. Technicians are back in positions of authority. The PLA is having a big say on industry in particular. Yet those experiences of the 1960s and early 1970s that were positive have not been dropped—cadres still do manual work, small-scale industry in rural outposts is still stressed, the barefoot doctors continue to be the backbone of the public health service. The *spirit* of current policy is a call for the old virtues—spurned by Mao for most of his last dozen years—of steadiness, obedience, and rational procedures.

If Mao later jettisoned the policies of the 1950s that are now being cited from Volume V of his *Selected Works,* will Hua be able to avoid having to do the same? Probably yes. Not that Hua is as able as Mao, but precisely that Hua is less bold and original than Mao.

Hua won't switch away from careful planning and the old virtues, because he is no more likely to start a Cultural Revolution than to write a symphony. Neither the Great Leap Forward nor the Cultural Revolution issued by logical necessity from the state of affairs that preceded them. They were shining pearls that one restless genius simply could not resist grasping for. They are now beautiful bits of history.

The third test will come in the struggle over priorities. Planning and the old virtues are not the whole of the matter. Someone has to tell the technicians how to divide up the available investment resources. That is a political decision, if one with few philosophic overtones.

Even without the presence in the Politburo of a utopian left, there will be sharp divisions over such decisions. Hua, Teng, and most of the PLA were united in abhorring the Gang of Four. But they are unlikely to see eye to eye on all issues of resource allocation.

At the national conference on industry held in May 1977, Defense Minister Yeh was blunt about military requirements. He even gently revised Mao's famous axiom that "Industry should serve agriculture." As the old marshal put it: "Basic industry must be speeded up to serve agriculture *and national defense* more effectively."

As for Hua and Teng, the trend of their thought is fairly clear. Hua favors more attention to the capital needs of agriculture than Teng does. He has consistently spoken up for things which rural leaders say they need. Teng has been industry's champion, as the case of the railways shows.

Nowhere was the fight between the Gang of Four and Teng more fierce than in the railroad bureaus. Teng said that the Gang were asking the railroads to perform on nothing more than "socialist enthusiasm." In the process they were neglecting safety standards and the need to give superior rewards to skilled workers. Efficient railroads seem to be a symbol of Teng's impatient desire to modernize China in a no-nonsense way.

Of course all demands must be relative and compromises are unavoidable. But if Yeh has a big ear for PLA requests, Hua has one for the farmers, and Teng for the needs of the advanced industrial sector of the economy. The Chinese consumer could probably use this triple rule of thumb to gauge how forthcoming political struggles will affect his pocketbook and the range of products it can buy.

The Ideological Picture.

The ideological problem of the post-Mao years stems in part from the very fact of the PRC's spectacular success. It concerns the changing role of class in Chinese society, and extends to how the problem of evil is handled.

Let me summarize the difficulty. Whenever something appears in Chinese society which does not accord with the ideal held by the leadership—a cynical play, some peasants spending too much energy on their private plots—the phenomenon is labeled "bourgeois" because the CCP does not find it a recognizable flower of the tree of socialism.

But the cynical play might not be "bourgeois" at all. It could have a motive and a meaning not linked in any way to class categories. By refusing to consider the possibility that such manifestations may be part of what socialism will be like, the Chinese Communist lifts socialism right out of the realm of men and history. He simply dismisses as "bourgeois" anything he does not like.

Such rigidity could hide from him the fact that he is pursuing phantoms—a more-than-human oneness among men; and a forced consensus which would muffle creativity as well as quirks. Or, alas, it may be a mere manipulation of words—in which case mass cynicism is the price that is paid.

Consider the ideological situation one year after the fall of the Gang of Four. Hope was rekindled during 1977 by blaming virtually all past evils on Chiang Ch'ing and her associates, and the exaggeration involved was massive. The problem is that such explanations are of diminishing utility. All fronts report a rosy state of affairs now the Gang have gone. But what about the next outbreak of corruption, plotting, wrong line? How will it be explained, without the Gang around as a convenient whipping boy?

A Chinese magazine made this comment on the literary scene in the summer of 1977: "Their minds at ease, thanks to the downfall of Chiang Ch'ing and her counterrevolutionary gang, old and young Chinese writers—professional and amateur alike—are going in for creative writing with vigor." The results may please Peking. But should they be disappointing, one more dent will have been made in the already battered official ideology.

Russia is no model in these matters, yet at least Moscow has tackled head on the issue of the decline of class struggle. In Marxist theory, of course, the fading of class is to be accompanied by the withering away of the state (the state, as an expression of class, loses its function as classlessness approaches). But the Soviet state shows no sign of withering. Faced with this granite fact, Soviet thinkers have come up with a new addition to the edifice of Marxist theory. They speak now of a "state of the whole people."

This phrase infuriates the Chinese. It replaces the dictatorship of the proletariat, and sets up an intermediary stage, prior to the long-delayed withering of the state. The Chinese argue that the state is always a class entity. Marx and Lenin indeed said so. However the Russians are perhaps being realistic. Class fades; the state does not. So the Marxian theory of the state ought to be adjusted. In this way the Russians have given themselves the makings of a post-class organizational theory. Relinquishing a little Marxian purity, they gain a little ideological credibility.*

The Chinese, meanwhile, are left with the dictatorship of the proletariat. Indeed the 1970s have seen more stress placed on this doctrine than any previous decade in the CCP's history. Since the Chinese state is a dictatorship of the proletariat, those who stand in its way are, by definition, "bourgeois."

But this doctrine no longer corresponds to the economic realities of China. It is a myth, and many Chinese must know it to be so. The Gang of Four further strained belief in a struggle between proletariat and bourgeoisie by indiscriminately calling anyone they didn't like "bourgeois." Yet such a way of talking persists (if in a muted fashion compared to the shrill excesses of the Year of the Dragon), despite the perils it carries.

---

* Alas, they have done nothing to create democratic political institutions appropriate to a "state of the whole people," and when Alexander Dubcek tried to do so in Czechoslovakia in 1968, Moscow crushed him.

That Peking is sensitive on this issue is indicated by repeated accusations against fallen leaders that they believed class was receding.

The Canton boss T'ao Chu, for instance, was said to have observed before his purge in 1967: "By and large the classes have now disappeared." Teng and Liu Shao-ch'i were attacked for uttering similar statements.

The Pakistani leftist Tariq Ali, interviewing an ex-Red Guard from Canton, enquired: "Did you really believe that Liu Shao-ch'i was a 'capitalist roader'—an agent of imperialism?" The young man replied: "Yes, I did. But we understood capitalism in a different way from Mao. We started from the viewpoint of being oppressed and suppressed. And for us, therefore, anyone who oppressed the masses *must* be a capitalist. Mao meant it in a different way of course."

In fact he didn't. The tragedy of Mao in the later years is precisely that he came to wield this simplistic, noneconomic, mud-slinging definition of capitalism. Of course it confused people. Of course it has brought on a crisis of ideological credibility.

How are the Chinese going to solve their ideological problem? Let us consider four possible future patterns for the politics of post-revolutionary China.

1. The first is "Caesarism," that is, the rule of a personal titan, who enjoys direct affective ties with the masses.

Mao from the time of the Great Leap Forward was such a Caesarist. He turned against his Party apparatus. He raised the gravest questions about the growth of bureaucracy. He put himself in direct touch with the masses, and he tossed them an exhilarating challenge to "rebel."

China is most unlikely to see such Caesarism in the 1980s and 1990s. No remaining Chinese leader can afford so grandly to lambast, and even eliminate, the intermediate levels between himself and the masses. Hua probably lacks the stature. Nor are the masses these days as likely—even if a titan existed—to play their child-like role in a Caesaristic setup. They are becoming too sophisticated to mistake politics for religion.

2. A second possible pattern is one of reduced state authority in the China of tomorrow. So there would be less government control and more reliance on social bonds.

The laws of the state and the customs of society constrain us. all, but in China the second has always had a special strength. The Westerner is not less struck in the 1970s than Leibnitz was two hundred years ago by China's "public tranquility and . . . social order." The key here is social discipline, distilled from dynasties of stress on the ethics of how people should live with each other.

The PRC has given China a strong state, such as has seldom been seen in Chinese history. But it is possible that the post-Mao state will weaken. This would be a consequence of trends already touched upon: the regions starting to assert themselves against Peking; Hua's lack of Mao's commanding intrinsic authority; a crumbling of the ideological cement that secures the edifice of power; reduced threat to China from outside, and a consequent undermining of the justification for hyper-strict authority.

If the balance between state and society tipped back a bit toward society, this might be a bad thing for China. Reduced state authority could lead to a loss of direction for the nation, an inability to lay down proper priorities and execute policies through to the end.

A sagging of state power would represent a return to a recurrent pattern in Chinese history. Lao Tzu, the Taoist philosopher, long ago adhered to an anti-state, pro-society posi-

Experiment in education: a class at a factory-based college in Tientsin. (*Photo by Ross Terrill*)

tion: "Ruling a big country is like cooking a small fish." And
a song about the peasant fulfilling his daily round in a self-
sufficient way regardless of machinations at the court goes
back to 2307 B.C.:

> When the sun rises I labor,
> When the sun sets I rest,
> I drink from the well I have dug,
> I eat from the fields I have tilled.
> What does imperial power matter to me?

A surge of anti-communism is not in question. A lighter
touch from Peking would not mean the unraveling of the socialist pattern of Chinese society. In this respect the China of
1976 was poles apart from the Hungary of 1956 (despite
Chinese fears of the parallel). A spill of power in Budapest
did lead to a sudden (if temporary) rollback of the socialist
social system. The Catholic Church reclaimed its land; the
aristocracy jumped out of the pit and made as if to resume its
old supremacy.

This would be quite impossible in China. The two severe
crises of power in the Year of the Dragon did not shake the
pattern of society. Factories did not return to private ownership. Buddhism did not revive. The schools went on teaching
Marx and Lenin and Mao as before.

The Year of the Dragon showed that China's national political system is not all that stable. This is partly because Mao
was a particularly subjective and bold Communist leader. It
may also be because there is no safety valve of widely expressed dissent that might enable the élite to discern moods
before they erupt into resistance. Political tension does not
stalk the country in Watergate style. It is bottled up at the top

in a few (literally) smoke-filled rooms—hence the potential for political zigzag.

But the *social* system is stable. Should there be a reduction in state authority, therefore, the daily life of the Chinese people would not be turned upside down. China would manifest less sense of overall purpose; some far-flung parts of the nation might carry on deviant policies. But hope should not rise in the breasts of the Kuomintang, or wishful-thinking Christians, or the Dalai Lama in exile in India.

Socialism in China, after twenty-nine years, is more than a "socialist" national political structure. The warp and woof of a socialist way of life among the citizenry may prove—in an echo of Chinese tradition—more resilient than the shaky political system itself.

And yet, on balance, one does not expect any sharp reduction of state power in China. Only a certain tilt away from Peking and toward the stronger regional bases, and a certain enlargement of the private realms of life at the expense of the tentacles of official ideology.

3. One way for China to solve the ideological problem would be simply to smother it beneath a neo-traditional bureaucracy. Mao was haunted by such a possibility. His successors may be less so. A combination of bureaucracy above, plus privatism below, could be a third possible shape of China's immediate future.

For years Peking scoffed at Milovan Djilas's *The New Class*, in which the Yugoslav writer described the Communist elite as equivalent to a ruling class. Yet there are now signs that the problem of bureaucratic careerism—a perennial one in Chinese history and in the briefer history of socialist governments—is of growing concern to the Chinese themselves. One of the last maxims Mao left behind touched on this problem.

"A number of Party members have moved backward and opposed the revolution," he observed in mid-1976. "Why? Because they have become high officials and want to protect the interests of high officials." Some Communist officials in Hong Kong, in a sharp reversal, have expressed keen interest in Djilas's idea of a "new class."

The tragedy of cynicism is that it is the handmaiden of bureaucracy. Chinese history is rich in examples of such a partnership. Although Confucianism is the most famous political philosophy of Old China, there were several others. Among them were two that seem as far apart as it is possible for political theories to be. "Legalism" was a theory of the absolute state, reminiscent of Thomas Hobbes's *Leviathan*. The Legalists were scientists of power, unconcerned with moral visions, unready to enfold the masses into a community.

"Taoism" (*tao* means way) was a religious world view oriented to nature. It was not a political theory as such—except in the potentially devastating sense that it disesteemed politics. The Taoist was typically a mystic, uninterested in structures, beloved of ambiguities, a man more at home in the mountains than in the magistrate's chambers.

Yet Legalism and Taoism often went hand in hand. Legalism, a theory of rule, competed with Confucianism as the political philosophy of the élite. Taoism, a way of living, was in general the philosophy of people opposed to or outside the establishment. Its critics called it escapism. Yet an apolitical Taoist public suited the Legalist bureaucrats perfectly.

Today, the official press confesses that various forms of escapism have grown up since the Cultural Revolution. People "evade responsibility"; they weary of "yet one more campaign." They reason, "If we do our own technical job well, then other people can take care of politics." This looks like neo-Taoism. If so, the reasons for its appearance lie partly in

the hyper-politicism of the Cultural Revolution—including
the tiresome overpoliticization carried on by the Gang of
Four—but also partly in the political theatrics that surrounded the Gang's fall.

Peking now says that the common people "long ago" knew
about the evils of the Gang of Four, but that they "feared
oppression" by the Gang if they spoke up about those evils.
That does not say much for China's political system. The fact
that the Gang "held a part of the power" is not a sufficient
explanation. Power in a socialist system is not mere possession of coercive capacity; it is generated only in constant
dialectic between the Party and the masses. How then could
fear of oppression hide basic truth for a decade? It sounds as
if the dialectic between Party and masses has seriously broken down, as if large segments of the people have been re-
treating into the privatism of neo-Taoism.

Is Legalism still alive? Very much so, apparently, and the
late Mao smiled upon it. A few years ago Mao reversed an
earlier position, to declare that Confucianism was utterly to
be condemned, and that Legalism was comparatively progressive. Praise was heaped upon Ch'in Shih Huang, the un-
Confucian dictator who briefly unified China with amoral administrative finesse 2100 years ago.

Mao was not a Legalist at heart. He was too much the
teacher, too much the man of doctrine, too concerned that
people not only obey but renovate their souls. Perhaps he
turned so implacably against Confucius because he felt the
philosophical idealism of the sage bubbling up in his own
mind.

Mao's heirs are better candidates for neo-Legalism than he
himself. A hallmark phrase of the Year of the Snake was
"control the realm" (*zhi guo*), a term with very traditional
overtones. Indeed the change in China since the fall of the

Gang of Four can be described with an analogy from the Chinese past. The neo-Confucians lost out to the neo-Legalists.

Was there not something Confucian about the Gang? They insisted that what is in people's minds—even more than objective circumstances—determines how people conduct themselves. They felt that political morality matters more than administrative rationality. They did not get carried away by the idea of fast economic growth. They believed in an all-encompassing official ideology, which should color every realm of life from the arts to family relations.

Is there not much that is Legalistic about the Hua-Yeh-Teng government? Certainly Hua's first slogan hit home with a Legalist thud: "Be meticulous in organization and direction." His every speech is an effort to show that doctrine should be subordinate to authority. Rules and regulations are back in favor. "Rebelling," "Going in the back door," "Being a helicopter," "Tossing around Chairman Mao's quotations," are all out of favor.

Meanwhile there has been a distinct resurgence of Soviet-educated bureaucrats of the Leninist stripe. These types form a generation. They tend to be in their forties or fifties, and to differ sharply in style both from officials twenty years older—who are likely to have had training or experience in the West—and from graduates of the Cultural Revolution—who are not always well trained but who are lively and un-bureaucratic. Diplomats in Peking who are seeking embassy staff know to request people in their sixties or seventies; indeed Chinese officials seem to understand the reasoning, for in offering an outstanding clerk or chef they will frequently point to his advanced age.

The Gang—and maybe Mao himself, as we have seen—believed that the bourgeoisie exists within the Communist

Party. This is a rather spine-chilling idea, yet the interesting implication is that debate and struggle are ongoing. The 1977–78 line is quite different. There is no bourgeois class within the Party. Citing Engels's attack on anarchists—the Gang were accused of being anarchists, too—the government maintains that the Chinese state is a "proletarian state." That rules out the bourgeoisie at the heart of things.

The message for the citizenry is fairly clear. They are to obey. The ship of state is in good hands; no fundamental questions need be raised. So much for the thrilling cry of the Cultural Revolution: "To rebel is justified." Rebel against what? Certainly not against the proletarian state!

4. A more hopeful possible future pattern than bureaucracy-plus-privatism is also a more likely one. It can be termed a "modified Rousseauism," that is, a community that is egalitarian, has a high degree of participation but little personal freedom. It would amount to a continuation of Maoism, but with less reliance on sheer spirit and more on settled political institutions.

It cannot be stressed too often that China was economically backward at the time of its revolution, and that it does not have a strong democratic tradition. This twin deprivation threw a tremendous problem into Mao's lap: how to achieve socialist political institutions, and do so in time to keep pace with socioeconomic development and cultural advance.

Mao's answer was to plunge the Chinese people periodically into a hothouse of forced, almost staged, democratic enthusiasm. The answer was not a solution. The Great Leap Forward and the Cultural Revolution have both been much criticized within China, and may be even more so in the future. They fell well short of remaking the Chinese people, and they did not change at all the basic way the Party runs the nation. The *spirit* of society was transformed, it is true, but only for a season. The institutions were not transformed.

It is not that the Chinese fail to understand the challenge of achieving socialist political institutions. Twenty-one years ago Lai Jo-yü, head of China's Federation of Trade Unions, observed boldly: "Some people seem to think that because the working class wields state power, the state as a whole will safeguard the interests of the working class, and the trade unions have lost their function as a protector of the workers' interests. This view is wrong."

Lai Jo-yü went on: "The reason is that classes have not yet been completely eliminated in our country, while various bureaucratic tendencies will inevitably continue to manifest themselves among us and it will take us a long time to overcome them. Under these circumstances, the material interests and political rights of the mass of workers and employees are not safe from damage by bureaucracy." Whether or not Lai's point about class retains importance, his point about bureaucratic tendencies surely does.

More than twenty years after Lai spoke, Chinese political institutions are still very paternalistic. Part of the problem is that Marxism is often treated in China as a metaphysic—as when Mao's Thoughts are called "spiritual assets"—instead of as a method of analysis.*

The view of Marxism as a metaphysic was expressed in all innocence by a Red Guard during the Cultural Revolution. "We will rebel," he cried, "against anyone who claims to oppose Chairman Mao and his Thought." That is dogma, not

---

* It is haunting to recall Mao's own warning, uttered in 1942, against treating Marxism as a metaphysic: "If we do not oppose the new formalism and new dogmatism today, the Chinese mind will be bound by the chains of another form of extremism." That sentence may be quoted one day in China.

politics; it is the language of children, not of socialist citizens. Even in a commonwealth of Maoist souls, democratic institutions will still be needed.

Mao long ago said that there are contradictions between any government and the people it rules. This is a valid starting point in the search for socialist political institutions that guarantee the rights of citizens. It will mean experimenting with elections at the local level; treating conflict as a clash among reasonable opinions rather than class warfare; tossing more issues out for public discussion without fear that Mao's Thoughts will be undermined by the outcome.

At the end of 1976 there came one small straw in the wind. "The Chinese people," stated *People's Daily*, when a hydrogen bomb test was announced in November, "firmly support the solemn and just stand which the Chinese government has consistently taken on the issue of nuclear weapons." What is this? How could the people *not* agree with the People's government? It is interesting, and most unusual, that the distinction was so baldly acknowledged.

Sociology to the Rescue.

Ultimately it is sociology itself that will probably help the Chinese to shape their political system. After much social change, China is far from what it was in 1949. As the poem written by the demonstrators at the Square of the Gate of Heavenly Peace in 1976 says: "China is no longer the China of yore,/And the people are no longer wrapped in sheer ignorance." The need for forced solutions may be ebbing.

Of the 35 million members of the CCP today, more than one-third have joined *since 1965*. These people are young moderns. From childhood they have existed in a sophisticated institutional environment of great complexity and specialization. They seem to be sincere Marxists; yet they are not "poor and blank"—Mao's famous phrase for the masses he undertook to mold into a revolutionary people.

These young moderns are the first generation who should be able to make socialist political institutions work. Dictatorship over them is inappropriate; they are not enemies. Politics as a quasi-religious festival is equally inappropriate; they are not naïve.

The Party members form only 4% of the nation as a whole, but the point has a wider import. Millions of urban workers and even the more advanced peasants are also becoming modernized in attitude and way of life. Take the case of the ex-Red Guards. Ten years after the Cultural Revolution they are now married, with children to feed and pacify, and a steady salary. The world does not seem the same to them as during the Cultural Revolution, when nothing was fixed and all things seemed possible.

Few of them retain utopian views. At the same time these millions have had a rich, if sobering experience. From 1966 until 1968 they took responsibility, made decisions, wrote resolutions, traveled the nation, looked power-holders in the face and often saw warts. They may now be sobered, but they are not sheep. They have settled down to routine chores, but they are not "wrapped in sheer ignorance."

Sociology can come to the rescue, then, by producing a new generation that finds it natural and essential to express Maoism in socialist political institutions.

The change is unlikely to be swift or dramatic. China is a very complex society and the previous three patterns I have mentioned will all be in evidence to some degree. Caesarism is not yet dead and some will try to put Mao's hat upon Hua's head; backward sectors of Chinese society will provide momentum for that attempt.

The reduced authority of Peking without Mao will make the status quo a powerful influence upon the future in far-flung parts of the land of 900 million. Equally, there is certain to be a great deal of bureaucracy in tomorrow's China, and a great deal of privatism on the part of the Chinese man in the street who knows how to sidestep the messy currents of affairs of state.

Yet the real choice is between bureaucracy-plus-privatism and steps toward genuine socialist political institutions. Individual freedom as the West knows it is not in the cards for China; the system does not permit it, and other values that are permitted seem more important in any case to most Chinese: economic security, pride in the nation, and a chance to participate in the cut and thrust of community life.

Nor is democracy around the corner, at least in the Western sense of a periodic choice between competing sets of leaders. The political monopoly of the Communist Party excludes it—and the Party is sufficiently respected that we cannot forecast its losing its grip.

The question is whether the CCP will encourage a more mature participation by informed citizens in the shaping of socialism, or whether the neo-Legalist solution of a Stalinist grip over a nation of sheep will prove more attractive.

Within that larger question—to which I do not know the answer—we see in China today a certain shift of emphasis as between equality and economic security. A full-blown Rousseauism would give full rein to the first. But the Cultural Revolution is widely thought to have tipped the scales too hastily toward strict equality (and nonstop participation). A modified Rousseauism would blend a structure of incentives with equality as a general value.

China will remain egalitarian. It will continue to be a high-participation society. Yet it is becoming more task-centered for the sake of economic progress. The emphasis for the time being is on modernizing the nation so that living standards can rise. Other values (e.g., equality) may have to give up a bit of ground as a result. The pattern will remain Maoist, but modifications to it will bring important changes in the life of the Chinese people.

9
America
and
֍ China ֍

Relations between the United States and China have reached a stage, like seeds when broadcast on the soil in changing weather, that must now lead either to growth or to a withering.

The Year of the Snake (1977) turned out to be a curious one for the Washington-Peking tie. Ever since the shadow of the 1976 election fell over Ford's China policy in the late summer of 1975, it had seemed that 1977 would be the year of opportunity. The two countries *still* had no full diplomatic relations. Would 1977 see an exchange of ambassadors?

Even as the Snake slithered in the prospects had already dimmed. The new U.S. President felt no passion on the China issue. He accepted the advice of both the State Department and the National Security Council staff to put the matter to one side at least until late 1977. History was repeating itself with extreme persistence. The few remarks Jimmy Carter did make on China, moreover, supported "independence" for Taiwan, and thus seemed to set normalization with Peking back rather than forward.

Hua Kuo-feng at festivities for May Day 1977, at Sun Yat-sen Park in Peking. (*New China News Agency Photo*)

But Carter's relations with the Russians did not go well in early 1977. And when Secretary Cyrus Vance returned from his unproductive Moscow trip in April, he paid increased attention to China. In Peking, meanwhile, a sense of anticipation about the new American President grew. In part this was in proportion to the souring of U.S.-Soviet relations. The Chinese had expected that Washington-Moscow ties under Carter would be more a story of "collusion" than "contention"—Peking's twin terms for superpower mutual dealings. Moreover the Chinese, thanks to Hua's fealty to Mao, still declined to play the Russian card. The hostility toward Moscow raged unabated.

So the United States generated some "movement"—as a series of small gestures is called by diplomats—toward China in the spring of 1977, and the Chinese were receptive in an unexcited way. Peking's envoy in Washington was courted in top-level sessions. Carter's son "Chip" was sent to Peking with a warm message. The post-Gang of Four mood in China helped. Heightened interest was shown in receiving specialized U.S. trade missions.

In May Carter made a striking statement at Notre Dame University in Indiana: "We see the American-Chinese relationship as a central element in our global policy, and China as a key force for global peace." And Vance made a speech to the Asia Society in New York which showed a sharp desire to carry forward the Shanghai Communiqué of 1972 and complete the task of normalizing relations. He announced a projected trip to China for November—but as a sign of the times it was brought forward to August.

By summertime the Taipei government was like an ant on a hot stove. 1976 had been one more year of reprieve for the plucky and lucky Nationalists. Squatting on their pretty island 100 miles from the China coast, they had already been saved from history's certain verdict by many twists of fate. In 1950 Pyongyang had come to their rescue. By moving on South Korea, Kim Il-sung provoked a 180-degree shift in U.S. policy toward Taiwan—from de facto abandonment to vigorous embrace. In 1975 it was Hanoi that came to their rescue. The Vietnamese Communists' drive on South Vietnam—as I will show in a moment—helped stymie the advance in U.S.-China relations.

The Year of the Dragon—such a tough year for China—was a good year for Taiwan in two ways. The U.S. election tied Ford's hands over China policy. And China's internal ructions cast a pall over the PRC's immediate future. Chou's death was a loss for Peking-Washington ties. Earthquakes took an economic toll, and were also an indirect military setback. The Gang threw sand into the machinery of China's links with the West.

Within the United States, friends of the Nationalists took advantage of the pause to raise endless fresh possible difficulties in the path of normalization. The most persuasive of these—the legal and legally related economic problems that would follow from "de-recognizing" Taiwan—caused concern in everyone's mind.

But by mid-year all Taipei's agonies were back. The remarks of Carter and Vance—and their studied failure to utter the three golden words "Republic of China"—brought cries of distress. All the reprieves had done nothing but nourish the Nationalists' illusions. A loser goes on sniffing victory until he is ushered from the ring. Could it really be true that the curtain still had not fallen on the Chinese civil war of the 1940s?

In fact the Vance trip to Peking in August 1977 brought no step forward toward normalization. At best—and Washington put the rosiest possible interpretation upon it—the trip kept semi-normalization in its post-1974 state of marking time. At worst—it was Peking that took the more pessimistic view—the Vance trip put a settlement of the Taiwan issue even further out of reach than it had been during the Ford administration.

By late 1977 Washington seemed to have turned aside from China policy, while pressing ahead once more with a range of negotiations with Russia. Carter had on his hands the difficult task of persuading Congress to ratify the Panama Canal treaties, and apparently felt that this made the Taiwan issue untouchable for the moment. Indeed Taipei might well have concluded that Panama saved them in 1977, as Vietnam had done in 1975 and Korea in 1950.

So many doubts crept into public discussion of the Sino-American connection in the mid-1970s that it is necessary to recall certain basic points.

In the first place, the relationship between the two nations is of great importance for several reasons:

• Because of what semi-normalization since 1972 has already achieved—an enormous reduction of the danger of war.

• Because China borders twelve nations, is the third largest military power in the world, has global concerns for the first time in its history, and is the most influential nation in Asia.

• Because the American and Chinese peoples are interested in each other, often get on very well with each other, have goods to trade and ideas of relevance to exchange with each other.

• Because both the United States and China have bigger problems with the Soviet Union than they have with each other, and share an interest in coordinating parallel strategies on some international issues.

• Because, for the United States, a good relationship with the PRC is a key to a creative policy in Asia as a whole, where world politics have increasingly focused since World War II.

In the second place, we should recall how far we have come since the dangerous days of Sino-U.S. hostility during the 1950s and 1960s. Three times in those years Washington threatened China with nuclear weapons. Not a single government official from either country visited the capital of the other.

In a Peking bomb shelter during 1973 I had a vivid reminder of the changed Sino-American atmosphere. The shelter belonged to the Peking Construction Tool Plant. "Who might attack China?" I asked as we toured the well-equipped tunnels. "Imperialists," the answer came back. But since the Chinese identify two types of imperialism—Russian and American—I decided to pursue my question through a back door. "Have any Americans visited your shelter?"

As I asked the question, my mind went back more than a decade. In 1964 when I first visited Peking, anti-Americanism was so tangible you could have cut it with a knife. Even the fact that I had once visited the United States made some Chinese wary of me.

But 1973 was another era. The director of the bomb shelter answered brightly: "Edgar Snow came here, and later on Joseph Alsop." That seemed to cover quite a wide political spectrum. Then I asked: "Have you had Russian visitors?" A stern face and a crisp reply: "This defense shelter is only for visitors from friendly countries." So much for which imperialism the Chinese fear. So much for distinctions between the political views of Snow and Alsop; both were Americans and that was all that counted. So much—at least for now—for the dark days of Sino-American hatred.

The new Sino-U.S. civility has reduced the danger of war in East and Southeast Asia, and produced a spurt in trade—especially in U.S. exports to China—and a slow but immensely worthwhile growth in cultural exchanges between two peoples who have much to offer each other. It has given the United States the possibility of extra leverage against the rising power of Russia.

Against these benefits I do not see any major costs. The four predicted by those Americans who opposed U.S.-China relations during the 1950s and 1960s have not materialized:

- Allies of the United States have not been deeply upset by Washington's opening to Peking; they have almost all established the same link themselves.
- Warnings that our dealings with Russia would be thrown off track by the Kremlin's shock at the end of Sino-U.S. isolation proved unsound; the Russian pique was a one-shot force whose impact did not outlast 1972.
- Peking's seating at the UN, which the new U.S.-China policy of July 1971 indirectly precipitated, has not after all resulted in Chinese efforts to "wreck" or "disrupt" the UN.
- China *has* paid its trade bills, and has *not* used its embassy to subvert America.

In fact, America's policy has changed more than China's policy since the 1960s. In November 1968, Richard Nixon said: "The world cannot be safe until China changes. Thus our aim should be to induce change; to persuade China that it cannot satisfy its imperial ambitions, and that its own national interest requires a turning away from foreign adventures and a turning inward toward the solution of its own domestic problems." But far from aptly analyzing China, Mr. Nixon was inadvertently predicting what America would have to do and has since largely done.

At any rate it is an immense gain that the governments, traders, sportspersons, scientists, and ordinary people of America and China have begun to meet each other. We have grown used to the tie with Peking. It is very hard now to imagine it not existing. But this does not mean we should forget the bitter past—because aspects of the past echo on into the present. Nor does it mean that we should take the tie for granted; in a world of flux a relationship is not a once-for-all achievement, but something that grows in the measure that it meets the challenges of its changing environment. We should no longer think of the tie with China as a merely negative gain—correcting an anomaly from the past—for the future's positive agenda beckons.

The present state of semi-normalization leaves the relationship starved in a hundred ways. There can be no direct banking facilities. There can be no Chinese trade exhibitions in the United States, nor Chinese ships or aircraft calling at American cities, since United States citizens with claims outstanding against the PRC (dating back to the rupture of 1949) could probably attach this Chinese property.

American media cannot establish news bureaus within the PRC. Chinese leaders will not pay visits to the States—only to the UN enclave at New York—and a marvelous opportunity to influence their thinking about America is lost. Students of the two countries cannot study in the other country. American businessmen miss large orders from China, especially for industrial equipment, because Peking gives priority to import sources that have diplomatic relations with the PRC.

Historically, Sino-American relations have been shaped by deeply felt values on both sides. In American minds, three were for a long time important:

1. A sense of American innocence. The United States felt different from Europe with its empires and its feudal past. America was a democratic and anti-colonial nation by birth.

2. A sense of having a mission in the world, and not least in Asia. The United States intended to extend its own virtues

to other nations. As Senator Wherry of Nevada vowed typically in the 1940s: "We shall lift Shanghai up, ever up, God
willing, until it is just like Kansas City."

3. Along with these feelings of purity and conviction of
mission went a Promethean spirit. Particularly after 1945, the
United States, standing in command of a shattered Japan,
felt an almost unlimited hope in what America could achieve
in Asia. This led unhappily to an arrogance of power. Thus
General Wheeler was able to say during the Vietnam years
that "The Far East has become our Far West," and a chief of
U.S. psychological warfare in Vietnam could declare with an
intention of magnanimity: "You can't kill all the people in the
world who disagree with you—you have to change some of
their minds."

These three mental starting points explain much about
American policy in China from the late nineteenth century
until the era of John Foster Dulles. There was much fascina-
tion with China, and enormous goodwill, and yet at the same
time an underlying effort to make China over in the image of
America—Christian, democratic, capitalist. The 1950s could
talk about the "loss" of China because earlier decades had
been so presumptuous in their plans for China.

The idealism of the United States was admired by many
Chinese, including Mao Tse-tung, but after World War II its
nature was twisted by marriage with power politics. Washington's policies in East Asia came to be based on a denial of
anti-colonialism and other progressive American traditions.

In fact, the semi-normalization of Sino-American relations
in the 1970s could take place only because these mental
starting points had been undermined by the defeat in Vietnam and by a new complexity in international politics.

After the United States struck trouble in Vietnam, China
knew that it would not give much trouble to China in the fu-

ture. It became clear to me during my second visit to China, in the watershed year of 1971, that Peking believed the tide of American expansionism in Asia had turned. China appreciated—and still does—the new realism in American policy. For we in America no longer bristle with a sense of innocence, which would hardly be possible after Vietnam. We have less of a sense of mission; are we sure we know what to offer to others? And our Promethean spirit has weakened—the dollar and the Marines cannot quite do today what they could twenty years ago.

Less well understood than the American starting points, though more important to grasp today because they have been more enduring, are four mental starting points on the Chinese side:

1. Mao Tse-tung and his régime inherited from the past a sense of China's centrality. To some extent this parallels America's sense of its own centrality. Both countries are vast continents. Both have been able to produce almost all of what they need. Both have been remarkably free from sudden intrusions of unwelcome outside forces.

Mao's "Middle Kingdom"* assumption was not the same as traditional China's. But he did take it for granted that China was important to America (maybe he overestimated this in the 1930s and 1940s). He did consider China the key to Asia's future. And he did adopt, for the most part, a "you come to us" attitude to all foreign countries except Russia.

2. The second point obtained its weight, in part, from the importance of the first. China's proud isolation had been shattered for the first time in the nineteenth century. Mao approached the United States with the sense of humiliation

---

* The name "China" (*Zhong guo*) means "Middle Kingdom," and in centuries past the Chinese did think of their country as the center of the world.

all Chinese patriots felt at the century of assault by Western nations from the Opium War of the 1840s onward. Here was a bitter recent past which the PRC was bent on leaving behind. China sought to become an equal with the major nations of the world, rather than merely an object of the policies of those more powerful than itself.

3. A vigorous aspiration to modernity is the third point. Mao made it clear long ago that a main aim of the CCP was to modernize and industrialize China. The United States is the leading modern industrial nation in the world. So although Mao's China was determined to shake free of Western control, it chose a path of development that leads it nearer to the levels and social experience of the West. In looking at the United States, the Chinese see some economic and technical aspects of their own future.

4. The fourth point is of course Marxism, which is composed of class analysis plus a theory of history. The Chinese Communists have always believed that imperialism will fall eventually from its own contradictions, and that socialism will everywhere in due course replace capitalism, just as surely as capitalism in its turn took over from feudalism. So they have a long-term perspective and an underlying optimism about the course of world history.

The Vietnam War seemed to the Chinese, as to many others, to mark the end of a quarter century of American militarist expansion in East Asia. And the difficulties of the dollar shortly after appeared to reinforce the idea of imperialism in retreat.

During that twenty-five-year period, the Chinese aim toward America was essentially a negative one. In the short term to forestall an attack from the United States. In the longer term to encourage the neutralism of a belt of small countries near China, so that they would not be bases for American military capacity that could threaten China.

These aims now have been largely achieved. It is not surprising that by the 1970s China should consider that Russia, with which it shares a 4,300-mile border, poses a bigger threat than a United States still strong but turning somewhat inward. Unlike seventeen years before, Peking found in 1972 that its offer to Washington to agree on the five principles of peaceful coexistence—a formula for equality and noninterference—was readily accepted by the American side.

We can sum up the significance of Mr. Nixon's thrilling trip to China in 1972 in this way. The danger of Sino-American war was more or less eliminated. So, too, was the luxury the U.S.S.R. had enjoyed of seeing its two main adversaries out of touch with each other. The trip "that changed the world" did change a few things. The international position of the Kuomintang government in Taiwan began to erode; since then it has lost its seat in the UN, recognition by more than sixty countries (leaving it recognized by only twenty-odd), and a good part of the American military presence on its soil. Japan and other allies of the United States were prompted to effect their own normalization with the PRC. And by no means least important, trade, cultural exchanges, and visits by ordinary people began again between China and the United States.

Public opinion in the United States quickly accepted what might well have been accepted earlier—that the conflict of interest between America and China is not great; that a world of two blocs has given way to more diverse patterns; that China has neither the will nor the capacity for far-flung military conquest; and that the ideological element in inter-

national relations is less prominent than many had considered it to be during the 1950s and 1960s.

However the new Sino-American relationship has made
less progress since 1974 than it did from 1971 to the end of
1973.

One reason has been the impact of the war in Indochina
and the way in which it ended. In 1972 Chou En-lai said to
Nixon: "There can be no understanding between us except
on the basis of settlement of the Vietnamese War first." Yet
in early 1975 the war in Vietnam and Cambodia still raged.
The United States even increased its military aid to the
Saigon régime, and made fresh, open-ended promises to the
Lon Nol régime in Phnom Penh. This made it difficult for the
Chinese side to maintain full momentum in Sino-American
relations.

By the summer of 1975, the essential victory of Marxist
forces all over Indochina made it difficult, in turn, for the
American side to do anything about the Sino-American tie
which could be construed as a "concession to communism."

An anecdote sums up the problem that arose. In the fall of
1975, Secretary Kissinger was sitting at dinner with Philip
Habib, Assistant Secretary for East Asia and the Pacific, and
another person who is interested in China. When asked by
this third person if the Taiwan issue might be settled during
Mr. Ford's forthcoming trip to China, Kissinger made a sour
reference to the fall, six months before, of South Vietnam
and Cambodia: "Habib has already lost two embassies from
his portfolio this year—he's not going to lose a third."

A second problem has been Taiwan. As the Shanghai Communiqué indicates, this issue is the chief obstacle to normalized U.S.-China relations.

The State Department has spoken at times of normalization as merely the extension of existing contacts with China.

But it is quite clear from the Shanghai Communiqué that "normalization" means the establishment of diplomatic relations, which cannot but involve a settlement in principle of the Taiwan issue as a factor in Peking-Washington relations.

The U.S. side has been slowly fulfilling its pledge at Shanghai to reduce and eventually eliminate its military presence on Taiwan. Yet at the same time a number of steps have been taken over the past two or three years which have actually cemented relations between America and the Taiwan régime: credits and assistance for massive military supplies (including Hawk ground-to-air missiles and large numbers of F-5E jet interceptors);* the sending of a senior ambassador to Taipei with a parting announcement that he was going to fill "one of the best posts we have"; agreement to the establishment of five new consulates for the Taiwan régime on U.S. soil; a string of ringing endorsements of the value and permanence of the official tie with the Republic of China by state legislatures; and repeated statements by U.S. leaders that relations between the Republic of China and the United States are secure from any future change.

Moreover a complacent "two-China" mood returned in certain influential American circles. Pro-Taipei sentiment appeared to grow particularly in the U.S. Congress during 1976 and 1977.

Meanwhile the Chinese government has made known its view that, in these circumstances, and given the continued, often-stated intention of Taipei to reconquer the mainland, a peaceful solution to the Taiwan issue is probably impossible. Actually it is hard to tell whether this is a serious forecast, or merely a way of reiterating that Taiwan is China's exclusive

---

* Total U.S. arms transfers to Taiwan rose from $196 million in 1974, to $215 million in 1975, and $293 million in 1976.

preserve (I will return to this in the next chapter). At any rate it adversely affects U.S. public opinion's view of the PRC.

To make matters worse, the Chinese government has not always made its determination to settle the Taiwan problem (as an issue in U.S.-China relations) clear to all branches of the U.S. government. It has even given some members of Congress the impression that the menace of the Soviet Union is of such overriding importance that no other issue, not even Taiwan, has high priority. The effect of this message, or of this misunderstanding if it is one, has not been helpful to the task of normalization.

Various theories could explain why the United States has not moved to disengage itself from the Taiwan régime. One is that Washington is quietly encouraging the idea of an independent Taiwan, either under Kuomintang or Taiwanese rule, with which the United States would continue to have diplomatic and military relationships while maintaining whatever link it could with Peking.

Another is that the U.S. government intends to move forward soon to full normalization with the PRC, and that its cozy support for Taipei is designed to give Taipei the best attainable bargaining posture for a negotiated settlement with Peking—which the United States will actively seek to bring about.

The third possibility is that the U.S. government does not intend to move ahead to normalization on the terms at present available, indeed that it envisages an indefinite continuance of its recognition of the régime in Taipei as the Republic of China.* This would mean a choice by Washing-

---

* This suits certain military strategists both in the Pentagon and in Taiwan who have revived the idea of Taiwan as a key base in U.S. Asia-Pacific strategy. The younger son of Chiang Kai-shek, General Chiang Wei-kuo, urges that Washington make Taiwan and Indonesia the twin bastions of its defense of the South China Sea and the Indian

ton among its commitments, giving a higher priority to the 1954 Security Treaty with Taipei than to the 1972 Shanghai Communiqué with the PRC.*

A final major obstacle to normalization since 1974 has been internal political flux in both countries. As the Watergate crisis swelled in early 1974, China began to doubt that Nixon could or would press forward with normalization. At the same time some circles in China were dubious about how fruitful the new tie with the United States had proven for China.

On the American side, finally, electoral pressures from within the Republican Party caught up with Ford by the late summer of 1975. Fearing the influence of Reagan, the Ford political forces decided by August to rule out any movement in relations with the PRC that could be criticized as "a concession to the Communists." Hence Ford went to China in December 1975 with very little in his briefcase.

The opportunity presented by the first six months of 1975, when Ford was fresh in office and the 1976 presidential election still distant, had been lost. This setback intensified, in turn, the doubts about the American connection which existed in certain Chinese circles: had not Nixon stated to Chou a firm U.S. intention to complete full normalization by the mid-1970s; do the dynamic Americans forget things so

---

Ocean. But such a role for Taiwan is precluded by the document Mr. Nixon signed in Shanghai.

* Such an order of priorities would please many in Congress, on grounds quite separate from the merits of the issue. Let me illustrate from an afternoon I spent before part of the House International Relations Committee in 1976. A leading congressman objected to my testimony: "You mean to say that you come here and urge full normalization of relations with Communist China?" I expected the congressman to go on to catalogue the evil aspects of the PRC. Instead he continued: *"Which would mean,* Dr. Terrill [at this point he looked fearsome], elevating the Shanghai Communiqué, signed only by the Executive Branch, *above* our Security Treaty with the Republic of China, which was ratified by Congress!"

fast that the Shanghai Communiqué has already become to them an inoperative relic of history?

The new U.S.-China tie had enabled Washington to slide away from Indochina without an appearance of disaster, but it had not yet helped Peking to solve its Taiwan problem.

During 1976 and 1977 many phantoms were let loose to try to frighten Americans away from this patient guest-in-waiting called normalization.

• It is said that we should not be hasty. Hasty after twenty-nine years! After all major nations in the world, including all the western European friends of the United States (and all the eastern European friends of the Soviet Union), have established full diplomatic relations with China. After China has become one of the three world powers in political and strategic influence. After two dreadful wars in Asia, which escalated from local civil wars largely because the United States and the PRC were hostile to each other. And after giving the Nationalists nearly three decades in which to make good their daily reiterated pledge to return to the mainland. ·

• It is said that we must keep our "commitments" to Taipei. Well, the Shanghai Communiqué of 1972 is a commitment too, and one that made more impact on both the Chinese and American peoples than the arrangement with Chiang Kai-shek in 1954.

Treaties are not written in concrete. Commitments change as the actual life of a society—for whose sake the commitments are made—evolves, and as the balance of international forces changes. The legal aspect is but one of many aspects of any nation's foreign policy. Lon Nol and Thieu could remind us—from sad exile—that for the United States to define the government of a given territory as an ally does not guarantee either a bright future for its people or a continuing American interest in their welfare.

It is not at all illegal, or contrary to any U.S. commitment, to terminate the 1954 treaty by giving one year's notice of this to Taipei—indeed Article X of the treaty provides for precisely that course of action. This would be a political decision based upon the realities of today's world, as foreign policy decisions must always be.

Finally it is important for the supporters of the continuance into the 1980s of the 1954 treaty with Taipei to understand the implications of what they propose. Do they actually mean that the United States should send troops to fight for the Nationalists against Peking in the event of war between the two? Which friends of the United States do they suppose would join it on the Nationalist side? And are they prepared for the gain which the U.S.S.R. would reap from war between the United States and the People's Republic of China?

• It is said the Russians would be "upset" by Sino-American normalization. This objection goes against both logic and experience. Of course Moscow would be made anxious; but why not, and what could the Russians do about it? The enduring impact on Moscow of Nixon's 1972 trip to Peking worked to American advantage. Anyone who has followed the SALT-I negotiations knows that the new Peking-Washington tie made the U.S.S.R. more disposed to an agreement than it would otherwise have been.

People who think that our China policy ought to be made in Moscow should recall that the politics of a triangle are not the same as the politics of an alliance. Interests are the basis of a triangle of relationships; leverage is its operating principle.

The Kremlin, sensibly, did not worry about "upsetting" the

United States when it walked hand in hand with China during the 1950s. Did that friendship reduce Russia's influence with the United States? Of course not; it added to Russia's influence. So will full Sino-American normalization add influence to the American side in Soviet-American relations.

• It is said that American public opinion is not in favor of normalizing relationships with the PRC and thus breaking official relations with the Taipei government. I do not believe it. The argument overlooks the impact of dynamic leadership. It is based on "public opinion polls" which are consistently emotive, and which consistently blur the distinction between official and unofficial ties between the United States and Taiwan.

The same voices of gloom said during the 1950s and 1960s that the American public was against any compromise—or even any dealings—with Peking. With a stroke of decisive leadership Mr. Nixon proved what nonsense that was in 1972. His trip to China, and the Shanghai Communiqué which issued from it, were approved by a vast majority. True some intellectuals have turned sour on China, but the ordinary American people are, more than ever before, open-minded about any fair case put to them on China.

Let us look more closely at these polls that some people regard as proofs that normalization would not be popular. Some of them are shocking indeed, less for their answers than for the initial questions. An NBC poll in 1974 asked: "Do you agree or disagree with the following statement: As a gesture of friendship to Communist China we should break off relations with Chiang Kai-shek and the Nationalist Chinese on Formosa." A *gesture of friendship* has got nothing whatsoever to do with why the relationship with Taipei ought or ought not to be broken. The point of breaking off relations with Chiang is to acknowledge that the government of China is in Peking—a historical aspect of the problem that was somehow overlooked in the NBC poll.

Consider a Gallup Poll taken in 1974. People were asked: "Do you feel it was just or fair, or not, that Nationalist China lost its membership in the UN?" And another question read: "The U.S. is bound by treaty to help defend Nationalist China in case of Communist attack. Do you think the U.S. should always honor this commitment or not?"

First, "honor" and "commitment" are very moralistic terms to put in a question of this kind. Second, in none of the five questions posed by the Gallup Poll is the People's Republic of China referred to by its correct name, but only by the ideological label "Communist China." Third, Nationalist China did not "lose its membership" in the UN. The seat of China was assumed by a new government of China; it was not a question of membership. (That Gallup Poll was quietly co-sponsored by the Republic of China, which may have had something to do with the wording of the questions.)*

The four-year lull in relations between the United States and China will probably come to an end in 1978. Either the relationship will move ahead once more, or it will fall back and lose importance for both nations.

The new leadership in both capitals will have to confront

---

* The most germane question in any foreign policy public opinion poll is that which gauges how important people think a particular country is, and will be, to the United States and in the world. A careful poll of Potomac Associates asked just this question in 1976 (*The Pursuit of National Security*, Washington, D.C., 1976, p. 29). The result shows massive potential support for any President who stresses policy toward the PRC. The American people see China, in the 1980s, as virtually on a par with the United States and Russia. They foresee "an increase in the power and importance of China over the next ten years, in contrast to a levelling off of the United States and the Soviet Union." And so on. This is far more meaningful data than that on how the public would handle the diplomatic technicalities of recognizing China at any point of time. Diplomatic technicalities are not the public's business; broad perspectives on what counts are.

the normalization issue squarely. The dust is settling in China after two years of change. In America, likewise, a new leader enjoys impressive authority and has at least two years of office still ahead of him.

The Chinese understood the pressures of election year. They were patient and did not push during 1976 for what they did not think they could get. Into 1977 they were preoccupied with laying down the line of their own new régime. 1978 is another story—probably the most crucial year since 1972 for Sino-U.S. relations.*

One hopes that Peking will give priority to its ties with the United States. From the U.S. side there are five reasons why Carter and Vance should resolutely seek to normalize.

First, it is never wise policy to cling to a discredited position rooted in a past that has disappeared; always better to face an illusion, cut some losses, and free the hands for the challenges of tomorrow.

Second, the Shanghai Communiqué is not only the carefully worked-out basis for the Sino-U.S. rapprochement of the past six years; it also forms a commitment that people around the world have identified as the serious core of a new Sino-American relationship. The Chinese still regard it as authoritative, so do most of the American people. It would be a disturbing piece of unpredictability for either side to turn its back on this charter of détente in the Pacific.

Third, there is no conflict of interest, between China and the United States, big enough to match the concern each has

---

*The U.S. national security chief Brzezinski said to a visitor in mid-1977: "The Chinese are very patient. We have to learn from them." That is either cynical or stupid. Normalization is as much in U.S. interests as it is in China's. Peking was patient in 1976 for a serious, particular reason. To interpret this as some endemic Oriental passivity would, I fear, be risky. The remark of a Peking official during 1976 should also be borne in mind: "What right does Kissinger have to say we will be patient?"

with the growth of Russian military and political power in many parts of the world. A flourishing Sino-U.S. relationship is one of the most effective ways available to check any excessive ambitions that the U.S.S.R. may have.

All over the world there exists a parallelism of strategic interests between the United States and China: in Africa, West Europe, Southeast Asia, the Indian Ocean, even in Indochina, which was so recently an obstacle to U.S.-China relations. A full diplomatic relationship is the minimum necessity for turning this parallelism into stable cooperation. Why leave fragile a relationship of such rich strategic promise?

Fourth, the current state of semi-normalization is not a stable one. If the Shanghai Communiqué is not fulfilled, that will mean it has been repudiated. Bitterness and disappointment would result, and new policy directions that might not suit us would probably emanate from Peking.

Finally, for the United States a rich and stable tie with China is, together with the Japan alliance, the foundation of a creative policy in Asia, where the U.S. now does more trade than it does in Europe. When relations with China were bad, war clouds hung over East Asia and/or Southeast Asia. When relations improved, the small lands of the region found a long-delayed chance to focus on the tasks of peace rather than those of war.

A militarist phase has ended in Asia. The peaceful development of societies for the well-being of their people can be the order of business for the rest of the century. The United States will not be less influential in peace than it was in war—whether we speak of intervention in Indochina or of intervention in the Chinese civil war.

And America will be at its best, and most faithful to its own traditions, by relying not on an endless prolongation of armed

hostility in the Taiwan Strait but on its vast economic resources and unmatched moral and diplomatic influence.

President Truman said in December 1945 that a strong
and united China is of the utmost importance to world peace.
It is still true today. And for China, a cooperative relationship
with America could be more important than any other foreign
relationship China has or could have.

10
The
Problem
⅌ of Taiwan ⅌

In a broad sweep over Sino-U.S. relations, the previous chapter raised the issue of Taiwan. Let me now focus directly on this major dilemma.

Taiwan is an island province of China which became separated from the motherland for half a century because of Japanese conquest. When the Chinese civil war was nearing its end, the Chiang Kai-shek forces went to that island, set up a mainland Chinese régime over the Taiwanese people, and thus introduced them into the fight between Mao Tse-tung and Chiang Kai-shek. That was the fate that overcame the Taiwanese.

Since 1949 they have been part of the Chinese civil war question. The U.S. commitment to them was not a commitment to the island as a polity, nor to the people of Taiwan, but to the régime of Chiang Kai-shek, with its claim to be the government of China.

Since Peking and Washington came to a limited agreement on the principles of the Taiwan issue at Shanghai in February 1972, some people say Taiwan is a sleeping dog which should be let lie. "Don't try to fix something that isn't broken," advises *The New York Times*. But in the light of overall world politics this would be unwise.

It is not beyond the limits of strong leadership on both sides to finish the construction of a Taiwan solution that was begun at Shanghai in 1972—provided that the idealism and rigidity that lie behind U.S. "commitments" to the Republic of China on Taiwan are modified alike by a sense of future strategic need and an awareness of history.

At the height of the Vietnam War, during the 1960s, the Poles told a story about Lyndon Johnson and Leonid Brezhnev. The two leaders stood in line dressed in striped pyjamas with a tin plate in hand at a camp not far from Peking. With a flash of weary irritation LBJ reproached his Russian fellow-in-distress: "You know, Leonid, I did keep telling you Berlin was not our major problem." The day may come when Jimmy Carter and Hua Kuo-feng will kick themselves for ever having thought that Taiwan was their major problem.

Russian power rises all over the world to change the color of familiar landscape; it is not easy to get used to the chilly new geography—from Angola to Laos. The United States (together with Japan and western Europe) must counter Soviet power in an era when nuclear weapons are unlikely to be politically decisive, economic issues preoccupy most nations, alliances melt like butter in the sun, and changes of social system are more likely in Europe than in Asia.

A solid and many-sided tie between the United States and the PRC is a logical means to do so. Here is one pressing reason why our link with China ought to be forged closer.

I am *not* suggesting that America should align with China against Russia. The best policy is a three-pronged one. In principle, treat the two red giants evenhandedly; in particu-

The succession, as seen by a French cartoonist. (*Le Monde*)

lar circumstances and spots around the world, lean now to one, now to the other. But since China is weaker than Russia, and since the U.S. tie with Russia has gone much further than that with China, start by making a compensatory tilt toward China in order to achieve a balance of power.

The problem of Taiwan has three parts. So long as there is a régime in Taipei that pants to recover the twenty-nine provinces it fumbled with and then lost, the Chinese civil war will smolder on. But this "two Chinas" pain has eased since 1972. The United States and Japan have acknowledged that there is only one China. Taipei's threats to invade the mainland lose credibility as new generations arise. Some fifty nations have stopped regarding the government in Taipei as the

Republic of China and begun to treat it as an entity with which there can be plenty of private—but no official—dealings.

A second part of the problem is the existence in Taiwan of U.S. soldiers and bases that were originally a by-product of the outbreak of the Korean War in 1950. A solution to this problem was laid down at Shanghai when the United States stated that "it affirms the ultimate objective of the withdrawal of all forces and military installations from Taiwan."

Since that time the United States has indeed withdrawn most of its military establishment from the island (much of it was in any case geared to the Indochinese wars rather than to the Chinese civil war), and U.S. officials say privately that withdrawal of the remaining planes and one thousand men does not pose a major problem from the American side.

A third part of the problem is the view held both in Taipei and Peking that Taiwan is a province that should be reunited with the mainland. Merger seems about as possible as mixing one unit of water with 55 units of whiskey (that is the population ratio of Taiwan and the People's Republic of China) and achieving a drink that differs in any noticeable way from pure whiskey. Yet I have subdivided the Taiwan problem for a reason which is important and lends hope.

As a matter of historical fact, the third part of the Taiwan issue was not an urgent matter until the first and second parts intruded. (Mao Tse-tung told Edgar Snow in the 1930s that Taiwan might or might not come back to China.)

The Taiwan question was turned into the emotional core of Chinese foreign policy, and the chief bilateral quarrel between Peking and Washington over twenty-nine years, by Chiang Kai-shek's claim that his remnant in Taiwan was the government of China, by the American backing for this claim, and by the decision of President Truman in June 1950 (reversing previous policy) that led to making the island a U.S. military base.

The United States once had a commitment to accept PRC sovereignty over Taiwan. The U.S. Secretary of State Dean Acheson said on January 5, 1950: "When Formosa was made a province of China nobody raised any lawyer's doubts about that. That was regarded as in accordance with the commitments. The United States is not going to quibble about the integrity of the position. That is where we stand."

The United States once had a commitment to avoid military links with the Nationalists on Taiwan. Said President Truman that same day in 1950: "The United States has no predatory designs on Formosa or any other Chinese territory. The United States has no desire to obtain special rights or privileges or to establish military bases on Formosa. . . . The United States will not provide military aid and advice to the Chinese forces on Formosa." Some commitments have a way of being forgotten.

It is a pity that memories tend to be short on the issue of Taiwan, not only for the sake of historical accuracy, but because the past gives important clues as to what Peking is likely to do in the future. In the mid-1950s Peking talked always of a peaceful solution to the Taiwan problem. Then came an announcement by the United States in the summer of 1957 that it would install Matador missiles (capable of carrying nuclear weapons) on Taiwan. Peking's line on Taiwan became tougher, and Chinese efforts at conciliation with the United States evaporated.

It was *our side* that helped destroy the hope of a peaceful resolution of the Taiwan issue. Forgetting this, some people as a consequence allow themselves to forget how horrendous in every way a *non*-peaceful solution would be from Peking's point of view.

Peking knows that it would be a big and risky task to integrate Taiwan with the southeastern provinces. The island has a higher standard of living than does the PRC. Its defense forces could cause a lot of damage if they chose to fight.

Far more important, there are few signs that public opinion in Taiwan is "turning red" in the way Peking has hoped for. This is the often-overlooked crux of the hope for peace in the Taiwan Strait. The Chinese are deeply attached to a concept of Liberation as a people's movement. A decade ago, Peking rather carelessly used the expression: "We shall surely liberate Taiwan," but friendly Taiwanese objected to it. The Taiwanese must basically liberate themselves, it was pointed out. Peking cannot be the prime mover.

Fortunately this is now the view in Peking. Today the PRC typically states: "The Chinese people [i.e., including those on Taiwan] shall surely liberate Taiwan," or "Taiwan shall certainly be liberated." This seems to rule out invasion and large-scale war.

All this suggests that once Taipei ceases to pose as the government of China, or is no longer acknowledged as such by Washington, and once Taiwan is no more the site of foreign planes and joint war games between U.S. and Taiwan forces, the question of Taiwan as a separated province may not be as urgent to Peking as many people now assume.

Does that mean that America should leave the Taiwan question as it stands? To do so would surely be to miss a promising opportunity. We should take the initiative on Taiwan for three important reasons:

1. The U.S.-PRC tie, given the ambitions of the clumsy but consequential Russian bear, will be critical in the 1980s.

2. The United States cannot go on forever pretending that

the government in Taipei is the Republic of China. Since 1972 America has been committed not to support a policy of "two Chinas." It is committed against an indefinite U.S. military presence in Taiwan. It is committed to go further down the path of normalized ties with the People's Republic of China. Fulfillment of all these commitments faces the stark obstacle that we continue to recognize the Republic of China.

3. Crucially, it is in U.S. interests to carry through on the Shanghai Communiqué while Peking continues to tilt so heavily away from Russia and toward America.

Under the hot winds of Russia-China hostility, Peking has already bent on Taiwan. During the 1950s and 1960s the Chinese always said there could be no normalization of relations with the United States without a settlement of the Taiwan question. Yet in 1972 they proved willing to begin the process of normalization with virtually no change "on the ground" in Taiwan and only a limited agreement on the principle of the thing.

China always used to say that it would be impossible to have Peking diplomats in Washington since they might bump into diplomats of the Chiang Kai-shek clique. Yet in 1973 Peking set up a big office in Washington even though Taipei still has an ambassador there (as well as more than a dozen Nationalist consulates all over the United States).

This bending by Mao and Chou, together with the fact that there are post-Mao voices in Peking which speak up for a more conciliatory line toward Moscow, should spur the United States to settle the Taiwan issue while Peking holds to an anti-Russian policy.

In fact, there is a chance of a full settlement of the principles involved over Taiwan (as an issue between Washington and Peking) that would leave the situation on the ground in Taiwan much as it is now for some time to come.

China says that full normalization with the United States will be achieved when three steps are taken: an end to diplomatic ties between Taipei and Washington; U.S. military withdrawal from Taiwan and an abrogation of the 1954 Security Treaty between the United States and Chiang's Republic of China. In other words, Peking seeks the de-internationalization of the Taiwan issue and asks that the United States not perpetuate the Chinese civil war. That is all the Chinese ask.

Of these demands, it is the treaty which is the sticky one. Military withdrawal is a stated goal of the United States and in fact it inches ahead. Since it is clear that the United States could keep an "unofficial" office in Taipei even after breaking relations with the Republic of China, the diplomatic switch is unlikely to be more momentous for Taiwan than was the similar step taken by Japan in September 1972. By 1977, *no less than eight of Taiwan's top ten trading partners* were among the ranks of countries that had established diplomatic relations with Peking.

Illusion and error always command a price, and the bizarre nature of the treaty cannot be overlooked. It is a treaty with a government that is not the government of the country that it claims to be. Can anyone deny that it was an error to continue to regard Chiang Kai-shek as the ruler of China for twenty-five years after he ceased to be so?

The treaty exists with a government—the Republic of China—that the United States would regard as superseded once it recognized the People's Republic of China, as it intends to do sooner or later. (The United States, by the way, already violated Article VII of the treaty—which requires that the disposition of forces in Taiwan be "determined by mutual agreement"—when in 1972 it announced unilaterally, in Shanghai of all places, that it was going to wind down its forces on Taiwan.)

But the treaty is not as important as the reality behind it, namely, U.S. concern for the welfare of Taiwan's inhabitants. If the situation on the ground in Taiwan today and tomorrow is what American public opinion is concerned about, the following could occur.

In the first place the United States would recognize the People's Republic of China and turn its liaison office in Peking into an embassy and its embassy in Taipei into a nongovernmental office. America would continue to wind down its Taiwan forces, which are for China, as John K. Fairbank has said, "more an insult than a menace," and which are not at all vital for U.S. interests in the region.

At the same time, Americans would keep a full range of economic and cultural relationships with various organs in Taiwan. At present one-third of Taiwan's exports go to the United States, and 220 American corporations have some $500 million invested in the island. There is no reason why this could not continue.

As for the treaty, Peking would take the view that it had ceased to exist. America would have to accept that it no longer had a treaty with "the Republic of China," but it could make a statement of American intent to defend the region in which Taiwan is located (e.g., "the Seventh Fleet and the area in which it operates"). No infringement of China's sovereignty would necessarily be involved, since there is a strip of international waters between Taiwan and the mainland.

Such a step need not reflect in any way on America's general reliability toward allies, because (unlike Japan, Australia, or South Korea) this ally has for twenty-nine years not been in control of its own territory.

The United States may wish to satisfy itself, in addition, that Taiwan could continue for the foreseeable future to obtain defensive arms supplies from outside Taiwan. Whether these originated in America or in other countries would matter little to the concrete welfare of Taiwan. I do not think Peking would make a fuss over this. The Chinese Communists, heir to Mao's doctrines of "men over weapons" and "war as politics," are the last to believe that weapons are likely to be the decisive element in determining the future of Taiwan. The U.S. side, particularly the Congress, may well believe otherwise. Let the future decide. A clash of concepts does not matter if the actual situation does not arouse division.

It is not a question of "abandoning Taiwan" or of "handing Taiwan over to Peking." Taiwan is not the fifty-first state of the United States; it has never been America's to "abandon," any more than China in the 1940s was America's to "lose." To suppose otherwise is to undermine the very Taiwanese people we mean to befriend. We should not "hand over" Taiwan, nor is Peking asking for that.

Does the Shanghai Communiqué "abandon Taiwan"? It does almost abandon a régime called the Republic of China; history already abandoned this régime in 1949. At stake is a phantom of yesterday, not the current livelihood of the people on Taiwan. By normalization the United States would be giving up not 17 million people but a myth. The Republic of China was an ideal of a past era: it failed to carry the Chinese people with it. The life of Taiwan today is a concrete reality of the present era.

Just as Taiwan has survived loss of recognition by tens of countries, and the loss of its peace treaty with Japan, so it would survive a similar step taken by the United States.

The friends of the Republic of China who talk about "abandonment" seem to have little confidence in the will and viability of the régime they champion. Let us separate the primary issue of Taiwan's future from the secondary issue of America's role in Taiwan's future.

Those who hope for a free and prosperous future in Taiwan, including non-Chinese who can do only a limited amount to ensure it, ought to put some trust in the flourishing entity which Taiwan presently is.

To underline this confidence, President Carter, after he has visited Peking and recognized the People's Republic of China, could visit Taiwan to pay his respects in various circles of Taiwan life and discuss economic and cultural ties. Nixon visited Peking when the United States had no diplomatic ties at all with the People's Republic of China; Carter would be in less of a limbo of protocol if he visited a Taipei that housed an unofficial American office.

People's Daily of Peking might blandly report the visit in four lines as that of a friendly foreign leader to an outlying province of China, which would not matter much since *People's Daily* has some experience in writing about what ought to be rather than what is. It would be more important that American TV networks would show Carter and a congressional entourage mingling with the people of Taiwan, who had not dropped into the sea as a result of Washington's recognition that the government of China is these days in Peking. The visit would dramatize the normalcy of the situation on the ground in Taiwan. For ordinary Americans the reality seen on the TV screen would be a good substitute for a treaty.

For Peking, to look the other way during Carter's visit to Taiwan would be to demonstrate the sincerity of Mao's statement to at least one foreign leader that the solution to the Taiwan problem will be "gradual" and "long-term."

What did Mao mean by this statement? It is the clearest possible pledge—consistent with Chinese insistence that in principle the issue is a domestic Chinese one—that the de-internationalizing of the Taiwan question will not be quickly followed by an attempt to take Taiwan. An invasion cannot be "gradual"; and when the Chinese say "long-term" they always mean a very long time indeed.

Indeed the Chinese have gone further. They have tied the issue of a peaceful solution to the issue of the three components of normalization: diplomatic relations with Peking, rather than Taipei; withdrawal of the military presence in Taiwan; and an end to the 1954 Security Treaty with the Chiang régime.

Teng Hsiao-p'ing spoke this way to New Zealand visitors in the fall of 1975. He reiterated the three points. Then he added: "If those three points are not implemented, then non-peaceful means cannot be ruled out." I don't think we can expect the Chinese to come closer than that to intimating that they will not use force against Taiwan once relations with the United States are normalized.

To be sure there could be risk in the policy here set out. In Peking a government could come to power that is not, like the present one, intent on a gradual and peaceful solution of the Taiwan question. But this almost presents us with a further reason for seeking a settlement with the present Hua government.

Political change may be spurred in Taiwan; uncertainty could take an economic and spiritual toll. But change could be for the better too. Certainly one change would be good for everyone concerned: Taipei should respond to the new facts of life by adopting a foreign policy of non-hostility to the PRC, and quiet Burma-style neutralism. It would join the Third World bloc of nations, vote on most issues with Peking in world forums, give up its role as lapdog of the West and its sterile drone on behalf of world anti-communism.

This change of foreign policy line would enhance the possibility of Taiwan existing for a long time as an individual entity with a social system of its own choosing. Giving up the daily-repeated aim of invading the mainland, Taipei would raise the moral barrier against aggression from Peking by a factor of thousands. Hopefully, one major fruit of U.S.-China normalization will be a new realism in Taiwan, and with it, a certain live-and-let-live stability in its relationship with the mainland.

If normalization is reasonably handled, not only will relations between Washington and Peking enter a more serious era, but Taiwan will probably be better off. To live on a myth is to live on the edge of a cliff. It is very likely that, as the year 2000 arrives, Taiwan will be living essentially its own life, if with growing bonds to the PRC. Our grandchildren will puzzle that the "Taiwan issue" should have bedeviled American foreign and domestic politics alike for thirty years.

Something will be required of all parties. Peking should be faithful to its own doctrine that Liberation cannot be forced upon a people. (For Taiwan, though theoretically a part of China, has developed a personality of its own.) Taipei should give up the Chinese civil war and acknowledge that a Communist-ruled China will be influential in Asia for a long time to come. Washington should continue its multifarious links with Taiwan society and also maintain its strength and diplomatic vigor in the whole of East Asia to deter sudden major power shifts.

To return to the two points with which this chapter began: a sense of future strategic need and an awareness of history are equally needed. A big issue is the growth of Soviet power, to which U.S. ties with China are an important counter. The time to develop them is now, before irresistible pressures arise in China for a thaw with the Soviet Union. A frozen position over Taiwan ought not to be allowed to stand in the way.

Then, too, a final American settling of accounts with the Chinese civil war is an historical imperative. Errors were made during the 1940s; hopes were dashed at the end of that decade. Time plus effortless American supremacy in the Far East built the errors and lost hopes into a half-believed tradition. But the circumstances that made it plausible have long since past. An entirely new order has replaced the Cold War order in Asia—witness the fact that hostility between Russia and China far outweighs that between any other two major actors on the scene. An American leader who can complete the task in Sino-American relations, and can handle it without bringing catastrophe upon Taiwan, will go down in history as a great statesman.

In resolutions of support for the present Taiwan government, scores of congressmen have declared that the United States should "do nothing to compromise the freedom" of our "ally, the Republic of China, and its people." Well, we have to separate the two aspects: There can be no future for an ally called the Republic of China. But there can be a rich future for the people in Taiwan and our practical ties with them.

If it means yielding a shadow and not substance, it is a bargain to put an end now to the Taiwan issue; to leave it finally to the Chinese people, on both sides of the Taiwan Strait, with a strong expectation that the Strait will not turn overnight into a bridge.

Some say that President Carter should not go to Peking, and if he goes should make no move at all on Taiwan. Others say that he should go to Taiwan and never budge on the island's future. I think he should visit both, settle the matter, and face tomorrow's issues instead of yesterday's.

11
A
Thaw with
🐉 Russia? 🐉

On September 13, 1976, the foreign minister of the Soviet Union drove up to the tomblike Chinese Embassy in the Lenin Hills district of Moscow. Accompanied by an array of Soviet ministers, Mr. Gromyko stepped inside the building and signed the book of condolence for the death of Mao Tsetung.

The day before, the Soviet Communist Party had sent a message of sympathy to Peking which was warm enough to include Mao's family and relatives. *Pravda* covered the plans for the funeral. That week it published analyses of international affairs which, amazingly for *Pravda*, did not criticize Peking. It did not even criticize the visit to China—and to Chinese military installations—of James Schlesinger, Moscow's bête noire and an advocate of U.S.-China military cooperation. What was going on behind the scenes? Could the Dragon and the Bear get together again and change the international landscape of the 1980s?

In defense capability, and by virtue of the political shadow it casts in Asia and the Pacific, China is part of the triangle of global power with the United States and Russia. But in economic terms (as we have seen) China is a Third World nation, possessing nearly one-quarter of the world's people but only 6 percent of the world's GNP. Peking needs time—time to develop its rich resources and so to match its great civilization with the all-round muscle of a world power. This is a long-term goal, and many a tactic will be employed on the way to reaching it.

Mao taught the Chinese to search for the contradictions in any situation, then seek to build a united front to meet the *principal* contradiction. In this process they take a long view, as if looking at the world through the reverse end of a telescope.

The big contradiction is seen to be between the control exercised by imperialists, as opposed to the independence of the small and medium-sized lands. Chinese strategy has been to support the "independence" of small nations against the "hegemony" of Russia and United States. The main idea is to gain time: for the poor and weak to become less so; for the acorn of independence to become the oak of socialism; above all, for China to become a modern industrial nation equal to any in the world.

Within this strategy the tactic is generally to favor one superpower at any one point. In the 1950s, Peking went arm in arm with Moscow and cursed the United States. During the Cultural Revolution of the 1960s, Peking called a plague on the houses of both giants and had little to do with either. In the 1970s, China veered openly toward America and declared Russia the greatest menace to China and world peace. What of the 1980s?

For the Communist world the Sino-Soviet dispute represents the most severe failure communism-in-power has ever known. It has also been the most potent fact in international politics for more than a decade.

Consider some of the consequences of the dispute: extra leverage for the United States against both red giants; room to maneuver for dissident Communist nations like Rumania; drastic setbacks to Communist insurgency movements in Asia (neither Moscow nor Peking wants to see Marxist victories that would work to the benefit of the other); and an end to the spiritual élan of communism as a united worldwide movement with clear aims.

No less potent would be the impact of the ending, or even merely the softening, of the dispute—not least for the United States. We would be ostriches not to weigh up the prospects. In fact the six months after Mao's death brought some gestures from Moscow that put the whole issue into clearer perspective.

What was on Mr. Gromyko's mind as he paid respect to Mao? The next few weeks gave an answer. On a verbal level, at least, Russia pursued an accommodation with post-Mao China. All criticisms of Maoism were stopped; polite messages went back and forth between Moscow and Peking. The drive came from the Soviet side, yet Peking contributed enough for some nibbling to go on through the austere grill of the world's bitterest major relationship.

Russia sent pleasant felicitations on the occasion of China's October 1, 1976, National Day. Peking said thank you, and, especially interesting, *Pravda* and *Izvestia* chose to tell the Russian people of the Chinese thanks.

A *Pravda* commentary on the occasion said that between Russia and China, "there are no problems that cannot be solved." It avoided polemic, and chose to dwell with nostalgia

on the 1950s, when the two countries were warmly allied—
an interesting emphasis in the light of Peking's own return,
during 1977, to that decade (by making Mao's writings of the
1950s the theme documents of the year).

When the U.S.S.R.'s fifty-ninth anniversary arrived a few
weeks later, Peking sent greetings that included one fairly
warm sentence: "The Chinese people have always cherished
their revolutionary friendship with the Soviet people." Peking's message also refrained from even mentioning the Sino-
Soviet border dispute, and spoke instead of the five principles
of peaceful coexistence. At Moscow's own commemorative
speeches on the Bolshevik Revolution in early November, the
references to China were so reasonable that, for once, the
Chinese officials present did not march out.

Then on November 27, the chief Russian negotiator in the
marathon border talks, Deputy Foreign Minister Leonid Ilyichev, came back to Peking for the first time since May 1975,
and his Chinese counterpart, Deputy Foreign Minister Yü
Chan, met him with striking cordiality at Peking airport. On
leaving Peking eighteen months before, Ilyichev had said he
would return to China only if there was a good chance of
substantive progress in the border talks.

Peking's diplomats in the United States, meanwhile,
seemed to have changed their tactics in discussing Russia-
China ties. One senior figure always used to answer a query
as to whether the feud could abate with a lecture saying this
was impossible. In late 1976 he chose a different reply to the
same question: "If the U.S.S.R. ceases its provocations near
the border, Sino-Soviet relations could improve. We know
that the U.S.A. has some anxiety about this."

Yet in the spring of the Year of the Snake, Moscow suddenly put an end to the honeyed words directed at Peking.
An eight-month period of fluidity came to an end in May

1977, when the Russians resumed all-out criticism of China, and for the first time attacked Hua Kuo-feng by name. The Chinese, in turn, had seldom been more vituperative about Russia than in mid-1977. What happened, and what does it mean for the future?

The nibbling showed the existence of a latent desire—especially from the Russian side—to improve the relationship. It also recalled the logic, in both bilateral and global terms, of doing so. This was a harbinger of things to come.

But a breakthrough failed to come about because the Russians were not prepared to match words with deeds. Many rounds of talks occurred between Ilyichev and Yü Chan. However, whereas the Russians wanted a rapprochement without preconditions, the Chinese insisted on a Soviet pullback of troops from the border to clear the air for any other business. (The Russians keep more troops on the Chinese border than on their entire European front.) Moscow was unready to begin with a pullback.

In addition, Hua upheld Mao in what the Russians were counting on as a post-Mao era. Hua is Mao's man in a period of pressures for de-Maoization. This extends to certain aspects of foreign policy, as well as domestic policy, and not least to China's attitudes toward Russia. True, Hua had got rid of the Gang of Four, who seemed more Maoist even than Mao, and he had done so with the support of some un-Maoist elements in the PLA and the state administration. Yet for the time being, at least, Hua held the line for Mao's behest of unremitting hostility toward Moscow.

Throughout the eight months of Soviet wooing, Teng was out of office. We do not know whether he considers the period one of missed opportunity. Certainly the hedging remarks of the Peking official in the United States about the prospects of change in the Sino-Soviet relationship (quoted

Ruling triumvirate: Hua Kuo-feng, Yeh Chien-ying, and Teng Hsiao-p'ing at the Eleventh Congress of the CCP, August 1977. (*New China News Agency Photo*)

above) suggest either a readiness to exploit those prospects for leverage against the United States, or a fluidity of policy resulting from high-level disagreements in Peking.

One factor on the American front strengthened Hua's hand. Peking had expected President Carter to "collude" with Moscow. By mid-1977 it was clear that "contention" was outweighing collusion. This suited the Mao-Hua line well. Carter seemed, after all, worth watching, and waiting for. This was a strong argument in favor of maintaining an anti-Russian, pro-American foreign policy.

So the approaches of 1976–77 stopped short of real progress. Brezhnev was too mean and Hua too Maoist. Yet our explanations for the failure themselves suggest that the Sino-Soviet feud may not go on much longer in its present obsessive form. The tide of objective forces, at least, seems likely to flow in the direction of Sino-Soviet détente.

After all, enmities between major nations seldom go on unabated for decades, certainly not forever. Mutual dislike is one thing; Russians and Chinese have that in abundance. But so do Poles and Russians, Koreans and Japanese, French and Germans, and each of those pairs is allied at present. Mutual popular dislike does not often stand in the way of the self-interest of states. Such evident dislike did not prevent the Sino-Soviet alliance of the 1950s. And it cannot be relied upon to keep relations between China and the Soviet Union in their current state of hostility.

Objective differences of historical experience and of culture—which are centuries old—form the background to the present rift. Even the CCP's disesteem for Soviet-style socialism goes all the way back to the 1920s, when Chang Kuo-t'ao, the only CCP leader to meet Lenin, went off to Moscow and was horrified by what he saw. But historical-cultural factors alone did not bring about the split.

The split occurred when it did because the two allies had differing opinions on important current policy issues. The main foreign policy issue was America. Could there be limited cooperation with Washington in the early 1960s? Moscow said yes; Peking believed that it was impossible. As a dispute on this second level developed, problems of the first level seemed to spring out from the background and arouse further passion.

The split then took on a third aspect: an overall fight over Marxist doctrine. Ideological letters flew back and forth between the two capitals during 1963. On many of these points of doctrine, Moscow and Peking had long disagreed—Stalin didn't understand the Chinese Revolution very well—but they had both chosen to keep quiet about the disagreement.

A fourth component is that of national security issues that divide the two giants, above all the border dispute. The border was never a problem until the split had occurred. It certainly was not a split over the border, though it has now become a split *about* the border among other things.

I think it is plain that the second point was the key one— the failure to agree on current issues that were urgent and vital. By the same token, if a new issue arises on which Moscow and Peking have the same interests, and see eye to eye, they will quickly do business with each other. Neither a 4,300-mile border, nor all the doctrines of Marx and Lenin put together, nor one of the biggest reservoirs of racism in the world, would be enough to prevent that.

On the Chinese side this leads us to Chairman Mao and to the PLA. Both have been intimately involved in the Soviet question. At times they did not agree with each other. And now the relation of both to Chinese politics has suddenly changed drastically. It is not a bit surprising that Moscow has taken a keen interest in the succession to Mao, and in the return of the PLA to the center of power in Peking.

There were, in fact, good reasons why Mao's death made an improvement in Sino-Soviet relations more likely than for a dozen years. Not only did Moscow find in Mao its chief bête noire. Many times Mao had to struggle with his own top colleagues over Russian policy.

Back in the 1920s, he split with the first secretary general of the CCP, Ch'en Tu-hsiu, by departing from Moscow's views to base China's revolution on the peasantry. He parted company with other CCP leaders by rejecting as suicidal the advice of Stalin to start uprisings in China's cities.

In the 1930s he bristled at the unoriginality of Chinese Communists who came back from Moscow spouting phrases from Soviet texts. The feuds were endless. Moving on to the 1950s, Mao got rid of Kao Kang—a regional boss from Manchuria who dealt directly with Stalin over Peking's head, and whom Khrushchev said Soviet leaders used to boast of as "our man in China." Mao also clashed with, and then demoted, Defense Minister P'eng Te-huai, the man who negotiated the agreement for Soviet nuclear aid to China. P'eng thought the Great Leap Forward a big slide backward and said so in eastern Europe.

In the 1960s Mao purged both his current second-in-command, Liu Shao-ch'i, who wanted to keep in touch with Russia in the face of the American threat in nearby Vietnam, and Lin Piao, P'eng's replacement as defense minister and Liu's as number two, who was apparently bold enough to say to Mao: "If you can ask Nixon to China, why can't I ask Brezhnev?"

Each time Mao won a battle, sometimes narrowly, against a senior associate who did not share his deep hostility toward Russia. But Mao is now in a crystal box and a process of de-Maoization, in fact if not in name, is under way beneath the orange-tiled roofs of Peking's palaces.

We have seen how important the PLA became in Chinese politics during 1977. Even before Mao died, there were signs of doubt in the army about his hard line on Russia and his soft line toward the United States. A number of high military officers who had been purged by Mao for being "soft on Russia" returned to top jobs in the PLA in 1975, when Teng Hsiao-p'ing was in effective control of the government. And after twenty-one months of detention as spies, the Soviet helicopter crew members were suddenly released that December, fêted, and declared not to have been spies after all.

Mao, in reaction, lambasted Teng (and maybe by implication his PLA supporters) for "capitulationism."

The point about the PLA can be simply summed up. It enjoyed a long period of cooperation with the Soviet Red Army, and does not think the Russians are all bad. It understandably sees defense cooperation with the Soviet Union of the kind enjoyed in the 1950s as highly attractive from a professional point of view.

All elements in Peking agree, and have said, that the danger from Russia is less today than it was a few years ago. Now that the PLA seems to have recovered from the disastrous effect on its prestige of the Lin Piao affair, it may be emboldened to embrace the logical conclusion that a businesslike relation with Moscow is now possible.

It is the United States, after all, which the PLA has had experience in opposing. Chinese officers have few reasons to feel chummy toward the West. Korea and the Chinese civil war of the 1940s were their last big battles, and in both of them the enemy was supplied and supported by America. We have proof—in the form of military documents that have reached the West—that some military men found Mao's sudden switch of enemies at the start of the 1970s puzzling indeed.

Had America so quickly changed its character? Were the Vietnamese all wrong still to view American imperialism as Asia's great problem? From a military man's point of view, what had Russia done to the PRC that was so bad, by the standards of the way powerful nations generally treat less-powerful neighbors?

In this light Hua's position is intriguing indeed. He tries to steer between the Scylla of Mao and the Charybdis of the PLA. Mao chose him. The PLA backed him (to say the least) in the crucial purge of the Gang of Four. On Russia, however, the legacy of Mao and the nudgings of the PLA push Hua in opposite directions.

Will Hua be a long-reigning chairman of the CCP? Will the Mao-Hua foreign policy last? Here Teng may be the key. When Teng snapped back into the limelight (again) in July 1977, photos indicated that Hua, Yeh, and Teng formed a newly minted triumvirate. One cannot say that Hua looks at ease in some of the celebratory pictures. Glancing at Teng, he appears decidedly sheepish. An imaginary caption might read (with apologies to Mao): "With you back I have worries."

Teng must pose a power challenge to Hua, and in some areas a policy challenge too. At Mao's funeral Hua summed up the Cultural Revolution as a triumph "over the counter-revolutionary revisionist line of Liu Shao-ch'i, Lin Piao and Teng Hsiao-p'ing." One wonders what Teng makes of that view of recent history and that way of paying tribute to Mao.

In fact Teng is a more weighty figure than Hua. The bullet-headed Szechwanese has more experience, wider bases of support, a greater record of meritorious deeds in the key events of the Chinese Revolution, a richer public image, seventeen years advantage in age, and probably more ability than his nominal superior.

Hua may turn out to be a long-lasting chairman of the CCP. Much depends on certain deals and currents of political influence about which we know little. What has Hua promised the PLA? And did Teng—from behind the scenes—have a say in the fall of the Gang of Four? On balance it seems to me quite likely that Hua will be only a transitional figure, a humble footnote to the era of Mao.

If Teng should live long enough—and two purges may have tempered him—to become Mao's true successor, he will surely modify Mao's policy toward Russia. This expectation is based on four considerations. First, Teng is far less cowed by Mao's "behests" than Hua—he must feel very unsentimental indeed by now about the man who twice cast him into the pit as a monster, sham Marxist, counterrevolutionary, and capitalist roader.

Again, Teng is deeply imbued with PLA influences. Whatever deals Hua did with the military, they cannot produce the mutual identification felt by Teng and the officers he served with for decades. He brought back to office, in his interval of power between 1973 and 1975, many PLA men whom Mao had purged as being tainted with the "purely military viewpoint" and with "revisionism" (that is, Russian ways). It speaks volumes that military leaders in southern China looked after Teng during his bout of disgrace in 1976.

Third, Teng's own record is that of a "revisionist" in the eyes of the later Mao. His pragmatism on domestic policy is well known from the Cultural Revolution attacks upon it. But his pragmatism on the Soviet issue is hardly less clear.

In the watershed year of 1965, Teng had revealed it fully. A debate raged over whether "unity of action" with Moscow was possible on Vietnam and other matters. In July 1965, after Mao had already decided to get rid of General Lo and President Liu (who both favored united action—Lo had even installed a high-frequency "hot line" for his communications with Moscow), Teng made a speech on the subject at the Ninth Congress of the Communist Party of Rumania. He backed united action. He still spoke of imperialism as being spearheaded by America. He criticized "revisionism" far more lightly than *People's Daily* was doing at the same time, and he criticized "dogmatism" far more severely than *People's Daily* was doing. It was a non-Maoist, non-Cultural Revolution speech that bent over backwards to keep the door open to Moscow.

People's Daily wrote in one of its 1976 attacks on Teng: "Class capitulationism and national capitulationism are interrelated." Mao himself had called Teng a class capitulationist; the link with selling out (as his critics viewed it) to the U.S.S.R. could hardly be made much clearer. Especially since the *People's Daily* article appeared just a few weeks after Teng's extraordinary gesture to Moscow of releasing and exonerating the long-captive Soviet helicopter crew. Teng's effective fall, in January 1976, was followed by a level of anti-Soviet rhetoric that was extreme even by Peking's most rip-roaring standards.

There was a neat symmetry to the fact that Hua, not Teng, received Richard Nixon on his return to China in February 1976. The sequence of events ran: (1) unproductive Ford-Teng talks in December 1975; (2) Teng's gesture to Moscow over the helicopter weeks later; and (3) as part of a new effort by Mao to stress relations with the United States, Hua talks with Nixon.

Moscow has often recognized in Teng a man less hostile to the Soviet Union than Mao and presumed Maoists such as the Gang of Four. The Soviet press gave a guarded welcome to the 1975 NPC meeting and its outcome, which marked the start of Teng's return to the summit of power. It deplored the fall of Teng before a left-wing gale in the spring of 1976. Peking was quick to recognize Moscow's pro-Teng posture in the Russian usage of the phrase "healthy forces" to describe those who lost out at the Square of the Gate of Heavenly Peace in April.

Of course the Russians are not infallible in their expectations of Chinese policy trends. Yet their preference for Teng over Hua is pronounced. When Hua, becoming premier in the very same gale that blew Teng from his perch, made his first speech as head of the government, he certainly reciprocated. Speaking of Soviet actions toward Egypt, Hua called the U.S.S.R. "ruthless and despicable." He referred to Moscow's "criminal plans," to "subversion" and "sabotage." He gave the Russians no chance to make overtures to him. He had made up his mind—and it was Mao's mind.

Meanwhile, Hua will have to give an answer to questions that have been raised about the high cost of the relentless vilification of Russia and the sharp tilt toward the United States, questions about the cost to China's friendships and to its budget.

Vietnam is dismayed by Peking's tirades against Russia's "social imperialism." The Angolan government sees South Africa, rather than the Soviet Union, as the enemy in its path. Cuba and other left-wing pockets in the Third World think China has chosen some odd bedfellows in making friends with anyone who is an enemy of Russia.

What can a Chinese say to Pyongyang when James Schlesinger, who has murmured about using nuclear weapons against North Korea, is embraced by Peking as a guru on the perils of détente with Russia? Just after the murder of President Allende of Chile in 1973, a motion was submitted to the ruling body of UNESCO declaring "grave concern at the events taking place in Chile." Only two countries did not vote for this motion: China and the United States. China's Third World friends sometimes wonder if the obsession with Russia has not blurred Peking's judgment.

The sharpest alienation has occurred with China's erstwhile closest ally. Albania has demurred at Peking's pro-American tilt ever since the fall of Lin Piao. This led Tirana (the Albanian capital) to hammer away at the slogan: "You cannot rely on one imperialism to oppose the other." It was diametrically opposed to Peking's actual strategy.

Tirana's slogan was close to Lin's thinking. An associate of

Lin's, the Albanian defense minister Balluku, went too far in opposing pro-Americanism, and Enver Hoxha purged him as "pro-Soviet" in 1974. But even Hoxha leaned to Lin's point of view. Tirana continued to quote Lin, even after his fall, and it maintained a frigid silence about Richard Nixon's visit to China in 1972. Still, the China-Albania embrace held on through the mid-1970s.

But after the fall of the Gang of Four, who wanted to keep both Russia and the United States at arm's length, Albania's alienation became serious and took practical form. Hoxha did not praise Hua. He did not join in the criticism of the Gang of Four. Chinese aid to Albania diminished in 1977. Through 1977 the Albanians attacked the principle—heart of Hua's foreign policy—that "My enemy's enemy is my friend." The Albanians cannot be accused of being soft on Russia—but neither does their obsession with Moscow go so far as to throw them into the arms of Washington.

Chinese officials who are concerned with China's economic modernization also see possible benefits in a moderation of the global rivalry with Moscow. Peking has spent billions of dollars, including more than half a billion on the railroad linking Tanzania with Zambia, in an effort to upstage Moscow (and the United States) in distant countries where actual Chinese interests are not very much at stake. Maybe the money could be better used at home.*

Chairman Mao Tse-tung believed that a twenty-five-year period came to an end when the United States, after failing to prevail in Indochina, became set on a downward course (of

---

* It was exceedingly interesting that during the campaign to criticize Confucius in 1974 some voices, making use of historical parallels, spoke of Wang An-shih (an eleventh century statesman) having been so concerned about the "northern border" that he neglected domestic development.

which the fall of Mr. Nixon was one symbol). He saw Soviet "social imperialism" taking over from U.S. "imperialism," just as the latter took over from European "colonialism" after World War II.

The delicate question is how boldly to play the one superpower off against the other, within what time frame to do so, and in what ways and areas China can stand in a united front with the United States (and Japan) against Russia as the principle foe. This is not merely a military question—in fact the moment of war danger from Russia may well have passed—but one of world power distribution that reaches far into the future.

For Mao and Chou En-lai, Peking's post-1972 link with the United States undercut the logic of any turn toward Moscow. They saw results in 1972 and 1973 and were satisfied. But other Chinese leaders later grumbled that Peking has gotten the thin end of the Sino-American stick.

Taiwan is as far out of Peking's reach as it was before the 1972 Shanghai Communiqué, in which Washington undertook to remove all troops from the island and to support "a peaceful settlement of the Taiwan question by the Chinese themselves." Chinese officials grew worried that American opinion was moving back toward a "two-China" line as Americans became confident that the United States can continue the present type of relationship with Taipei and Peking indefinitely.

How, voices in Peking quietly ask, will China ever regain Taiwan if Peking is so obsessed by the problem of Russia that no issue is worth a chopstick unless it is part of the anti-Moscow struggle? Why not instead treat the two superpowers evenhandedly, these same voices ask, and thus gain more leverage with both? These questions Hua will have to answer during 1978 and 1979—if Sino-American normalization does not come about.

* * *

In contemplating the prospect of China recovering from its deep obsession with Russia, it is important to recall the setting in which the split occurred.

Sino-Soviet bitterness was born of Peking's inferiority complex and Moscow's arrogance. A backward China could not approve of Khrushchev's "goulash communism"; Peking's purse, after all, was too slim to allow material standards to be made a test of socialist achievement. A vulnerable China wanted Russia's help with nuclear weapons—until Peking could stand no more of Moscow's interference and decided to walk the nuclear path alone. When Peking was fearful that the Vietnam War might expand into a Sino-U.S. conflict, China's leaders found it necessary to debate whether or not to trust in "joint action" with Russia to defend Hanoi—and perhaps Peking as well.

Repeatedly, the problem was that of a weak partner which smarts at its weakness. But times and circumstances change, and by now China's inferiority complex has ebbed.

Since the split with Moscow in 1960, the Chinese have gained stature and influence in the world. They have their own nuclear weapons, they have entered the United Nations, they have established relations with nearly seventy additional nations, they have become the spiritual leaders of the Third World. Today Peking can face Moscow with a confidence it never had in the 1950s.

I am not suggesting that the two red giants will return to their intimacy of the 1950s or that they will find agreement on Marxist doctrine or rattle the saber at the United States. A relaxation of tensions is all the term "détente" means, and hard-headed interests will form its basis.

The Communist "church" is split once and for all, and "Protestant" and "Catholic" have developed distinct socioeconomic ways. But ideology is going to matter less to foreign policy—even China's—than it did when Mao became out-raged by Khrushchev's ideas of "peaceful coexistence" and "goulash communism." Hence one great obstacle to Sino-Soviet thaw—what would happen to the claim of each to be the fount of revolutionary truth?—is far less of an obstacle in an era of lowered ideological temperatures than it would have been a decade ago.

In a word, China's new strength precludes a return to the past Sino-Soviet tie. But the same strength puts a business-like, give-and-take relationship with Moscow within reach. Much depends, of course, on Moscow's attitude toward the government of Hua, Yeh, and Teng. If the Russians do not try to meddle in China's affairs and if they give Peking half a chance, détente may not be so far off in Sino-Soviet relations.

Russia would have to make a historic decision to give up trying to influence Chinese politics so as to produce a lapdog pro-Sovietism in Peking. Powerful nations confronted by ris-ing nations have often faced such a challenge—and have always found it unpleasant.

As for the Chinese, they would have to state their terms. So far Peking has not really wanted to mend fences with Russia—hence the concentration on abuse plus broad pro-posals for final total solutions to all problems. A *New York Times* reporter asked a high Chinese official during 1977 what the border dispute was all about, if, as Peking claims, the key area of Russian expansionism is not in Asia but in Europe. "Even if the Soviet Union occupies all the disputed border areas," replied the official with a broad smile, "that will not give it world hegemony."

The reply showed that China is playing a long-term and global game. It needs time, as I said at the start. But in the meantime it cannot really blame Moscow for the nonsolution of problems—such as the border—which China would rather leave smoldering. If the Peking leaders were thinking in purely regional terms, I think they would state their terms and achieve a border settlement with Russia (as they have done with half a dozen other nations). But no, they bid to match this superpower in an all-round way. It is an intangible goal, and a non-negotiable one.

If Hua and Brezhnev do sit down together before Hua sits down with Carter, the consequences will be ticklish for the United States and its friends.

To be sure, détente with Moscow would not lead Peking to cut off its ties with Washington. China and the United States have no direct major conflict of interest, apart from Taiwan. No reason exists for a return to the old enmity now that Washington views China as a given fact of life, rather than a crimson phantom of the imagination.

The politics of a triangle are, after all, not the same as the politics of ideological blocs. Leverage and balancing acts are the hallmarks of a triangle. (Thus the Russian anxiety at a gathering U.S.-China rapprochement in 1970 spurred Moscow to attain détente with Washington.) Trust will of necessity be limited. No two parties to the triangle can truly align with each other, for that would make the third party too desperate. Nor can any two parties rationally fight each other, for that hands too much of a triumph to the third party. This means, I think, that into the 1980s no flank of the United States–U.S.S.R.–China triangle will show intimacy or alignment, but no flank will erupt into war either.

Any improved Moscow-Peking relationship would occur against the background that today, unlike during the Cold War, each has a permanent, give-and-take, working relationship with Washington. Indeed Hua's government could not expect any equal and mature tie with Russia—and no other kind would be acceptable in the Forbidden City—unless Moscow understood that détente between Peking and Washington was to continue.

Further, China must go on looking to the West and Japan for trade and expertise. Thirty years ago Stalin remarked that the Soviet and Chinese economies do not "fit" together, and this is still true. Both need advanced technology from the West. The U.S.S.R., in its eastern zones, needs the same kind of investment for development that China does. No improvement in the Peking-Moscow atmosphere, in a word, is going to reverse the westward trend of China's international economic involvement.

Détente between Russia and China would express itself in an easing of the border problem. The issue is not about large amounts of territory, actually, but about the principle of whether czarist treaties are valid or not. Peking says they are not. But Peking does not ask back 98 percent of the land which the Czars wrung from the old China.

Moscow has often chosen to confuse the principle with the package of territory. Yet, during 1976, the Russians quietly acknowledged that China is not asking for 580,000 square miles—the land China lost—but only the 12,700 square miles which Russia took over and above the "unequal" treaties.

If the will is there, this border squabble could quickly simmer down, and the logic of triangular politics may generate the will.

One of two outcomes would result. An agreement (such as China made in its Senkaku Islands dispute with Japan) to shelve the issue for the time being. Or a partial settlement on the Amur and Ussuri rivers section, where the territory in-

volved is very minor (in western Sinkiang, the second disputed border area, large tracts are at issue and delicate ethnic
tensions make everyone jumpy). In either case a pullback of
troops from near the border would also occur.

Along with a stabilizing of the border issue would come a
softening of the Sino-Soviet global confrontation. Peking and
Moscow might not ever cooperate much, except on behalf of
small Marxist nations which cannot afford to offend either,
but they would cease to perceive every trouble spot through
the lens of an obsession with each other.

The détente could be ushered in by a Hua-Brezhnev summit, although a likely prior sign would be fresh steps on trade
and technical links and toward harmonized policies for the
benefit of some small Marxist state. Peking might test the
water with one of Russia's satellites, perhaps Poland or
Mongolia, before trying to come to terms with the Bear itself.

From the Chinese side, the departure of Brezhnev from the
scene could provide a suitable opportunity for an adjustment
of policy. If desired, it could readily be said that Mao was absolutely correct about the Khrushchev and Brezhnev eras,
but that the post-Brezhnev trend is to recover some lost socialist virtues and turn back from the path of imperialism.

One thing is sure. If a thaw comes, both sides will insist
that no big change has occurred. That is the habit of nations.
Nixon said U.S. policy was unchanged when he stepped off
the plane after visiting Peking in 1972. Moscow and Peking
would blandly point out that the Russian and Chinese "peoples"—glossing over "governments"—have always been
bosom brothers.

The United States has benefited from the Sino-Soviet split,
and President Carter would find its healing unpleasant. No

longer would Washington enjoy the luxury of having better relations with both Moscow and Peking than they have with each other. It follows that both Russia and China would gain leverage with Washington in bilateral dealings.

There might be other results. Some nations friendly to the United States would be sorry to see an end to efforts by Peking or Moscow to woo them as part of an effort to isolate the Communist rival. Thailand and Malaysia would fear for an increase in Communist insurgency. Japan would be squeezed if Peking felt more relaxed about its northern border, and Tokyo might find its economic interest in Asia hemmed in by sharper Chinese political influence. In the same way, those East European countries most open to the United States—notably Rumania and Yugoslavia—might feel a more chilly breeze from Moscow.

A few benefits could accrue. Chances would rise that the four powers concerned with Korea—the United States, Japan, China, and Russia—could coax Seoul and Pyongyang to settle some issues and damp down others. Peking might join in arms control talks if it no longer felt that every Soviet move was a plot to isolate China or tie China's hands. Optimists might even see a "triangle of détente" as the start of a kind of "structure of peace," within which international problems will be tackled rather than merely tossed around.

On balance, though, it seems that a flirtation between the Bear and the Dragon would be a setback for the West.

A triangle of relationships does not really exist at present, and we overlook this fact at our peril. Remember that the top Soviet and Chinese leaders have had no contact with each other for nine years.

And if one side of the "triangle" is almost a vacuum, neither are the other two sides equal; one wonders whether

Carter would agree to a suggestion by Hua to meet in Sin-kiang, near the Russian border, as Ford agreed to Brezhnev's idea of a meeting in Vladivostock, on China's disputed door-step.

The truth is that the United States benefits from the lack of relationships along one side of the triangle, and that it has chosen to make the U.S.S.R.-U.S. bond a fuller one than the bond with China. We could happily go on like this if it were not for the probability that the pseudo-triangle will become a real triangle.

Why bother with U.S.-China relations, some people say, if China and the U.S.S.R. will soon be back in each other's arms? The answer is, first, because Russia and China will not return to their old intimacy and military partnership. And second, because the immense influence of the United States could greatly delay and modify a Sino-Soviet thaw, if it is ex-erted to consolidate the U.S.-China bond on the basis of mutual interest *before* the propitious moment for a Sino-Soviet thaw arrives.

I am not against détente with Russia—indeed there is no alternative to it—even though I agree with James Schle-singer that in the eyes of the Russians "détente itself is a *con-sequence* of the growth of Soviet power." To try to manage and modify our disagreements with Moscow must be our top foreign policy priority. In the long run, world civilization may not survive unless the arms race between the United States and Russia is stopped, and unless steps are taken soon to-ward building international structures that reflect the grow-ing interdependence of nations.

But in the short term it is urgent for the United States to show clear strategic purpose, and to exercise innovative dip-lomatic leadership, in order to counter the rise in Soviet power which will probably be the key trend in world politics during the 1980s.

The United States and China do not disagree on whether to stand up against any Soviet expansion, but since 1974 they have failed to sharpen the one great weapon they jointly possess for the task. I mean the building up of the Sino-U.S. relationship. It is putting the cart before the horse for Peking and Washington to argue about the merits of détente. They could undercut most of their argument if they took practical steps toward a tacit partnership.

It is not a question of an alliance, but of making the Sino-U.S. side of the triangle a solid fact of political life on the world scene. The American tie with Rumania shows, in a smaller way, how a link across the chasm of different social systems can have political importance; in this case as a curb on Russia, an encouragement to southeastern Europe generally, and as a bridge between the United States and China during 1970–71. An effective partnership for peace with China, plus existing alliances with western Europe and Japan, would form a massive quadripartite barrier to Soviet expansionism.

Let me sum up what U.S. policy ought to be. The better American relations with China and with the U.S.S.R., the closer they are in terms of interlocking ties and the more nearly equal in value, then the less damaging any new liaison between Russia and China would be. The United States already is far better placed than it was in the 1950s, when Washington knew nothing of what Peking and Moscow were up to together and little even of the thinking of each about America. An evenhanded policy toward Russia and China can defuse the impact of a better Russia-China tie.

For America, good relationships with Third World countries, and with its own allies, could also set a limit on the headway that a China and a Russia no longer hostile to each other could make around the world. Most important, if President Carter is able soon to settle the issue of Taiwan insofar as it affects our relationships with China, the temptation in Peking to turn to Russia should recede.

12
China's Struggle to
᪥ Join the World ᪥

The issue of China "joining the world" is an old one. There have long been contacts between China and other civilizations, yet the Middle Kingdom was for most of the time either superior or passive (or a bit of both) toward others. Europeans for their part, once they had discovered Chinese civilization, often took China for fantasy rather than reality. Voltaire, like the foreign self-styled Maoists of today, tried to join China to the world philosophically by finding preferred universal values there, using reluctant China as a distant lever against his own society which he disliked.

If the question of China joining the world used to be one for armchair theorists of culture, today it is a hard political, strategic, and economic issue. We need to know how far China will try to stay under the banner of "self-reliance" in order to assess the prospects for global interdependence. Mao laid the foundations for a modern China—thus in touch with the world. But he insisted too on a China true to itself—and thus apart, at least in spirit, from the world. Where will the emphasis lie tomorrow?

China as a world: a poster in Kwangsi Province depicts a group representing China's various nationalities. The slogan, first in Chinese and then in five minority tongues (Mongolian, Tibetan, Uighur, Korean, and Kazakh), with a romanization at the bottom, reads: "Unite to Achieve Still Greater Victories." *(Photo by Ross Terrill)*

Consider what is at stake:

- The People's Republic of China has nuclear weapons instantly deliverable to most of Asia and most of the Soviet Union.
- The entire shape of Southeast Asia's future will to a great extent depend on whether or not China sustains cooperative relations with the smaller countries around it and with Japan.
- The American anxiety over the power of the Soviet Union would be intensified by any Chinese initiative leading to détente between Moscow and Peking, equally so by any forced or voluntary withdrawal from the international scene on the part of a defeated or shattered China.
- Chinese policies on international trade, finance, aid, and environmental issues have all become of substantial international concern.

China's cherished principle of self-reliance was evident after the terrible earthquake around Tangshan in 1976. All foreign offers of help were declined, including one from the International Red Cross. Was this the correct spirit which alone can lead to development with dignity, or was it a macabre and backward-looking nationalistic celebration?

Self-reliance was also lavishly used during the Year of the Dragon to justify the fall of Vice Premier Teng, who was accused during the spring of wanting to "give up China's independence" (by making a deal with Russia?) and of wanting to "sell out China's natural resources" in order to buy high-technology capital goods from Japan and the West. But soon the chief leftist accusers of Teng were themselves dismissed from office and criticized for errors of line and conduct, and by July 1977, Teng was back in office, in a new leadership combination with Hua and Yeh. How then will self-reliance fare under the new government?

The PRC's principle of self-reliance seems to have four sources.

1. In the period of the Manchu Dynasty's encounter with the West, after 1840, China became subject to the will of foreigners. Having known the pain of dependence, the Chinese breathe with determined pleasure the air of total independence. Moreover, the methods by which the CCP led the Chinese people to "stand up" again owed little even to the U.S.S.R., which was supposed to be revolutionary China's sponsor in beating back the West.

2. Self-reliance owes something to China's long tradition of cultural self-containment. China knew an isolated greatness centuries before the coming of the European nation-state or the Industrial Revolution. As late as Voltaire's day, even an educated Chinese did not know, or feel the need to know, where Britain or France or America was. Mao's success within the CCP during the 1920s and 1930s was due largely to his modification of European Marxism to accommodate Chinese cultural traditions and the social realities of peasant China.

3. A key tenet of the Marxism to which history and culture pushed Mao is that internal factors are always decisive in a nation's affairs. The people and only the people are the motive force in history, said Mao, thus laying the foundation for a socialism of national self-reliance. Revolution cannot be exported; foreign aid can only be a marginal force in development; neither foreign bases nor bombers coming from afar can tip the scales of war against an army that moves among the people as fish in water.

4. The objective facts of China's ponderous size and agri-

cultural economy have made self-reliance in part the rationalization of necessity. Even a loan ten times the meager U.S. $300 million which Mao wrung from Stalin in 1950 would only have been a drop in the bucket of China's investment need. It is very difficult, too, to conceive of any foreign nation credibly guaranteeing to defend effectively China's 3.6 million square miles against aggression. As for food, China has no option but to provide its own; to import more than a tiny percentage of the needs of 900 million people would not be possible. Such a quantity of extra grain is not available in the world and China could not pay for it even if it were.

Now the first three of these four sources of self-reliance are not immutable. In fact self-reliance is being severely modified economically and politically, though not as yet militarily.

During the 1970s China's trade with the world rose very sharply in value. It quadrupled between 1969 (U.S. $3.86 billion) and 1975 (U.S. $15 billion), before falling off slightly during the traumas of 1976, then picking up again by 1978. China is obtaining short-term loans by buying complete plants from western Europe, Japan, and the United States, on schemes of "deferred payment" which provide for 20 percent down, the balance to be paid over a five-year period starting from the date of completion of the imported plant. Peking also pays 8 percent interest to overseas Chinese who open time accounts in Chinese yuan at Bank of China branches in Hong Kong and elsewhere.

At the same time a certain institutionalization of China's international economic involvement appears to be taking place. Ports and other foreign-related communications facilities are being greatly improved. Some 1,200 foreign technical personnel are living in China (shades of the Russian presence in the 1950s, but the current helpers are from Europe, Japan, and the United States). Futures premiums in yen and dollars are now offered to traders with China who wish to protect themselves against changes in the value of the Chinese yuan. Some sixty trade exhibitions in China over the past six years have introduced millions of Chinese people to the idea of China using and even relying on non-Chinese products.

Peking trading corporations also have recently taken some belated steps toward international trade practices. They have agreed to write contracts in U.S. dollars, have granted more sole agencies, and have started to take style more seriously in garments and other consumer goods. They have inaugurated mini-fairs to allow more specialized trade dealings, and permitted some foreign sellers to have direct contact with the Chinese end-users of their products. They now allow foreign buyers to have a label put on goods—alongside the Chinese label—stating that the article was "made in China exclusively for X."

Behind all these developments lies an apparent rejection of strict self-reliance in the sense of buying only what cannot be made and selling only what is left over, in favor of a tentative acceptance of the law of comparative advantage in international economic relationships. Thus China has exported cotton cloth and rice even though they are rationed at home; goods have been bought from Thailand which China seems hardly to need; copper has been imported from Chile which China could produce at home if it chose to invest more in mining.

China has also become a major donor of foreign aid. In an aid program that began modestly in 1956, Chinese engineers, agriculturists, and medical personnel have fanned out to dozens of Third World countries. By the early 1970s, Peking's aid (excluding that to Communist countries) totaled about U.S. $500 million per year. In some years it has been larger than comparable Soviet aid. In terms of percentage of GNP, China's nonmilitary aid has been almost as big as America's.

The type and style of Chinese aid has won praise. Loans are generally interest-free. Technical assistance is given free and not included in the stated value of the aid package. Chinese aid personnel live simply, make few demands on the receiver country, and do not try to use aid as a thin end of the wedge for wider influence.

China itself receives no foreign aid. It was not always so. Quite a bit of Soviet aid came during the 1950s. At first China regarded this as compatible with Chinese control of its own pattern of development; but when the tension between the two powers became great, the Chinese did without Soviet aid. China's aid to the Third World indicates that Peking does believe in nations helping and also influencing each other, and sees this as beneficial so long as no domination is involved. In the case of its own receipt of aid from Moscow in the 1950s, when domination occurred, this removed its justification. But the Chinese are by no means opposed to foreign aid.

A certain acceptance of an interdependent world is also evident at the political level. The PRC has since 1971 played a more constructive part in international organizations than most governments during the 1950s and 1960s predicted it would. Peking diplomats have not "disrupted" the United Nations; indeed Chinese newspapers devote a great deal of space to telling the people about the UN. Peking has not sought to establish any rival international organizations. It voted at Stockholm in favor of an international fund for the environment, and has supported other measures devoted to tackling problems on a world level. It accepts, as one might not expect of a régime with an autarkic tradition, the validity of a search for a "new international economic order."

China's tacit reliance on the forces and vibrations of the triangle of global power is also a departure from the tenet of self-reliance. Chou En-lai publicly stated that new links with the United States made China feel more secure in the face of threats from the Soviet Union. China's concern to oppose Russia all over the world has led it to modify Mao's principle that each people can defend itself and to approve of American and other Western foreign bases.

So Peking relies on the United States against the U.S.S.R.; and it takes as the fulcrum of its foreign policy, not the national autonomy of each small country, but rather a tacit grouping of whoever will resist Russia by whatever means.

The Chinese leadership has not been completely united, however, about these various departures from self-reliance. Over recent years three strands of dissent have been evident.

A surge of hinterland chauvinism appeared during the Cultural Revolution, and traces of it still exist. (Oddly enough, it has sometimes been found in one city far from the hinterland—Shanghai—as if some elements there are still trying to deal with guilt about Shanghai's wicked imperialist past.) Some Red Guards called for an immediate takeover of Hong Kong, saw no need for Chinese embassies abroad, supported the right of ethnic Chinese in Rangoon to wear Mao badges and offer allegiance to Mao.

The hinterland chauvinist is reluctant to view China as merely one nation among others. He clings to wisps of the old Middle Kingdom understanding of China as co-terminous with civilization. That the hinterland chauvinists of the 1960s—and the Shanghai ultra-leftists of the 1970s—were youthful means we should not declare this strain of thinking extinct, although the fall of the Gang of Four has ended its high-level influence for now.

A more recent view holds that China should not rely on one superpower to help ward off another. Related to this is a fear that to play an active part in the global triangle is to risk a loss of revolutionary principle. China should be even-handed toward Russia and the United States, this view runs, and call a plague on both their houses. This would mean either having very little to do with either superpower or having similar dealings with both.

The victims of recent purges—Lin Piao, Teng, the Gang of Four—all apparently thought Mao had moved too far toward the United States. Differences of opinion in Peking over the 1975 purchase of Spey aircraft engines from Britain suggest that some in the Politburo were uneasy about turning to the West for military help against the Soviet threat. As for the danger to revolutionary principles in playing the global triangle, Angola is just one of several issues over which China has lost sympathy in the left-hand corner of the Third World.

A further note of unease at such departures from self-reliance was sounded in debates during the Year of the Dragon about the proper way to modernize the nation. In this and earlier debates we find three interpretations of China's relation to the world economy:

- self-reliance as complete uninvolvement or isolation;
- self-reliance as freedom from outside influence;
- self-reliance as freedom from outside control.

Of these, no one in Peking now favors total uninvolvement in international economic relationships; not many of Teng's critics, and certainly not Mao, thought China should never buy and sell abroad. So all voices in the debate are on a spectrum from "freedom from foreign influence" to a more relaxed position of "freedom from foreign control."

The issue between these two positions is *where do the norms come from*. Those who are wary of foreign influence (as the Gang of Four were) start with a Chinese vision of the modernized future and then ask if anything necessary for its achievement must come from outside China.

Those who insist only on no foreign control (e.g., Teng) believe that a full vision of a modernized China itself involves learning from others. "We should modestly study all advanced foreign things," Teng wrote in a document of 1975 that infuriated the Gang of Four, "and import specific foreign technology to accelerate the development of the economy."

A related tension exists over the speed of development in advanced sectors of the Chinese economy. Some Chinese spokesmen stress the rate of growth and cut a few corners of socialist theory in doing so. Others stress the moral concerns of egalitarianism even at a certain cost to the rate of growth.

How serious are these three doubts concerning China's departure from self-reliance likely to prove into the 1980s? As a framework, I suggest that the PRC's basic drives since 1949 have been to recover from the past and to recover from poverty.

The past means feudal China: Confucian hierarchy; women as chattels; an ignorant peasantry cut off from culture; no idea of progress but rather belief in a Golden Age long since gone. It has not been easy to throw off.

The past also means the one-hundred-year period after 1840 when this rigid Old China encountered the West and was carved up like a melon by foreign intruders, resulting in loss of control, racist insults, and an economy twisted to suit the interests of far-off rentiers and traders. That century of troubles laid bare a terrible gap between the pride of China as a civilization and the abjectness of China as a feeble nation.

The dull weight of feudalism; the national nightmare of imperialism—flight from these twin demons has given New China its magnificent sense of purpose.

Recovery from poverty is equally central to the Chinese Revolution. None of the Chinese leaders, whether "pragmatists," or PLA officers, or remnants of the left, romanticizes backwardness. Making the revolution has called for firm values. But the point of the revolution is to modernize China.

Arguments flare about *how* to do so. Yet no careful reader of China's press could deny that its preeminent topic is development: finding new oil; a bridge completed; health care in the villages; making colleges serve China's tangible needs; new soft drink machines and other consumer items in the cities.

Development is the name of the game. A very large factor behind the China-Russia split has been the economic gap between the two nations. Peking officials become passionate when relating how the Russians mocked at China's backwardness ("Khrushchev even said: 'These Chinese you know—five of them share one pair of trousers.' "). And "goulash" as a yardstick for successful socialism is mainly annoying to those socialists who feel relatively short of goulash.

The point is that recovering from the past has an ambiguous relationship to recovering from poverty. The first is a political task; the second is largely economic. You see the ambiguity in China's attitude to the West. The West exploited China, so China had to oppose it. Throwing the West off was a way of dealing with the past. Yet the West was rich and modern, and the Chinese Communists chose a path of modernity that the West already traverses in an economic and technical sense. Recovery from poverty means drawing nearer to the levels and social experiences of the West.

Ever since the start of the Cultural Revolution, political

values and economic tasks in China have had a tendency to tug against each other. Was the evil against which the Cultural Revolution was directed a hangover of Old China? Mao said yes. When he disagreed with Liu Shao-ch'i on priorities he declared Liu a "bourgeois." Mao saw himself as driving a few last nails into the coffin of China's feudal past. Liu on the other hand saw the issues in shades of gray, as organizational problems rather than as black and white class judgments.

Can Chinese youth be trusted to grow up as sturdy pines of socialism? Mao had his doubts. They live an easy life; the heroic deeds which were a daily routine for the makers of the revolution are for these young moderns only items in a history book. But the young have their own measuring rod of virtue. A Canton boy whose father was a worker is convinced he was "born red." To imply he is a weak socialist because he did not make the Long March seems like telling a Christian he is a fake because he did not live in the time of Jesus. The boy probably respects performance at a given task more than ideological labels written during past battles.

Has Russia's social system become Fascist? Mao thought so. While at the start of the Cultural Revolution the U.S. threat to China was the key foreign issue, by its end the Soviet threat had largely replaced it. Instead of debating whether Moscow could still be of any help in meeting an American attack, as in 1965, the dominant Chinese leaders were starting to ask, by 1969, whether Washington might be an indirect help against the Soviet danger. Mao viewed Russia in the time-tested framework of imperialism.

But some PLA officers have found it difficult to accept that Russia has suddenly replaced the United States as the primary menace to world socialism. Some leftists worry that supporting "stability," wherever the alternative may be increased Russian influence, means selling out on anti-colonialism and world revolution. Is not the chief remaining neo-colonial issue in Asia the separation of Taiwan from China; and who else but America is responsible for it?

Can China advantageously mount cultural exchanges with the West without becoming itself tainted? Economic officials, who mostly focus on recovery from poverty, think it can. China has recovered enough from past political weakness, they feel, to engage with the West free of danger to either its sovereignty or its psyche. Besides, China needs know-how from foreign sources.

But some people on the left, in public security organs, or with long historical memories, have been dubious about the number of people-to-people delegations going to and fro. They argue that the era of anti-imperialism must still be sustained. They feel a greater urgency about the politics of recovering from the past, it seems, than about the economics of recovering from backwardness. You can be red and backward, they maintain, but if you are not red you are nothing.

Should China accept foreign credits in order to be able to import capital technology? Yes, say trade officials who have bought U.S. $3–4 billion worth of complete ("turn-key") plants from abroad in the last four years. They would like to accelerate China's promising oil industry by "deferred payment" imports of equipment.

No, say the ideologues and hinterland chauvinists who place a "no foreign influence" interpretation on self-reliance. They would, if pressed, rather cling to the long-resonant but now strained slogan "No debt abroad or at home" than push the rate of GNP growth up from 6 to 8 percent.

How many hours a week should the student of chemistry or Japanese spend reading Engels's *Anti-Dühring* and Lenin's *State and Revolution*? Once more the answer hinges on the changing meaning of, and the relation between, recovering from the past and recovering from poverty.

With the Gang of Four calling the tune in culture, students over the past decade often spent one-quarter or more of their class time on Marxist texts. Marxist ideas were viewed as a weapon against class enemies who try to use intellectual activity as a means of capitalist restoration.

But the pragmatic Marxists around Teng think that the Cultural Revolution sapped the quality of Chinese higher education. Turning colleges into worker-peasant-soldier study groups set back the modernization of China by years, they believe, and may even detract from China's self-reliance by forcing it to import expertise that could have been developed at home. "Those ignorant of a profession," said some pragmatists in a swipe at the idea of redness as panacea, "cannot head departments." Teng felt that political study had become ritualistic, and he complained that "scientists today are not given time for research."

Our framework suggests that, over and above questions of faction or personality, China's relations with the world will be influenced by the working out of two contradictions. Recovery from the past is largely accomplished, but recovery from backwardness is not. In the political-strategic realm China is a kind of superpower, whereas in the economic realm it is still a Third World nation.

Having become a major political-military power, China will have to modify principles that drew their point from its weak and exploited condition.

Certain specific natural and sociopolitical factors will also bear on the fate of self-reliance in China's struggle to join the world.

246 The Future of China

1. Nature itself may play a part through drought, flood, and earthquake. Such natural disasters affect export capacity, as was the case after the Tangshan earthquake, although they can produce the kind of unity stemming from a sense of siege that was also evident at Tangshan.

2. Future weapons development by China and other nations will play a role. The possession by China and its most likely enemies of long-range missiles has probably called into question some military postulates derived by the PLA from "people's war." Do the younger Chinese defense strategists believe that Mao's idea of drawing the enemy in and surrounding him is applicable to missile warfare? Or that of waiting for a moment of one's own choosing for a counterattack? In fact there are signs that they do not. Recent articles on defense strategy—disguised as historical flashbacks to the civil war of the 1940s—suggest that the PLA is no longer opposed to fighting big pitched battles at the place and moment of an enemy's intrusion. These articles also stress the need for sophisticated weaponry far more than CCP writings have ever done before.

3. Within five years, at most, there will probably be a degree of détente between China and Russia (as I argued in Chapter 11). Peking need not construe this as a sacrifice of self-reliance, but on the contrary as a welcome end to the risks of relying on America to ward off Russia. Nor would it bring a sharp change in Chinese international economic policies. The Soviet and Chinese economies do not fit each other's needs. China must continue to look to the West and Japan for high-technology capital goods, and to the Third World for sale of its light manufactures.

But a return to Sino-Soviet civility—ideological intimacy will never return—would signal in China, whether as cause or consequence of an improved relationship with Moscow, a less distinctive Maoist path of development and less reliance on the idea of "people's war" in military strategy. Sino-Soviet détente would also ease the pinch on resources for China's agricultural mechanization and industrial modernization. It would make China less interested than during the mid-1970s in importing defense-related equipment from western Europe. It would probably be accompanied by a greater selectivity in Third World activism: Peking might well focus mainly on Asia, and less on Latin America, Africa, and the Middle East.

4. A kind of middle class has started to assert its interests and express its opinions. I have shown how events surrounding the fall of Teng in 1976 saw informed public opinion play a new role in China. The period of 1975–77 equally brought insistent pressure from skilled workers for higher rewards, and the Hua government eventually had to offer wage increases to most industrial workers. Additionally there is a growing Chinese élite that has gained recent international experience in trade, diplomacy, and cultural and technical exchanges.

All this means that methods of Party decisionmaking may have to become more democratic, that the economic demands of sophisticated workers will bulk large in debates on allocation of resources, and that breathtaking changes of line in any sphere of Chinese policy may become less frequent than in the era of the Great Helmsman above and the undifferentiated masses below.

5. In the balance between the centralized power of Peking and the power of leading provinces and regions, the general trend has recently favored the periphery. There are already signs that the death of Mao, as expected, has accentuated this trend by virtue of the reduced authority of Hua's central government.

The issue of the center versus the periphery is politically a complex one. The Cultural Revolution left, for example, favored a China that was economically decentralized but ideologically centralized. Regional PLA commanders often differ on this issue from central military administrators in Peking. The main points are that an internationally involved Chinese economy must needs be a rather centralized one; that Teng was criticized for trying to increase central control of the economy; that this criticism of Teng brought at least a temporary timidity to some of China's international economic dealings during 1976; and that the wiping out of the Cultural Revolution left in October 1976 followed by the return of Teng in July 1977 set in motion a steady retreat from the anti-Teng line.

At the same time the deep institutional trend is toward decentralization—much as Hua tries to blunt it—and this could indirectly make China's relations with other countries more complicated. We can rule out any breakup comparable to the warlord period half a century ago. Most of the endemic causes of such breakup have already been eliminated: famine, absence of transportation, lack of linguistic communication, lack of a sense of the nation.

But even Mao found the pressures of the strong regions hard to resist; one reason he brought Teng back in 1973 was to get his help in controlling the regional military leaders. And Hua has less power of command and resistance than Mao had. One sign of the times during 1977 was an easing up of Peking's long-standing drive to abolish regional dialects. "The various dialects," said a Peking paper in a major concession to those who can't speak Mandarin, "will still be used by the people of different localities for a long time to come."

Potentially more momentous, General Hsu and First Secretary Wei, the leading figures in Canton, began to speak out and throw their weight around as if South China was (as it has often been in history) an entity with rights, views, and a voice of its own. If this trend goes further it will certainly affect foreign policy, for the world does not look quite the same viewed from Canton or Kunming as it does from Peking or Shenyang.

6. The PLA has kept its fingers mostly out of politics during the 1970s because it burned them doing the opposite in the Lin Piao era. It did not play a big role in the fall of Teng. It was not the army but the leftist militia, with Shanghai as its model, that took the lead in putting down the Peking demonstration in April 1976.

But after the Tangshan earthquake, at the time of Mao's funeral and especially during the first year without Mao, the PLA came to the fore again. Should the PLA quickly become the major voice in the Chinese government, détente with the U.S.S.R. might come sooner rather than later (with consequences already summarized), and the army officers, being less sophisticated modernizers than Chou or Teng, might wish to press on with international economic relationships but nevertheless show less skill in doing so.

One note of caution is that by the end of the 1980s, the PLA leaders will no longer be the old veterans of the field armies and the pre-Liberation struggles. They will have fought in Korea and have emerged in various "model-soldier" drives. About no Chinese group do we know less than about this rising generation of military men, but they seem oriented to professionalism and technology, and to have some leanings toward Soviet ways.

What is the likely future balance between self-reliance and interdependence? China's involvement in the world economy

will continue to lag behind its role in world politics and strategy. Recovery from the past has proceeded further than recovery from economic backwardness. Peking is no longer
merely passive but diplomatically active. The scope of its concerns has become global and no longer merely national in the
minimum sense of keeping the world out.

Even in China's international economic relations the
steady trend is away from self-reliance. This is because the
principle of self-reliance is in large part a self-protecting
mechanism for the relatively weak—and China is ceasing to
be weak even in economic terms.

Moreover a complication arises from the fact that the international economic world that China must deal with ceases to
be merely a string of sovereign states. To an important degree the multinational corporation has entered the picture.
The national unit cannot be the lynchpin of a doctrine of self-
reliance if the international connections of business have already qualified the sovereignty of the national unit.

China likes to deal with nations on an individual basis, but
the realities do not always permit this. To deal with a buyer
or seller in New Zealand, for instance, may be to deal with an
arm of a multinational corporation for which New Zealand is
a mere arena of operations. To this extent it will be difficult
to keep foreign policy and foreign economic policy as tightly
linked with each other as in the past.

China's involvement in international economic relationships will go ahead steadily, though with adjustments as
to direction. Trade will grow further; grain imports are likely
to taper off, but China will buy large amounts of sophisticated high-technology capital goods. Since Peking's strategy
is import-substitution, the nature of such goods will change
over time—less chemical fertilizer- and textile-related equipment may be bought into the 1980s, and more transportation

technology. Steel imports may fall, although specialty steels will not.

To pay for its imports, China will sell increasing quantities of oil, as well as metals and minerals, and a steady quantity of farm products. The great market for China's burgeoning light industrial products will not be either the West or Japan, but the Third World. The electronics, textiles, bicycles, that used to come mainly from Japan will come more and more from China (where labor costs are far lower than in Japan).

As for trade between the United States and China, there is every reason to expect the two-way volume to rise toward U.S. $2 billion or so soon after normalization. (The present outrageous tariff discrimination against Chinese products having then been removed, China will sell more to the United States and be ready, in turn, to buy far more.) When politics does not intrude, Chinese importers tend to prefer American high-technology goods to others available. Particularly promising are the fields of telecommunications, oceanography, data processing, extractive construction, and medical technology.

I have referred to self-reliance as a mechanism. Indeed the Chinese term itself indicates a method, and not a goal; *zi-li geng sheng* means literally "regeneration through one's own efforts." It can be distinguished from *du-li zi-zhu,* which means "independence" or "autonomy." Self-reliance is a method with moral and even embattled overtones; independence or autonomy is, of course, the description of a condition.

An ideological principle such as self-reliance must be viewed in a specific sociological context; the principle changes as the situation changes. Ideology is not merely a decoration without impact on policy; nor, however, is it to be equated with policy. It relates in important and complex ways to policy. It changes over time, and more nearly equates with policy at certain periods and in certain spheres than in others. Self-reliance is not a fixed aim, then, but a principle of struggle for a specific situation of China's relative weakness that is already passing.

There was a threat to China's control of its own affairs in the economic ties Peking had with Moscow during the 1950s. Such a danger is much less in China's new ties with the West during the 1970s, in part because China is now stronger and more experienced. Today's links with America do not play tricks with Chinese sensitivities to anything like the degree that such links would have done in the 1950s.

Most of the sources of the principle of self-reliance have dried up. The era of imperialism that dates back to 1840 is largely spent as far as China is concerned. Unlike even the strong dynasties, the CCP has succeeded in modifying China's cultural aloofness and has accepted that China's history is part of world history. Even Mao's nativistic principles may soon be elevated to the level of a general ethic and thus cease to be the actual source of policy.

The objective factors of China's size and agricultural character appear to be the most persistent, and will continue to act as the major constraint against any clear-cut abandonment of self-reliance. Yet the very success of the CCP in its pursuit of the modernizing task—the reason for existence of all Marxist régimes—chips away at what the generation of the Long March would recognize as self-reliance. Mao's Party, which in defiance of Stalin took China back into its own rural depths, has also set the agenda for China to join the world as a great industrial power.

This task Hua Kuo-feng now presides over. He has no roots in Old China. Nor did he taste much of the century of

humiliation that began with the Opium War and ended just
as Hua joined the CCP. The same is true of many of the people gathering around him.

By the time the Hua government assumed office, China
had become, objectively speaking, linked in important and ir-
reversible ways with other nations and with international institutions. Within China, memory of uninvolvement with the
world fades fast. Young people take it for granted that their
country is a great power, which should forcefully declare its
views on global issues, which has to be consulted before international problems can be solved, which buys and sells
with one hundred or more other nations.

To that extent domestic China is no longer a drag upon
China's struggle to join the world. And outside China there is
an acceptance of the weight and role of this massive nation
that eases Hua's task. At the time of Mao's death, it was plain
that China had entered the consciousness of the entire globe.

I was in a small Moroccan town the day after Mao died.
Half the population was on the beach. I was with a citizen of
Thailand. A Moroccan student broke away from his group of
friends and approached the Thai: "We in Morocco are very
sad to hear of the death of your president," he said. Asia may
be shadowy enough to Moroccans for anyone from east of
India to be taken for a Chinese; yet Chairman Mao was
famous on that beach.

Citizens of an African town so small that it has no newspaper felt that a man from China was part of Africa's concern.
And high-school students on the rim of the Sahara knew
enough about the Long March of Mao to compare it with the
War of the Riff of Morocco's own hero Abdel Krim. Similar
stories were reported from dozens of countries on all continents. Chairman Mao had become a global household
name—Chinese history had taken its place in world history.
The Chinese present was part of our time, not merely, as for

Voltaire, a lever to wield in the West's own domestic churnings.

Yet the road to international involvement runs through a landscape of constant change, with challenges ahead for a China that lacks a long tradition of dealing on equal terms with the rest of the world. In particular, in the era of Hua, Yeh, and Teng, foreign policy becomes linked in two fresh and complicating ways with domestic realities.

China's place in the world will soon come to be defined, less by imperialism and the struggle against it, than by two more subtle bonds. Economics will link the life of the Chinese people to the international community. In achieving a better standard of living, the Chinese will lean on foreign trade and technology. And as they achieve it they will feel a deeper, more permanent interest in the world beyond the Middle Kingdom. This is a road of no return. As people's life-in-society changes, so their outlook changes. In that respect socioeconomic change is a tyrant.

The second link is vaguer, more controversial, yet of enormous importance. It is the growing moral unity of the world as barriers of distance and unfamiliarity go down. A verse from the Middle Ages puts it well: ". . . *si est de nos: ne vos sans moi, ne moi sans vos.*" (It is that way with us: neither you without me, nor me without you.)

Ordinary people in China are learning about the non-Chinese world as never before in Chinese history. Their own way of life will cease to be, in their own minds, a sealed box with no lines out to the sealed boxes of other civilizations. Because such connections will be made, the Chinese government will not be able to continue to treat diplomacy as a realm of top-secret conversations plus elaborate symbolism. With brilliant skill—and a style reminiscent of Europe at the time of Disraeli and Bismarck, before democracy arrived to complicate international relations—Peking has kept foreign policy as a professional realm apart from the masses (how Henry Kissinger loved them for it!).

It would be intriguing if a Nobel Prize for literature were suddenly to be awarded to Pa Chin or Mao Tun. These two fine writers, almost like Solzhenitsyn when he won his prize, have for years not been in high official favor within their own country, where they still live.* If the Nobel Committee were to decide that one or other of them is among the great writers of the age, how would Peking react? What would it say to the Chinese people? Would it accept the challenge to bring domestic Chinese opinion into dialogue with international opinion?

Despite favorable trends, then, the nuts and bolts of joining the outside world will be complex and sometimes painful for China. Hua, heir to an office from which great deeds were accomplished, must evolve a new basis for Chinese perceptions of their place in a post-imperialist world. He will have to fix on an equilibrium for China's external relationships that allows for China's particularity but at the same time prepares it for the truly international existence that most people in the world will be leading one hundred years from now.

The stakes are high, for China counts today. If Hua's new regime fails, what will become of the 900 million Chinese; and if he succeeds, how will the rest of us adjust?

---

* Though, interestingly, some of Pa Chin's writings have just been republished in Peking after a long interval of nonavailability.

Appendixes—
From Mao to
Hua in Documents

1. RIOT IN PEKING
Chinese Journalists' Report

(a) Under the headline: "Counterrevolutionary Political Incident at Tien An Men Square [the Square of the Gate of Heavenly Peace]," worker-peasant-soldier correspondents and *People's Daily* staff filed this report on the mêlée of April 5, 1976.*

Early April, a handful of class enemies, under the guise of commemorating the late Premier Chou during the Ching Ming Festival, engineered an organized, premeditated and planned counter-revolutionary political incident at Tien An Men Square in the capital. They flagrantly made reactionary speeches, posted reactionary poems and slogans, distributed reactionary leaflets and agitated for the setting up of counter-revolutionary organizations. By means of insinuation and overt counter-

---

* English translation of this report and the following two decisions from *Peking Review*, April 9, 1976.

revolutionary language, they brazenly clamoured that "the era of Chin Shih Huang is gone." Openly hoisting the ensign of supporting Teng Hsiao-ping, they frenziedly directed their spearhead at our great leader Chairman Mao, attempted to split the Party Central Committee headed by Chairman Mao, tried to change the general orientation of the current struggle to criticize Teng Hsiao-ping and counterattack the Right deviationist attempt to reverse correct verdicts, and engaged in counter-revolutionary activities.

The counter-revolutionary activities culminated on April 5. At about 8 a.m., a loudspeaker car of the municipal Public Security Bureau was overturned, the body of the car and its loudspeakers smashed. After 9 a.m., more than 10,000 people gathered in front of the Great Hall of the People. At its maximum the crowd at Tien An Men Square numbered about 100,000 people. Except for a handful of bad elements who were bent on creating disturbances, the majority of the people were passers-by who came over to see what was happening. Some of the people were around the Monument to the People's Heroes; the majority were concentrated on the west side of the square near the eastern entrance to the Great Hall of the People. A dozen young people were surrounded and beaten up by some bad elements, receiving cuts and bruises on their heads with blood trickling down their swollen faces. The hooligans shouted: "Beat them to death! Beat them to death!" An army guard who tried to stop the hooligans by persuasion had his insignia pulled off, uniform torn and his face beaten to bleeding. The bad elements exclaimed: "Who can put this situation under control? Nobody in the Central Committee can. Should he come today he would not be able to return!" Their counter-revolutionary arrogance was unbridled to the extreme. The masses were infuriated and many of them said: "Ever since liberation, Tien An Men Square has always been the place where our great leader Chairman Mao reviews parades of the revolutionary masses. We'll absolutely not tolerate such counter-revolutionary acts happening here!" Several hundred worker-militiamen who went up the flight of steps leading to the Great Hall of the People to stand guard were broken up into several sections by the hooligans. The latter repeatedly shouted reactionary slogans and savagely beat up anyone in the crowd who opposed them. Some of those who got beaten up were dragged to the monument and forced to kneel down and "confess their crimes."

At 11:05 a.m., many people surged towards the Museum of Chinese History on the east side of Tien An Men Square. In front of the museum, a woman comrade who came forward to dissuade them was immediately manhandled. At this moment, a bunch of bad elements besieged a People's Liberation Army barracks by the clock tower in the southeast corner of the square. They crushed the door, broke into the building and occupied it. A few bad elements, sporting a crew cut, took turns to incite the people, shouting themselves hoarse through a transistor megaphone. Towards noon, some of the trouble-makers proclaimed the inauguration of what they called "committee of the people of the capital for commemorating the Premier." A bad element wearing spectacles had the impudence to announce that the Public Security Bureau must give a reply in ten minutes. He threatened that if their demands were not met, they would smash the public security department.

At 12:30, the P.L.A. fighters on guard duty at Tien An Men Square marched in formation towards their barracks to guard it. The bad elements who were making disturbances shouted in instigation: "The people's army should stand on the side of the people!" and "Those befuddled by others are innocent!" Later, they overturned a Shanghai sedan car and set it on fire. The firemen and P.L.A. guards who came to the rescue were blocked, and a fire-engine was wrecked. These bad elements said that putting out the fire meant "suppressing the mass movement." Several members of the fire-brigade were beaten to bleed.

At 12:45, a detachment of people's police came as reinforcement. But they too were taunted and stopped. The caps of several policemen were snatched by the rioters and thrown to the air. Some even threw knives and daggers at the people's police. Several policemen were surrounded and beaten up.

In the afternoon, the sabotage activities of this handful of counter-revolutionaries became still more frenzied. They burnt up four motor vehicles bringing water and food to the worker-militiamen on duty or belonging to the public security department. Around 5 o'clock in the afternoon, this gang of bad elements again broke into that barracks, abducted and beat up the sentries, smashed the windows and doors on the ground floor and looted everything in the rooms. Radios, quilts, bed sheets, clothing and books were all thrown into the fire by this gang of counter-revolutionaries. They also burnt and smashed dozens of bicycles of the Peking worker-militiamen. Black smoke rose to the sky amid a hubbub of counter-revolutionary clamours. Nearly all the window panes in the barracks were smashed. Then they set the barracks on fire.

The revolutionary masses showed their utmost hatred for this counter-revolutionary political incident. Yet the handful of bad elements said glibly: "It manifests the strength of the masses." They went so far as to claim brazenly that "the situation has now got out of hand and it would be of no use even if a regiment or an army was called in," and so on and so forth, showing their unbridled reactionary arrogance.

See how these counter-revolutionaries use extremely decadent and reactionary language and the trick of insinuation to viciously attack and slander our great leader Chairman Mao and other leading comrades on the Party Central Committee:

"Devils howl as we pour out our grief, we weep but the wolves laugh. We spill our blood in memory of the hero; raising our brows, we unsheathe our swords. China is no longer the China of yore, and the people are no longer wrapped in sheer ignorance; gone for good is Chin Shih Huang's feudal society. We believe in Marxism-Leninism, to hell with those scholars who emasculate Marxism-Leninism! What we want is genuine Marxism-Leninism. For the sake of genuine

Marxism-Leninism, we fear not shedding our blood and laying down our lives; the day modernization in four fields is realized, we will come back to offer libations and sacrifices."

The clamours of these counter-revolutionaries about combating "Chin Shih Huang" and demanding "genuine Marxism-Leninism" were out-and-out counter-revolutionary agitation in the same vein as the language used in Lin Piao's plan for a counter-revolutionary coup d'etat, *Outline of Project "571."* By directing their spearhead at our great leader Chairman Mao and the Party Central Committee headed by Chairman Mao, and lauding Teng Hsiao-ping's counter-revolutionary revisionist line, these counter-revolutionaries further laid bare their criminal aim to practise revisionism and restore capitalism in China.

In the past few days these elements not only wrote reactionary poems but put up reactionary posters. They lauded Teng Hsiao-ping and attempted to nominate him to play the role of Nagy, the chieftain of the counter-revolutionary incident in Hungary. They raved that "with Teng Hsiao-ping in charge of the work of the Central Committee, the struggle has won decisive victory" "to the great satisfaction of the people throughout the country." They uttered vile slanders, saying that "the recent so-called anti-Right deviationist struggle is the act of a handful of careerists to reverse verdicts." They openly opposed the great struggle initiated and led by Chairman Mao to repulse the Right deviationist attempt to reverse correct verdicts; their counter-revolutionary arrogance was inflated to the utmost.

However, the time when these counter-revolutionary elements ran rampant coincided with the day of their downfall. Going against the will of the people, they were extremely isolated. As these bad elements were making disturbances, perpetrating acts of violence and sabotage, many revolutionary people courageously stepped forward to denounce their counter-revolutionary acts and struggled against them. The Peking worker-militia, people's police and army guards on duty at the square and the revolutionary people present at the time worked in close co-operation, and fought bravely in defence of Chairman Mao, the Party Central Committee, Chairman Mao's revolutionary line and the great capital of our socialist motherland.

When the handful of bad elements again set fire to the barracks at 5 p.m., the army guard put out the fire at the risk of their own lives. To safeguard the Great Hall of the People, more than 100 Peking worker-militiamen were injured, a dozen of them seriously wounded. Six army guards were abducted and many wounded. Risking dangers, the people's police persevered in fighting. Although the barracks was besieged and fire was engulfing the first floor, leading comrades of the Peking worker-militia command post persevered in the struggle on the second floor. At this critical moment, the switchboard operator calmly reported the news to leading departments concerned.

At 6:30 p.m., after Comrade Wu Te's speech was broadcast, most of the onlookers and the masses who had been taken in quickly dispersed. But a handful of counter-revolutionaries continued their desperate resistance and again posted some reactionary poems around the Monument to the People's Heroes. Three hours later, on receiving an order from the Peking Municipal Revolutionary Committee, tens of thousands of worker-militiamen, in co-ordination with the people's police and P.L.A. guards, took resolute measures and enforced proletarian dictatorship. In high morale, the heroic Peking militiamen valiantly filed into Tien An Men Square and mounted powerful counterattacks. They encircled those bad elements who were still creating disturbances and committing crimes in the vicinity of the Monument to the People's Heroes. They detained the active criminals and major suspects for examination. In the face of powerful proletarian dictatorship, the handful of rampant rioters could not withstand even a single blow. They squatted down, trembling like stray dogs. Some hurriedly handed over their daggers, knives and notebooks on which they had copied the reactionary poems. Several criminals who pulled out their daggers in a vain attempt to put up a last-ditch fight were duly punished. The revolutionary masses and people of the whole city heartily supported and acclaimed the revolutionary action of the Peking worker-militia, the people's police and P.L.A. guards.

The Political Outcome

(*b*) Very swiftly the CCP announced two major leadership decisions:

RESOLUTION OF C.P.C. CENTRAL COMMITTEE ON APPOINTING COMRADE HUA KUO-FENG FIRST VICE-CHAIRMAN OF C.P.C. CENTRAL COMMITTEE AND PREMIER OF STATE COUNCIL

On the proposal of our great leader Chairman Mao, the Political Bureau of the Central Committee of the Communist Party of China unanimously agrees to appoint Comrade Hua Kuo-feng First Vice-Chairman of the Central Committee of the Communist Party of China and Premier of the State Council of the People's Republic of China.

The Central Committee of the
Communist Party of China
April 7, 1976

RESOLUTION OF C.P.C. CENTRAL COMMITTEE ON DISMISSING TENG HSIAO-PING FROM ALL POSTS BOTH INSIDE AND OUTSIDE PARTY

Having discussed the counter-revolutionary incident which took place at Tien An Men Square and Teng Hsiao-ping's latest behaviour, the Political Bureau of the Central Committee of the Communist Party of China holds that the nature of the Teng

Hsiao-ping problem has turned into one of antagonistic contradiction. On the proposal of our great leader Chairman Mao, the Political Bureau unanimously agrees to dismiss Teng Hsiao-ping from all posts both inside and outside the Party while allowing him to keep his Party membership so as to see how he will behave in the future.

The Central Committee of the Communist Party of China April 7, 1976

2. SAYINGS OF TENG

Although most of these remarks were revealed by Teng's critics, their essential authenticity is not to be doubted.

- "The main thing is to solve the problem of food. Black cat or white cat—it's a good cat if it catches mice."
- "One mustn't always talk with ready terms, but should say something new."
- "One should not talk of class struggle every day. How can there be so much class struggle? In real life, not everything is class struggle."

Criticizing the Cultural Revolution:

- "Now there are some people who are afraid to write articles. The New China News Agency receives only two articles every day. In movies only the part of soldiers is acted and the background is always war. How can we find movies always so perfect? Neither this role nor that role is allowed to be played."

At a Red Guard rally in Peking, December 27, 1966, held to struggle against Liu Shao-ch'i and Teng:

- "My thinking and conduct ran afoul of Mao Tse-tung Thought. My divorce from the masses demonstrated clearly that

I was not fit for leadership work entrusted by the Central Committee.

"The mistakes I committed during the Cultural Revolution show that my petty bourgeois and intellectual ideology has not been thoroughly remolded, that my bourgeois world outlook had not, in essence, been remolded, and that I am not a good socialist.

"As my ideological and political elements stand now, I am ill-suited for a leadership job in the Central Committee.

"I am sincerely willing to dedicate myself to reform and hope to be a glorious personage."

After his first rehabilitation in 1973:

• "What is the meaning of one following a mistaken line? When you become a provincial committee secretary, you simply have to listen to the party central. If you don't, you are being anti-party. But when things go wrong as you follow orders, how can you be blamed? Let bygones be bygones. Those dismissed from office should be reinstated. Can shouting, yelling . . . be called revolution? It can cheat nobody except yourself."

• "Don't criticize the theory of productive forces any more. If there is more criticism, nobody will dare to grasp production."

Remarks on Gang of Four types:

• "Young leading cadres have risen up by helicopter; they should really rise step by step."

Criticizing radical "helicopters":

• "Some people tend to criticize others in order to achieve fame, stamping on others' shoulders to move up to key positions. They have a half understanding of others, but when they get wind of a mere trifle, they will criticize it for so long. This is because they have a lust for fame."

Of left-extremists:

- "They sit on the toilet yet do not manage a shit."
- "If they tell you that you're a capitalist roader, it means you're doing a good job."

Of education in the wake of the Cultural Revolution:

- "Hou Pao-lin [a comic dialogue entertainer] once very aptly remarked that primary school pupils carry one pen, high school boys carry two, college students carry three, and illiterate ones carry four. Most college students now carry nothing but one brush for wall poster writing. They can't do anything else."
- "Schools are unnecessary if they only aim to turn out workers and peasants."
- "Professors are after all professors. You have to admit that if they are capable. If you are good, go ahead and be professors. I am not the material. That's why no one says Teng Hsiao-p'ing is a professor. You have to trust intellectuals before you can employ their service. Scientists today are not given time for research. How can they create or invent things?"

Declining to go to one of Chiang Ch'ing's theatrical pieces:

- "For her drama reform I would raise my two hands to show approval, but I would not care to watch the show."
- "With the model operas today, you just see a bunch of people running to and fro on the stage. Not a trace of art. No sense bragging about them. Foreigners clap them only out of courtesy, not because they appreciate the show."

After a performance of the Vienna Symphony Orchestra:

- "This is what I call food for the spirit. Revolution must have art in it. Only artistically talented persons can really appreciate the substance of revolution. The model operas nowadays are no more than gong-and-drum shows. Go to a theater and you find yourself on a battlefield."

His sole words when confronted at a student meeting in the spring of 1976 with a list of his errors and a demand for a self-criticism:

- "I am an old man, and my hearing is not very good; I don't hear a word of what you say."

At the Eleventh CCP Congress in August 1977, in his first speech after being rehabilitated a second time:

- "There must be less empty talk and more hard work."

3. DEATH OF MAO
Message from the Government to the People

Within a few hours of Mao's death in the early hours of September 9, 1976, this message was issued. It was entitled: "MOURNING WITH DEEPEST GRIEF THE PASSING AWAY OF THE GREAT LEADER AND GREAT TEACHER CHAIRMAN MAO TSE-TUNG."*

MESSAGE TO THE WHOLE PARTY, THE WHOLE
ARMY AND THE PEOPLE OF ALL NATIONALITIES
THROUGHOUT THE COUNTRY

---

* English translation of this message and the following announcement from *Peking Review*, September 17, 1976.

From
The Central Committee of the Communist Party of
    China,
The Standing Committee of the National People's
    Congress of the People's Republic of China,
The State Council of the People's Republic of
    China, and
The Military Commission of the Central Commit-
    tee of the Communist Party of China

The Central Committee of the Communist Party of China, the
Standing Committee of the National People's Congress of the
People's Republic of China, the State Council of the People's
Republic of China and the Military Commission of the Central
Committee of the Communist Party of China announce with
deepest grief to the whole Party, the whole army and the people
of all nationalities throughout the country: Comrade Mao
Tsetung, the esteemed and beloved great leader of our Party,
our army and the people of all nationalities in our country, the
great teacher of the international proletariat and the oppressed
nations and oppressed people, Chairman of the Central Committee of the Communist Party of China, Chairman of the Military Commission of the Central Committee of the Communist
Party of China, and Honorary Chairman of the National Committee of the Chinese People's Political Consultative Conference, passed away at 00:10 hours on September 9, 1976 in Peking as a result of the worsening of his illness and despite all
treatment, although meticulous medical care was given him in
every way after he fell ill.

Chairman Mao Tsetung was the founder and wise leader of
the Communist Party of China, the Chinese People's Liberation
Army and the People's Republic of China. Chairman Mao led
our Party in waging a protracted, acute and complex struggle
against the Right and "Left" opportunist lines in the Party,
defeating the opportunist lines pursued by Chen Tu-hsiu, Chu

Chiu-pai, Li Li-san, Lo Chang-lung, Wang Ming, Chang Kuo-tao, Kao Kang-Jao Shu-shih and Peng Teh-huai and again, during the Great Proletarian Cultural Revolution, triumphing over the counter-revolutionary revisionist line of Liu Shao-chi, Lin Piao and Teng Hsiao-ping, thus enabling our Party to develop and grow in strength steadily in class struggle and the struggle between the two lines. Led by Chairman Mao, the Communist Party of China has developed through a tortuous path into a great, glorious and correct Marxist-Leninist Party which is today exercising leadership over the People's Republic of China.

During the period of the new-democratic revolution, Chairman Mao, in accordance with the universal truth of Marxism-Leninism and by combining it with the concrete practice of the Chinese revolution, creatively laid down the general line and general policy of the new-democratic revolution, founded the Chinese People's Liberation Army and pointed out that the seizure of political power by armed force in China could be achieved only by following the road of building rural base areas, using the countryside to encircle the cities and finally seizing the cities, and not by any other road. He led our Party, our army and the people of our country in using people's war to overthrow the reactionary rule of imperialism, feudalism and bureaucrat-capitalism, winning the great victory of the new-democratic revolution and founding the People's Republic of China. The victory of the Chinese people's revolution led by Chairman Mao changed the situation in the East and the world and blazed a new trail for the cause of liberation of the oppressed nations and oppressed people.

In the period of the socialist revolution, Chairman Mao comprehensively summed up the positive as well as the negative experience of the international communist movement, penetratingly analysed the class relations in socialist society and, for the first time in the history of the development of Marxism, unequivocally pointed out that there are still classes and class struggle after the socialist transformation of the ownership of the means of production has in the main been completed, drew the scientific conclusion that the bourgeoisie is right in the Communist Party, put forth the great theory of continuing the revolution under the dictatorship of the proletariat, and laid down the Party's basic line for the entire historical period of socialism. Guided by Chairman Mao's proletarian revolutionary line, our Party, our army and the people of our country have continued their triumphant advance and seized great victories in the socialist revolution and socialist construction, particularly in the Great Proletarian Cultural Revolution, in criticizing Lin Piao and Confucius and in criticizing Teng Hsiao-ping and repulsing the Right deviationist attempt at reversing correct verdicts. Upholding socialism and consolidating the dictatorship of the proletariat in the People's Republic of China, a country with a vast territory and a large population, is a great contribution of world historic significance which Chairman Mao Tsetung made to the present era; at the same time, it has provided fresh experience for the international communist movement in combating and preventing revisionism, consolidating the dictatorship of the proletariat, preventing capitalist restoration and building socialism.

All the victories of the Chinese people have been achieved under the leadership of Chairman Mao; they are all great victories for Mao Tsetung Thought. The radiance of Mao Tsetung Thought will for ever illuminate the road of advance of the Chinese people.

Chairman Mao Tsetung summed up the revolutionary practice in the international communist movement, put forward a series of scientific theses, enriched the theoretical treasury of Marxism and pointed out the orientation of struggle for the Chinese people and the revolutionary people throughout the world. With the great boldness and vision of a proletarian revolutionary, he initiated in the international communist movement the great struggle to criticize modern revisionism with the Soviet revisionist renegade clique at the core, promoted the vigorous development of the cause of the world proletarian revolution and the cause of the people of all countries against imperialism and hegemonism, and pushed the history of mankind forward.

Chairman Mao Tsetung was the greatest Marxist of the contemporary era. For more than half a century, basing himself on the principle of integrating the universal truth of Marxism-Leninism with the concrete practice of the revolution, he inherited, defended and developed Marxism-Leninism in the protracted struggle against the class enemies at home and abroad, both inside and outside the Party, and wrote a most brilliant chapter in the history of the movement of proletarian revolution. He dedicated all his energies throughout his life to the liberation of the Chinese people, to the emancipation of the oppressed nations and oppressed people the world over, and to the cause of communism. With the great resolve of a proletarian revolutionary, he waged a tenacious struggle against his illness, continued to lead the work of the whole Party, the whole army and the whole nation during his illness and fought till he breathed his last. The magnificent contributions he made to the Chinese people, the international proletariat and the revolutionary people of the whole world are immortal. The Chinese people and the revolutionary people the world over love him from the bottom of their hearts and have boundless admiration and respect for him.

The passing away of Chairman Mao Tsetung is an inestimable loss to our Party, our army and the people of all nationalities in our country, to the international proletariat and the revolutionary people of all countries and to the international communist movement. His passing away is bound to evoke immense grief in the hearts of the people of our country and the revolutionary people of all countries. The Central Committee of the Communist Party of China calls on the whole Party, the whole army and the people of all nationalities in the country to resolutely turn their grief into strength.

We must carry on the cause left behind by Chairman Mao and persist in taking class struggle as the key link, keep to the

Party's basic line and persevere in continuing the revolution under the dictatorship of the proletariat.

We must carry on the cause left behind by Chairman Mao and strengthen the centralized leadership of the Party, resolutely uphold the unity and unification of the Party and closely rally round the Party Central Committee. We must strengthen the building of the Party ideologically and organizationally in the course of the struggle between the two lines and resolutely implement the principle of the three-in-one combination of the old, middle-aged and young in accordance with the five requirements for bringing up successors to the cause of the proletarian revolution.

We must carry on the cause left behind by Chairman Mao and consolidate the great unity of the people of all nationalities under the leadership of the working class and based on the worker-peasant alliance, deepen the criticism of Teng Hsiaoping, continue the struggle to repulse the Right deviationist attempt at reversing correct verdicts, consolidate and develop the victories of the Great Proletarian Cultural Revolution, enthusiastically support the socialist new things, restrict bourgeois right and further consolidate the dictatorship of the proletariat in our country. We should continue to unfold the three great revolutionary movements of class struggle, the struggle for production and scientific experiment, build our country independently and with the initiative in our own hands, through self-reliance, hard struggle, diligence and thrift, and go all out, aim high and achieve greater, faster, better and more economical results in building socialism.

We must carry on the cause left behind by Chairman Mao and resolutely implement his line in army building, strengthen the building of the army, strengthen the building of the militia, strengthen preparedness against war, heighten our vigilance, and be ready at all times to wipe out any enemy that dares to intrude. We are determined to liberate Taiwan.

We must carry on the cause left behind by Chairman Mao and continue to resolutely carry out Chairman Mao's revolutionary line and policies in foreign affairs. We must adhere to proletarian internationalism, strengthen the unity between our Party and the genuine Marxist-Leninist Parties and organizations all over the world, strengthen the unity between the people of our country and the people of all other countries, especially those of the third world countries, unite with all the forces in the world that can be united, and carry the struggle against imperialism, social-imperialism and modern revisionism through to the end. We will never seek hegemony and will never be a superpower.

We must carry on the cause left behind by Chairman Mao and assiduously study Marxism-Leninism-Mao Tsetung Thought, apply ourselves to the study of works by Marx, Engels, Lenin, and Stalin and works by Chairman Mao, fight for the complete overthrow of the bourgeoisie and all other exploiting classes, for the establishment of the dictatorship of the proletariat in place of the dictatorship of the bourgeoisie and for the triumph of socialism over capitalism, and strive to build our country into a powerful socialist state, make still greater contributions to humanity and realize the ultimate goal of communism.

Long live invincible Marxism-Leninism-Mao Tsetung Thought!

Long live the great, glorious and correct Communist Party of China!

Eternal glory to the great leader and teacher Chairman Mao Tsetung!

Funeral Announcement

There soon followed this announcement:

ANNOUNCEMENT

by

The Central Committee of the Communist Party of China,

The Standing Committee of the National People's
Congress of the People's Republic of China,
The State Council of the People's Republic of
China, and
The Military Commission of the Central Commit-
tee of the Communist Party of China

To express the boundless respect and admiration and deepest
mourning of the whole Party, the whole army and the people of
the whole country for our great leader Chairman Mao Tsetung,
it is hereby decided:

(1) Mourning services will be held at the Great Hall of the
People from September 11 to September 17. Members and Al-
ternate Members of the Central Committee of the Communist
Party of China, leading members of the central Party, government and army organizations and of various departments of
Peking municipality, and representatives of workers, peasants,
soldiers and the masses of other circles will attend the mourning services to pay their respects to the remains of Chairman
Mao lying in state.

Members of all government organizations, army units, factories, mines, enterprises, shops, people's communes, schools,
neighbourhood communities and all other grass-roots units will
hold memorial services in their own units.

(2) A solemn memorial rally will be held in Tien An Men
Square at 3 p.m. Peking time on September 18.

Live transmissions of the memorial rally in Tien An Men
Square will be carried by the Central People's Broadcasting Station and the Peking Television Station. All government organizations, army units, factories, mines, enterprises, shops, people's communes, schools, neighbourhood communities and all
other grass-roots units should make arrangements for the
masses to listen to or watch the broadcasts and express their
condolences.

All localities at or above the county level across the country should arrange meetings of representatives of workers, peasants, soldiers and other circles at 3 p.m. on September 18 to listen to the live transmission of the memorial rally in Peking, after which memorial speeches will be delivered by the principal leading members of the local Party, government and army organizations.

(3) From September 9 to September 18, the national flag will be flown at half-mast in mourning throughout the country and at the embassies, consulates and other organizations of China stationed abroad. During this period all recreational activities will be suspended.

(4) At 3 p.m. sharp on September 18, people in all government organizations, army units, factories, mines, enterprises, shops, people's communes, schools and neighbourhood communities and all those moving outdoors, with the exception of those whose work cannot be interrupted, should stand at attention wherever they are in silent tribute for three minutes. At 3 p.m. sharp on September 18 all places and units with sirens, such as trains, ships, military vessels and factories, should sound their sirens for three minutes in mourning.

(5) To the governments, fraternal Parties and friendly personages of foreign countries who want to come to China to take part in the mourning, the Chinese embassies and consulates in these countries should express deep gratitude and inform them of the decision of the Central Committee of our Party and the Government of our country not to invite foreign governments, fraternal Parties or friendly personages to send delegations or representatives to take part in the mourning in China.

Hence the announcement.

September 9, 1976

4. THE MAO MEMORIAL AND
VOLUME V OF HIS *SELECTED WORKS*

The first government decisions to be announced following Mao's death concerned a Mao Memorial and the further publication of Mao's writings.*

DECISION ON THE ESTABLISHMENT OF A MEMORIAL HALL FOR THE GREAT LEADER AND TEACHER CHAIRMAN MAO TSETUNG

Adopted by
The Central Committee of the Communist Party of China,
The Standing Committee of the National People's Congress of the People's Republic of China,
The State Council of the People's Republic of China, and
The Military Commission of the Central Committee of the Communist Party of China

October 8, 1976

To perpetuate the memory of Chairman Mao Tsetung, the great leader of our Party, our army and the people of all nationalities in our country and the great teacher of the international proletariat and the oppressed nations and oppressed people, and to educate and inspire the workers, peasants, soldiers and other labouring people to carry out Chairman Mao's behests, uphold Marxism-Leninism-Mao Tsetung Thought and carry the cause of proletarian revolution through to the end, it is hereby decided:

---

* English translation of both decisions from *Peking Review*, October 15, 1976.

(1) A memorial hall for the great leader and teacher Chairman Mao Tsetung will be established in the capital Peking.

(2) Upon the completion of the memorial hall, the crystal coffin containing the body of Chairman Mao Tsetung will be placed in the hall so that the broad masses of the people will be able to pay their respects to his remains.

DECISION ON THE PUBLICATION OF THE "SELECTED WORKS OF MAO TSETUNG" AND THE PREPARATIONS FOR THE PUBLICATION OF THE "COLLECTED WORKS OF MAO TSETUNG"

Adopted by the Central Committee of the Communist Party of China

October 8, 1976

In the past half century and more, the great leader and teacher Chairman Mao Tsetung, basing himself on the principle of integrating the universal truth of Marxism-Leninism with the concrete practice of the revolution, inherited, defended and developed Marxism-Leninism in all respects and enriched the treasure house of Marxist theory in the course of leading China in the great struggle to accomplish the new-democratic revolution and carry out the socialist revolution and socialist construction, in the great struggle against the Right and "Left" opportunist lines within the Party and in the great struggle against imperialism, against modern revisionism with the Soviet revisionist renegade clique at the core and against the reactionaries of all countries. Chairman Mao's works are immortal Marxist-Leninist documents. The publication of these works is of great immediate importance and far-reaching historic significance for the people of all nationalities of our country in carrying out Chairman Mao's behests and carrying through to the end the proletarian revolutionary cause and for the cause of the liberation of the proletariat and the oppressed nations and oppressed people the world over. The publication will be a great event in the annals of the development of Marxism and we must exert ourselves seriously and earnestly and carry it out well. The Central Committee of the Communist Party of China hereby decides:

(1) Volume V of the *Selected Works of Mao Tsetung* will be published at the soonest possible date, with other volumes to follow. While the selected works are being published, active preparations are to be made for the publication of the *Collected Works of Mao Tsetung.*

(2) The work on the publication of the *Selected Works of Mao Tsetung* and the *Collected Works of Mao Tsetung* will be under the direct leadership of the Political Bureau of the Central Committee of the Communist Party of China headed by Comrade Hua Kuo-feng, under which a committee for the editing and publication of the works of Chairman Mao Tsetung will take charge of the work of compiling, editing and publishing.

(3) The General Office of the Central Committee of the Communist Party of China will be responsible for collecting and keeping all the manuscripts of Chairman Mao's works.

The Central Committee directs the Party committees at all levels to send to the General Office of the Central Committee as soon as possible all of Chairman Mao's manuscripts kept in their localities or their units, including the original scripts of articles, documents, telegrams, written directives, letters, poems and inscriptions, and the original minutes of Chairman Mao's speeches. The General Office of the Central Committee should make duplicate copies and send them to the units or persons that have provided the originals, for their own keeping.

The C.P.C. Central Committee calls on the whole Party, the whole army and the people of all nationalities throughout the country to bring about a new upsurge in studying works of Marx, Engels, Lenin and Stalin and of Chairman Mao and energetically help collect the originals of Chairman Mao's writings. It hopes that Marxist-Leninist Parties and organizations and progressive organizations and friendly personages of various countries will offer their help to make a success of the work of collecting the originals of Chairman Mao's writings.

5. CELEBRATING HUA'S RISE AND THE GANG OF FOUR'S FALL

To celebrate the fall of the Gang of Four and the accession of Hua to the chairmanship of the CCP, the three leading Peking newspapers published on October 24, 1976, a joint editorial entitled "GREAT HISTORIC VICTORY": *

Red flags are flying over the mountains and rivers, everywhere in the motherland, and the faces of our 800 million people glow with joy. Hundreds of millions of people in all parts of our country have held mammoth demonstrations in the last few days. One million armymen and civilians yesterday met in a grand rally in Peking, the capital. They warmly celebrated Comrade Hua Kuo-feng's assuming the posts of Chairman of the Central Committee of the Communist Party of China and Chairman of the Military Commission of the C.P.C. Central Committee, hailed the great victory in smashing the plot of the anti-Party clique of Wang Hung-wen, Chang Chun-chiao, Chiang Ching and Yao Wen-yuan to usurp Party and state power, and denounced with great indignation the towering crimes of the "gang of four." The whole Party, the whole army and the people of all nationalities throughout the country are determined to rally most closely round the Party Central Committee headed by Chairman Hua Kuo-feng, carry out Chairman Mao's behests, and carry the proletarian revolutionary cause through to the end.

Comrade Hua Kuo-feng was selected by the great leader Chairman Mao himself to be his successor. Chairman Mao proposed Comrade Hua Kuo-feng for the posts of First Vice-Chair-

---

* English translation from *Peking Review*, October 29, 1976.

man of the Central Committee of the Communist Party of China and Premier of the State Council in April 1976. Then, on April 30, Chairman Mao wrote to Comrade Hua Kuo-feng in his own handwriting: "With you in charge, I'm at ease." In accordance with the arrangements Chairman Mao had made before he passed away, the October 7, 1976 resolution of the Central Committee of the Communist Party of China and Chairman of the Military Commission of the C.P.C. Central Committee. This represents the common aspiration of the whole Party, the whole army and the people of the whole country and was a great victory in smashing the plot of the "gang of four" to usurp Party and state power. It was a joyous event of immense historic significance. Comrade Hua Kuo-feng, in whom Chairman Mao had boundless faith and whom the people throughout the country deeply love, is now the leader of our Party, and our Party and state have a reliable helmsman to continue their victorious advance along Chairman Mao's proletarian revolutionary line.

The Party Central Committee headed by Comrade Hua Kuo-feng crushed the plot of the "gang of four" for a counter-revolutionary restoration and got rid of a big evil in our Party. Wang Chang-Chiang-Yao had long formed a cabal, the "gang of four," engaged in factional activities to split the Party. The great leader Chairman Mao was aware of this long ago and severely criticized and tried to educate them again and again. And he made some arrangements to solve this problem. Chairman Mao criticized them on July 17, 1974, saying: "You'd better be careful; don't let yourselves become a small faction of four." Again, on December 24, Chairman Mao criticized them: "Don't form factions. Those who do so will fall." In November and December of the same year, as the central leading organs were preparing to convene the Fourth National People's Congress, Chairman Mao said: "Chiang Ching has wild ambitions. She wants Wang Hung-wen to be Chairman of the Standing Committee of the National People's Congress and herself to be Chairman of the Party Central Committee." On May 3, 1975, at a meeting of the Political Bureau of the Party Central Committee, Chairman Mao reiterated the basic principles of "three do's and three don'ts," and warned them: "Practise Marxism-Leninism, and not revisionism; unite and don't split; be open and aboveboard, and don't intrigue and conspire. Don't function as a gang of four, don't do it any more, why do you keep doing it?" That very day Chairman Mao, on this question, gave the instruction that "if this is not settled in the first half of this year, it should be settled in the second half; if not this year, then next year; if not next year, then the year after." Toward Chairman Mao's criticism and education, the "gang of four" took the attitude of counter-revolutionary double-dealers who comply in public but oppose in private. Not only did they not show the slightest sign of repentance, but on the contrary they went from bad to worse, further and further down the wrong path. During the period when Chairman Mao was seriously ill and after he passed away, they became more frantic in attacking the Party and speeded up their attempts to usurp the supreme leadership of the Party and state. We faced a grave danger of the Party turning revisionist and the state changing its political colour. At this critical moment in the Chinese revolution, the Party Central Committee headed by Comrade Hua Kuo-feng, representing the fundamental interests and common aspiration of the whole Party, the whole army and the people of the whole country and with the boldness and vision of the proletariat, adopted resolute measures against the "gang of four" anti-Party clique, smashed their plot to usurp Party and state power, and saved the revolution and the Party. Thus the proletariat won a decisive victory in counter-attacking the onslaught by the bourgeoisie.

The "gang of four," a bane to the country and the people, committed heinous crimes. They completely betrayed the basic principles of "three do's and three don'ts" that Chairman Mao had earnestly taught, wantonly tampered with Marxism-Leninism-Mao Tsetung Thought, tampered with Chairman Mao's directives, opposed Chairman Mao's proletarian revolutionary line on a whole series of domestic and international questions, and practised revisionism under the signboard of Marxism. They carried out criminal activities to split the Party, forming a factional group, going their own way, establishing their own system inside the Party, doing as they wished, lording it over others, and placing themselves above Chairman Mao and the Party Central Committee. They were busy intriguing and conspiring and stuck their noses into everything to stir up trouble everywhere, interfere with Chairman Mao's revolutionary line and strategic plans and undermine the socialist revolution and socialist construction. They confounded right and wrong, made rumours, worked in a big way to create counter-revolutionary opinion, fabricated accusations against others and labelled people at will, and attempted to overthrow a large number of leading Party, government and army comrades in the central organs and various localities and seize Party and state leadership. They worshipped things foreign and fawned on foreigners, maintained illicit foreign relations, betrayed important Party and state secrets, and unscrupulously practised capitulationism and national betrayal. Resorting to various manoeuvres, they pursued a counter-revolutionary revisionist line, an ultra-Right line. Chairman Mao pointed out: "You are making the socialist revolution, and yet don't know where the bourgeoisie is. It is right in the Communist Party—those in power taking the capitalist road. The capitalist-roaders are still on the capitalist road." Wang Hung-wen, Chang Chun-chiao, Chiang Ching and Yao Wen-yuan are typical representatives of the bourgeoisie inside the Party, unrepentant capitalist-roaders still travelling on the capitalist road and a gang of bourgeois conspirators and careerists.

Our struggle against the "gang of four" is a life-and-death struggle between the two classes, the two roads and the two lines. By forming a narrow self-seeking clique to usurp Party and state power, the "gang of four" sought to change fundamentally the proletarian nature of our Party, change its basic line for the entire historical period of socialism and restore capitalism in China. If their scheme had succeeded, it would have meant serious disaster for the Chinese people. The crushing of this anti-Party clique has removed from the Party a bunch of hidden traitors, rid the country of a big scourge and redressed the grievances of the people. The Party, the army and the people are all jubilant. This is a great example of putting into practice Chairman Mao's great theory of continuing the revolution under the dictatorship of the proletariat. It is of tremendous immediate importance and far-reaching historic significance to our adhering to the Party's basic line, combating and preventing revisionism, consolidating the dictatorship of the proletariat, preventing the restoration of capitalism, building socialism, upholding the principles of proletarian internationalism and carrying out Chairman Mao's revolutionary line and policies in foreign affairs. It is a great victory for the Great Proletarian Cultural Revolution and for Mao Tsetung Thought.

Chairman Mao pointed out in 1971: "Our Party already has a history of 50 years and has gone through ten major struggles on the question of Party line. There were people in these ten struggles who wanted to split our Party, but none were able to do so. This is a question worth studying: such a big country, such a large population, yet no split. The only explanation is that the people, the Party and the entire Party membership are of one mind in opposing a split. In view of its history, this Party of ours has a great future."

Summing up our Party's experience in the ten struggles on the question of Party line, Chairman Mao pointed out that "the correctness or incorrectness of the ideological and political line decides everything" and put forward the three basic principles "Practise Marxism, and not revisionism; unite, and don't split; be open and aboveboard, and don't intrigue and conspire." These principles are our criteria for distinguishing correct from erroneous lines and our sharp weapon for identifying the bourgeoisie inside the Party. The whole history of our Party shows that only by adhering to the three basic principles can our Party march in step, win wholehearted support from the masses of the people and organize a mighty revolutionary contingent, and only by so doing can our revolutionary cause thrive. Whoever goes against the three basic principles betrays the cause of proletarian revolution and the vital interests of the Party and the people, inevitably loses the confidence of the people and brings ruin and shame upon himself. On ten occasions in the past, the chieftains of opportunist lines tried to split our Party, but they all failed. The present Wang-Chang-Chiang-Yao "gang of four" anti-Party clique, too, has come to an ignominious end because it practised revisionism and splittism, engaged in conspiracies to usurp Party and state power, and thus completely forfeited the confidence of the people and became extremely isolated. Historical experience has time and again shown that our Party cannot be easily destroyed. Our Party is worthy of its reputation as a Party founded, tempered and nurtured by Chairman Mao himself, as a politically mature Marxist-Leninist Party and as a great, glorious and correct Party.

While acclaiming our Party's great historic victory, the whole Party, the whole army and the people of all nationalities throughout the country, under the leadership of the Party Central Committee headed by Chairman Hua Kuo-feng, are determined to hold high the great red banner of Marxism-Leninism-Mao Tsetung Thought, persist in taking class struggle as the key link, adhere to the Party's basic line and persevere in continuing the revolution under the dictatorship of the proletariat. We must thoroughly expose the vile crimes of the Wang-Chang-Chiang-Yao anti-Party clique, penetratingly criticize their counter-revolutionary revisionist line and eradicate its pernicious influence. It is imperative to draw a strict distinction between the two different types of contradictions and handle them correctly, earnestly implement Chairman Mao's principles "Learn from past mistakes to avoid future ones and cure the sickness to save the patient" and "Help more people by educating them and narrow the target of attack," so as to unite with all those that can be united with. We should continue to criticize

Teng Hsiao-ping and repulse the Right deviationist attempt to reverse correct verdicts. We should enthusiastically support socialist new things, consciously restrict bourgeois right and consolidate and develop the achievements of the Great Proletarian Cultural Revolution. We should grasp revolution, promote production and other work and preparedness against war, go all out, aim high and achieve greater, faster, better and more economical results in building socialism and continue to develop the excellent situation.

Having eliminated the "four pests," our Party has become even more united, even stronger and even more vigorous, and the dictatorship of the proletariat in our country is more consolidated. The masses of the people are in high spirits and militant; everywhere in our motherland, orioles sing and swallows dart. Before us arises "a political situation in which there are both centralism and democracy, both discipline and freedom, both unity of will and personal ease of mind and liveliness." Since we have such a great Party, army and people, no difficulty whatsoever can stop our triumphant advance. Under the leadership of the Party Central Committee headed by Chairman Hua Kuofeng, we are able to continue our advance in the socialist revolution in accordance with Chairman Mao's line and policies and, in accordance with the grand plan Chairman Mao mapped out, accomplish the comprehensive modernization of agriculture, industry, national defence and science and technology and build China into a powerful socialist country before the end of the century, so as to make a greater contribution to humanity and work for the final realization of communism.

6. DISSIDENTS ASK FOR DEMOCRACY AND THE RULE OF LAW

The following are excerpts from a 20,000-word unauthorized wall poster put up in Canton during 1974. It was signed 'Li I-che,' a pseudonym for three youths. The writers are by no

means anti-Mao or anti-Communist. They are enthusiastic
for the aims of the Cultural Revolution, which they believe
Lin Piao betrayed. Their concern is with democracy and the
rule of law. Their poster is dedicated both to Mao and to the
Fourth National People's Congress (eventually held in
1975).*

> The freedom of speech, the freedom of press, the freedom of as-
> sociation, which are stipulated in the Constitution, and the free-
> dom of exchanging revolutionary experience, which is not sti-
> pulated in the Constitution, have all been truly practiced in the
> great revolution and granted with the support by the Party Cen-
> tral headed by Chairman Mao. This is something which the
> Chinese people had not possessed for several thousand years. It
> is something so active and lively. It is one extraordinary
> achievement of the revolution.
>
> But this Great Proletarian Cultural Revolution has not ac-
> complished the tasks of a great proletarian culture revolution,
> because it has not enabled the people to hold firmly in their
> hands the weapon of extensive people's democracy.
>
> In the summer of 1968, the socialist legal system "suddenly
> became inoperative," while, on the other hand, "the state power
> is the power to suppress" became operative. All across the land,
> there were arrests everywhere, suppressions everywhere, mis-
> carriages of justice everywhere. Where did the socialist legal
> system go? Allegedly, it was no longer of any use because it
> belonged to the Constitution established by the old People's
> Congress whereas the new People's Congress was not convened
> yet. Now, there was no law and no heaven!
>
> This was a rehearsal of social-Fascism in our country; and
> the commander-in-chief of the rehearsal was Lin Piao.

---

* Chinese text available in the Hong Kong monthly *Zhan Wang* (Look), No. 332. In
preparing an English version I have relied heavily on a translation in the Taipei journal
Issues and Studies, January 1976.

The masses of people are not A-tou [nickname of the crown prince of the State of Shu in the period of the Three Kingdoms, who was notorious for his ignorance and good-for-nothingness]. They are fully aware of the source of their misfortune. The cutting edge of their attack is directed at the Lin Piao System. No one of them has manifested hatred of Chairman Mao's revolutionary line and policies. On the contrary, they hate Lin Piao— the one who distorted and hindered this line and these policies—and those who enjoy vested interests from the Lin Piao System. They demand democracy; they demand a socialist legal system; and they demand the revolutionary rights and the human rights which protect the masses of people. "What? You demand democracy? You are reactionaries! Because you are reactionaries, we'll give you no democracy." They talk loudly and fluently; and are fond of quoting Chairman Mao's passages in connection with the people's democratic dictatorship.

Whether or not acknowledging that there is emerging in China a Soviet Union type of privileged stratum (of which Liu Shao-ch'i and Lin Piao, etc., were the political agents only) is the fundamental theoretical question of affirming or negating the Great Proletarian Cultural Revolution.

Whence are . . . the shockingly high-class luxuries? Whence are the disguised heritages of children of high-ranking cadres who have matter-of-factly enjoyed the rights of possessing property? What are the recourses of the mode of possession of the new bourgeois class and the political measures which protect this mode of possession? In literature and art, in education, in the "May 7 Cadre School," in Going up to the Mountains and down to the Countryside, in Getting Rid of the Stale and Taking in the Fresh, in attending universities, and in cultivation of the successors, in short in almost everything which is called a "newborn thing," the privileged can use their divine presence and demonstrate their divine power.

May we not say that the Soviet Union's change [to revisionism] began with the practice of a high-salary system for its high-ranking cadres, which was intended to keep up with the levels of bourgeois experts? In our China, even if the tradition permits, and the people do not object to, the practice of providing certain preferential treatment to the veteran cadres who have allegedly shed much blood and sweat for the revolution, can we thus belittle its corruptive effects on the regime as well as its influence over the new social relations?

We are not Utopian socialists; therefore, we acknowledge that there exist in our society at the present stage various kinds of differences which cannot be eliminated by a single law or decree. But, the law governing the development of the socialist revolutionary movement is not to enhance the differences but to eliminate them, and even more, not to allow these differences to be expanded into economic and political privileges. Special privileges are fundamentally opposed to the interests of the people. Why should we be so shy about the criticism of special privileges? . . .

"Who gives us the power?" The people do. Thus, our cadres should not be Mandarins but errand runners of the people. However, power is the most corruptive agent of men. A man's ascension in status is the most trying test to see if he is working for the benefit of the majority, or for the benefit of a minority. Whether or not one can preserve his spirit of serving the people is chiefly dependent upon the revolutionary supervision by the people, in addition to his own efforts; whereas the mass movements are the richest sources for a revolutionary to preserve his revolutionary spirit.

How should the rights of revolutionary supervision of the masses of people over the leadership at various levels in the Party and the state be stipulated? And how should it be explicitly stipulated that when certain cadres (especially the high-ranking cadres in Central organizations) have lost the trust of the broad masses of people, the people "can dismiss them at any time"?

The "4th National People's Congress" should answer these questions. . . .

Are the people's democratic rights not written in our Constitution and Party Constitution and Central documents? Yes, they have been written down. Not only that, but there also are the stipulations of "protecting the people's democracy," "not allowing malicious attack and revenge," and "forbidding extracting a confession by torture and interrogation." But, these protections have been, in fact, always unavailable, while, on the contrary, Fascist autocracy has been "allowed" to be practiced. . . .

The 9th Party Congress in 1969 already announced that "the current main task is the concrete fulfillment (of policies)." Since then five years have passed; and Lin Piao has been destroyed for three years. Why have so many important proletarian policies not been concretely fulfilled?

Moreover, in recent years the policies have been changed frequently, even to the degree that "orders issued in the morning are changed in the same evening." In addition, there has been an endless emergence of local policies, which make the people very much confused, even to the degree of doubting the Party. . . .

Has the Constitution of 1954 also not made stipulations of the people's democratic rights? Has Chairman Mao not said many times that: "Without extensive people's democracy, the dictatorship of the proletariat cannot be consolidated?" But, partly because there exists the anti-democratic force which was represented by Lin Piao, and partly because the masses of people have seldom made use of these democratic rights (owing to the deeply entrenched feudalist tradition in China, and a lack of democratic spirit resulting from our country's comparatively backward production and the limited cultural level of the people), the objective of "creating a lively and vigorous political situation" brought forward by Chairman Mao many years ago has been very far indeed from being achieved.

7. THE MILITARY PRESS LAUDS HUA

Liberation Army Daily, the PLA Newspaper, published this remarkable editorial on October 29, 1976, under the heading: "COMRADE HUA KUO-FENG IS OUR PARTY'S WORTHY LEADER."*

Chairman Hua Kuo-feng, dressed in a green army uniform, stood on the rostrum atop magnificent Tien An Men Gate. Armymen and civilians in their hundreds of millions across the country heartily cheered and sang at the top of their voice. They cheered because the great Communist Party of China again has a leader of its own and sang because the great Chinese People's Liberation Army again has a supreme commander of its own.

While the great leader and teacher Chairman Mao was seriously ill and after his passing, the anti-Party clique of Wang Hung-wen, Chang Chun-chiao, Chiang Ching and Yao Wen-yuan stepped up its moves to usurp Party and state power. We were confronted with the real danger of our Party turning revisionist and our country changing its political colour. At this grave historical juncture the Party Central Committee headed by Comrade Hua Kuo-feng, with the boldness and vision of proletarian revolutionaries, shattered at one stoke the criminal plot of the "gang of four" to usurp Party and state power, thus saving the revolution and the party and winning a victory of decisive significance for the proletariat in its counterattack against the onslaught of the bourgeosie. By leading our Party from danger to safety through tempestuous storms, Comrade Hua Kuo-feng averted a major retrogression in Chinese history and a great disaster for our people, thereby winning the complete trust and wholehearted affection of the whole Party, the whole army and the people of all nationalities throughout the country. Comrade Hua Kuo-feng is indeed a worthy successor selected

---

*English translation from *Peking Review,* November 5, 1976.

by Chairman Mao himself, a worthy helmsman to steer Chairman Mao's cause forward, and a worthy wise leader of the Communist Party of China founded by Chairman Mao.

In this life-and-death struggle between the two classes, the two roads and the two lines, it is of extremely great immediate importance to review Lenin's theory of the relations between leaders, political parties, classes and the masses. Marxism-Leninism holds that "the people, and the people alone, are the motive force in the making of world history." (Mao Tsetung: *On Coalition Government.*) The making of history by the people implies affirming the role of leaders who represent their interests and will and the role of the people in their millions. The masses are divided into classes; classes usually are led by political parties; political parties, as a rule, are directed by more or less stable groups composed of the most authoritative, influential and experienced members who are elected to the most important positions and are called leaders. In order to become a genuine battle headquarters for the proletariat, a proletarian revolutionary party must have leaders who have come to the fore in class struggle and in the revolutionary movements of the masses, who are loyal to the masses and maintain flesh-and-blood ties with them and who are good at concentrating their ideas, persevering in them and carrying them through. Such leaders are generally acknowledged by the masses and are genuine representatives of the proletariat. The presence of such leaders in a proletarian party is a manifestation of its political maturity and the hope for the triumph of the proletarian cause. Without such leaders, "the dictatorship of the proletariat, and its 'unity of will,' remain a phrase." (Lenin: *A Letter to the German Communists*). The great victory won by the Party Central Committee headed by Comrade Hua Kuo-feng in smashing the plot of the "gang of four" to usurp Party and state power is proof of the great role of Party leaders at critical turning points in history.

Great revolutionary struggles produce great persons. Leaders of a proletarian party are recognized by the masses in the course of struggle and practice; they are not self-appointed. The leading role of the great leader and teacher Chairman Mao in the whole Party was established in the course of the great struggle of the Chinese revolution, through revolutionary storms and after overcoming many difficulties and hazards, and was acknowledged by the whole Party, the whole army and the people of all nationalities throughout the country. Summing up both the positive and negative experiences of the Chinese revolution and the international communist movement, Chairman Mao put forward the five requirements for successors to the revolutionary cause of the proletariat and, in the acute struggle between the two lines within the Party, personally selected Comrade Hua Kuo-feng to succeed him as the leader of our Party. The period in which Comrade Hua Kuo-feng became First Vice-Chairman of the Central Committee of the Communist Party of China and Premier of the State Council was the most difficult period since the founding of New China because of serious natural disasters and because the "four pests" were rampant. Under the leadership of Chairman Mao, Comrade Hua Kuo-feng withstood the adverse current, did away with interference, overcame difficulties and correctly and appropriately handled a series of important domestic and international questions. Chairman Mao wrote in his own handwriting "With you in charge, I'm at ease," which expressed his boundless trust in Comrade Hua Kuo-feng. After the death of the great leader and teacher Chairman Mao, the Party Central Committee headed by Comrade Hua Kuo-feng, in order to carry out Chairman Mao's behests and defend the purity of Marxism-Leninism-Mao Tsetung Thought, promptly made the wise decisions on the establishment of a memorial hall for Chairman Mao and on the publication of the *Selected Works of Mao Tsetung* and preparations for the publication of the *Collected Works of Mao Tsetung,* and exposed the Wang-Chang-Chiang-Yao anti-Party "gang of four." All this demonstrates still more the noble qualities, outstanding ability and revolutionary boldness and great far-sightedness of Comrade Hua Kuo-feng as leader of our Party. It further proves that the decision Chairman Mao made before his death was extremely wise, that Chairman Mao's cause has a worthy successor and that our socialist motherland has an infinitely bright future.

A major point in practically every struggle between the two lines in the history of our Party has been the struggle waged by the proletariat to defend the status of its party leader against the plots of bourgeois conspirators and careerists to usurp the supreme leadership of the Party. Such were the soul-stirring struggles against the setting up of a bogus central committee by Chang Kuo-tao, against the counter-revolutionary *Outline of Project "571"* of Lin Piao, and against the plot of the "gang of four" to usurp Party and state power! The essence of these struggles is whether to uphold the correct Marxist-Leninist line, persist in making revolution, persevere in going forward and lead China to a bright future or to push an erroneous opportunist and revisionist line, oppose the revolution, cling to retrogression and drag China down into darkness. A great victory has been won in the current struggle: The proletariat has once again defeated the bourgeoisie, socialism has once again triumphed over capitalism and Marxism has once again prevailed over revisionism. We have boundless trust in the leadership of the Party Central Committee headed by the Party's leader Comrade Hua Kuo-feng and have full confidence in the prospects of future struggles.

Love for our Party, our state, our army and our people finds concentrated expression in love for our leader. Every Communist Party member and every revolutionary fighter should with a high level of consciousness love, support and defend the leader of our Party. Comrade Hua Kuo-feng's becoming the leader of our Party conforms to the needs of the revolution and is an inevitable historical outcome; it is the common aspiration of hundreds of millions of Chinese people and a reliable guarantee that our Party and state will continue to advance triumphantly along Chairman Mao's proletarian revolutionary line. We will resolutely fight to the end against anyone who dares to oppose

Marxism-Leninism-Mao Tsetung Thought and the Party Central Committee headed by Chairman Hua Kuo-feng.

8. CHINESE VIEWS OF AMERICA

(a) What *People's Daily* had to say about Nixon and Kissinger wasn't all that was said about these two in China. In the summer of 1971, just after Kissinger's first trip to Peking, some foreign visitors photographed these two poems on the literary bulletin board of a factory in the city of Sian: *

Poem one
Nixon's Personal Statement

Blazing fires of revolution burn the world over
Boiling oil is poured on the Pentagon
The raging fire in Coconut Grove startles the universe
War drums along the Equator shake the heavens
As the economy takes a further downward turn every day
The tide of rebellion rises up in waves
A visit to China is the only way out
For a brief respite from blazing flames that singe the eyebrows.

Poem two

For next year's national presidential elections
Two promises made have not at all been redeemed
The key to capture votes is a visit to China
He will not hesitate to use grease paint and to peddle his sex-
    appeal
The C.I.A. brains trust is at its wits' end

---

* English translation based on that of Dr. Cornelis Schepel of the University of Leiden, changed in places by myself after perusal of the Chinese text and consultation with Dr. Ch'en Li-li of Tufts University.

The Ping-Pong game let through a glimmer of hope
Kissinger's trip to Peking brought a joyful message
He drinks fine wine and eats crab's legs, pulling his happiest
grinning face
That Nixon may go down in history, the most famous president
in two hundred years
With painted face-mask, disguised as a beauty, he comes to ne-
gotiate
But the demons-demasking-mirror in the city of Peking is truly
inexorable
A fear grows that his true image will be revealed and his great
cause will fail
There is no way out but to go to church, and in profound wor-
ship
Pray to high heaven and beseech God: "Protect me through this
difficult passage!"

(b) A journalist from Shanghai who is an acquaintance of
mine, Wang Cheng-lung, visited San Francisco in 1973;
translated here are excerpts from his report printed in *Literary Currents* [Shanghai], August 13, 1973.* It is typical of
many articles in the Chinese press about visits to America.

FRIENDSHIP ON THE OTHER SIDE OF THE PACIFIC
—Account of a Visit to San Francisco's Number Eighty Dock

On the morning of June 11, our delegation of Chinese journalists visited Dock Eighty. Riding in a silver-gray bus, we
passed through San Francisco's Chinatown, crossed over the
hanging Golden Gate Bridge, negotiated hilly streets, shot along
a turnpike . . .
It's an old dock right on the Pacific. Many buildings of irregular shape lend an air of antiquity. There are shabby concrete
walls; layers of dirt on the windows; exhaust from automobiles

---

* English translation by myself, with the assistance of my student, Liang Tsan-tang.

has even blackened some areas. Opposite the dock are small shops and bars. The high part of the walls and the roofs are crowded with dazzling advertisements.

At this time the street was deserted. Only seagulls jumping on the concrete dikes and the pavements, and a few workers with bags moving briskly toward the Work Agency, colored the scene.

The Work Agency of the dock is situated in a one-story building at an intersection. At the door is a weather-beaten board covered with English words. Lots of people were pressing by the main gate, jamming each other, creating much hustle and bustle. . . .

[Amid the welcoming crowd] stood an old lady, with a little girl on tiptoe. The one with a smile, the other with an upturned innocent little face, ardently waved at us. The dock seethed with the enthusiasm of the American people.

I was deeply moved and touched by the spectacle. Suddenly there ran out from the crowd a big strong American friend. His face one enormous smile, he came with large steps, his hand in position long before he reached me, and he yelled: "How are you, good sir*!"

"Oh, it's you, good sir*—it's Austin."

Austin, son of a dock worker, was wearing a 70 percent new Sun Yat-sen jacket.** Its collar was open, revealing his husky neck. He stood out from the crowd for his exceptionally vivacious spirit.

As I looked at his well-built physique, scenes of his visit last fall to Shanghai with an American Labor delegation moved through my mind. . . .

While we immersed ourselves in recalling past friendship, we walked with other delegates to the gate of the Work Agency.

---

* The Chinese term used here is the formal *nin,* rather than the ordinary word for you, *ni.*

** What Americans call a "Mao jacket" is known in Mao's China as a "Sun Yat-sen jacket."

. . . The place for obtaining a "work ticket" was a booth surrounded by a glass wall. . . . Facing us were two great and striking slogans, written both in English and Chinese: "TEN THOUSAND YEARS TO THE FRIENDSHIP OF THE AMERICAN AND CHINESE PEOPLES," and "WARMLY WELCOME THE JOURNALISTS DELEGATION FROM THE PEOPLES REPUBLIC OF CHINA."

Austin explained to me: "On the docks of San Francisco, there are about 1500 workers—excluding some electrical artisans—who line up here every day to ask for work tickets. It is very difficult to find a job at these docks. Especially since the introduction of many mechanical labor-saving devices, there has been little work offered—only a few are getting tickets." . . .

Since I'd never seen a work ticket before, I hoped to take a look at one. Austin understood this, and turned around to borrow one of these small tickets. He explained to us thoroughly the meaning of all the English words written on it. . . .

It was 8:40 a.m. when we finished visiting the Work Agency, and we crossed the road to a nearby restaurant to have breakfast. Austin related to me, as we ate, things that had happened since his visit to China. "When I told my co-workers about conditions in China, everybody was warmly receptive, and extremely interested in the working conditions of Chinese dockers." . . .

After breakfast we went to visit the loading section of the dock. . . . "Bulk loading" is a rather up-to-date technique. Yet most dockers prefer to unload ships from lands which do not possess this advanced technique. In this way there are more job opportunities for workers.

The "bulk-loading" technique has brought much profit for capitalists, but a shrunken chance for jobs on the part of workers. Moreover it undercuts the chance for workers to develop their own new techniques. Such is the characteristic feature of a modernized American dock.

After our host had explained things to us, he said in a pas-

sionate tone: "We hope in the future to have ships at this dock
from the Peoples Republic of China, and also our ships at Chinese docks."

(c) According to sources in Taiwan, this speech (excerpts
here) on Sino-American relations was given on August 24,
1976, to a gathering of young Chinese diplomats, by Keng
Piao, a high Peking official who is director of the International Liaison Department of the CCP.*

"With respect to our relations with the United States, some
gogetters and adventurists do not see correctly the dual nature
of the U.S. ruling circle. Most people see only its reactionary
side and put stress on struggle. They have failed to see its weak
side which could be made use of, thus negating the thinking of
making necessary a struggle against and taking advantage of
the weak side of the United States.

"No matter from what angle we look at it, we must have a
correct concept on the question of our U.S. policy. To wit: (1)
The United States is still an imperialist country; (2) In accordance with the development of the situation, we must positively
improve Sino-U.S. relations in some aspects. These two points
contain the philosophy of both unite and struggle—a practice of
established fundamental policies and flexible tactics.

"So long as we fully recognize the dual nature of the U.S. imperialism we can easily understand our U.S. policy, which
seems to be contradictory but actually is not. For example, on
the one hand, we denounce the continuing presence of U.S.
imperialist troops in some countries. But, on the other hand, we
support the presence of U.S. troops in Western Europe and in
the Philippines. There is nothing strange after we make an explanation. Though the continuing presence of U.S. troops in
Western Europe cannot hold off the aggressive ambition of the

---

* English translation from *What's Happening on the Chinese Mainland* (Taipei), January 15, 1977.

Soviet revisionist new tsar, at least it can bring about a temporary stability and serve as a deterrent to defer the timing of war.

" 'Deferring' is favorable to us and to the whole world. In fact, it is our consistent foreign policy to oppose the presence of U.S. troops in other people's territories. However, we are in favor of the continuing presence of U.S. troops in some areas. This is a flexible application of tactics under the major premise. On the contrary, if we push the United States to side with the enemy and treat it as we treat the Soviet Union, apparently, we will be attacked both from front and rear and will plunge ourselves into a difficult situation."

* * *

"Taiwan has little political influence in the world today. But, it is impossible to settle the Taiwan problem within a short period. It may last one or two decades, or even longer. Liberation of Taiwan won't be realized immediately after the completion of the normalization of Sino-U.S. relations, but in no case shall we abandon the assertion that Taiwan is a part of Chinese territory and allow a big country as the United States to promote the 'two Chinas' theory at will. So we say that the prerequisite for the United States to establish diplomatic relations with China is to recognize the Government of the 'People's Republic of China' as the sole legitimate government and withdraw its Ambassador from Taiwan. We will not object to the United States maintaining trade and people-to-people contacts with Taiwan after the establishment of diplomatic relations.

"The mounting atmosphere in the U.S. ruling circle to 'make detente with the Soviet Union' is an important matter which calls for our concern. Nixon and Ford have visited here. Members and leaders of the U.S. Congress and former U.S. Secretary of Defense Schlesinger are to be invited to visit here. More influential Americans in military, political and social circles will also be invited. There is only one purpose—to tell them repeatedly our views of the situation and make clear that to make detente with the Soviet Union is impracticable. It is to capitulate and turn back. It is not a positive way to solve world problems but a way to bring harm to all."

9. VOICES FROM THE STREET

Some people in the West still believe that the Chinese people never commit crimes and that all think alike and behave precisely as the CCP urges them to. This has never been the case; today less than ever. The three documents below—seen by me on walls in the streets of Shanghai—lift a corner of the veil from a China less formal than that reflected in *People's Daily* and seen on the conducted tour.*

(a) *Notice About Bicycles*

Comrades, with the industrialization of our socialist society, coupled with the unceasing rise in the people's living standard, the use of the bicycle becomes daily more popular.

But there is a small minority who feel a tremendous urgency for a bicycle, and also some out-of-towners without an understanding of the bicycle marketing supply regulations of Shanghai, who violate the law and buy unregistered vehicles on the black market. In this way it is easy to be deceived and duped. Let's hope that we will all heighten our revolutionary alertness, and carefully abide by the following points:

I. Do not freely buy or sell, exchange, or ask someone else to buy for you, bicycles or bicycle parts on the black market, but only through regular stores. If you do, you not only violate the law but you also will be easily deceived. The Ministry of Taxes will not honor the transfer of these bicycles. The Office of Public Security will investigate, and will not respect property rights in its investigation.

---

* English translation by myself, assisted by Liang Tsan-tang.

II. Do not park your bicycle carelessly any old place. They will be easily lost this way. Be sure to use a lock. At night, be sure to park it in a safe place.

III. Everyone should cooperate to support these marketing supply regulations. The Ministry of Commerce should enforce these regulations ever more diligently, and we should all support these efforts to combat bicycle thiefs and those who buy bicycles and bicycle parts contrary to these regulations.

(b) *Tips on Using the Telephone*

Use the phone whenever necessary, and only when necessary.

Make sure you have the correct number, then when you hear the dial tone, carefully dial the number.

Always answer the phone as soon as it rings.

Make your phone conversations as brief as possible.

Replace the phone in its correct position when you have finished using it.

PLEASE DO NOT INSTALL OR TRANSFER A TELEPHONE PRIVATELY.

(c) *A complaint by a citizen of Shanghai*

(This takes the form of a wall poster—in the text I have used the literal translation "big-character poster"—which complains that an earlier poster by the same citizen was torn down. Unfortunately I do not know the contents of the earlier poster. The writer is evidently a worker in the Shanghai Machine Repair Factory—it is not clear what relation he has to the Metallurgy Bureau, against which his grievance is directed. This second poster remained on a wall in central Shanghai throughout my five-day visit to the city in August 1975. Scores of people stood reading it for much of each day. The poster is in two parts. The first is addressed to the Party Committee of the Metallurgy Bureau; the second is addressed to the public at large.)

To the Party Committee of the Metallurgy Bureau
You used strongly to advocate not only the use of the big-character poster, but also the acceptance of big-character poster criticisms and comments from the ranks of the people. Rivers and mountains have not changed, but you have changed. Only superficially are you enthusiastic. In fact you have been apathetic, and you have even opposed a poster that was designed to advise you. In an attempt to hide your wrong-doings, you removed my poster. . . . This act is truly one of ugliness built upon ugliness! You are concerned to save face, not to save the correct policy! How long can this go on?

> *Shanghai Machine Repair Factory*
> *Chai Pao-yao*

Desperate Plight of the Big-Character Poster
Big-character posters are a form of struggle of great usefulness to the working class, and very bad for the capitalist class. They are a powerful means for both revealing and resolving conflicts. By writing a poster, one can snap a kind of seemingly placid, but actually explosive atmosphere which can occur.

Chairman Mao called the big-character poster a fine new weapon. He said it may be used in any public place—whether a city, village, factory, school, store, cooperative or whatever. The National People's Congress even made the right to put up big-character posters the law of the land—including it in the Constitution of the People's Republic of China.

Lu Xun* said it was rare to find such an excellent form of expression as the big-character poster. Forty years have passed. The old problem of the gap between words and deeds is still not well handled.

This past July, I put up a big-character poster. But some influential and privileged man gathered the people's militia to

---

* Lu Xun (1881–1936) was an influential left-wing writer and social critic much admired by Mao.—R.T.

take it down. They came with brooms and buckets and washed my poster off the wall. . . .

Later, because of my writing the big-character poster, I was very ruthlessly, and quite irrationally, beaten up by the militia in an underground shelter.

If I am really a poisonous weed, then the Metallurgy Bureau should be out to get rid of me. Why have they not dared to do so? Because I am not a poisonous weed.

You labeled me as a rumor-spreader. Yet Comrades Ho and Chu testified to the truth of my statements at the Big Debate Meeting of Number Three Factory Party Committee. Moreover, none of the committee members questioned the truth of my statements.

Does my poster divulge important, classified national information? No it does not. The comrades of the people's militia all agree that putting up big-character posters is a good practice. The real problem is that my poster did not serve a certain person's interests, and it revealed his surreptitious doings. That made him determined to have the poster taken down.

The idea of the big-character poster was created by the Chinese people. It was designed by them as a sharp weapon for socialist revolution. Being advocated by Chairman Mao, it has been used all over the world. Even in Ethiopia the revolutionaries made use of the big-character poster.

Yet the big-character poster has been in deep distress in its own homeland. It has been considered a needle in the eye of those who are only superficially Mao's followers. They speed up its extermination. They even imprison those who put up posters. These superficial Mao-followers are the very ones who are supposed to guarantee the Chinese people's free use of big-character posters.

I myself, as an ordinary worker, living in the city which is the birthplace of the Communist Party of China, in an era when Chairman Mao is still alive, have actually tasted their type of "guarantee" many times.

I have witnessed in action the revival of Lin Piao's principle,

"political power is the power to repress the people." It has over-
whelmed my right to expression. Alas, alas, the big-character
poster is being buried!

> *Shanghai Machine Repair Factory*
> *Chai Pao-yao*
> *1975. 8.22*

10. TENG DOES A DOUBLE LAZARUS

In July 1977, the Central Committee of the CCP met. It confirmed Hua as CCP chairman; not less significant, it rehabilitated Teng. The following is the relevant excerpt from a joint
editorial entitled "Historic Meeting" which summed up the
event.*

The Third Plenary Session of the Tenth Central Committee of
the Communist Party of China has been successfully held. As
the glad tidings spread all over China, hundreds of millions of
people are holding rallies and demonstrations, beating drums
and gongs and setting off firecrackers to acclaim the tremendous success of the session, and they are expressing their
hearty support for the resolutions it adopted. The whole Party,
the whole army and the people of all our nationalities are jubilant.

The Third Plenary Session of the Tenth Central Committee
was a very important meeting in the history of our Party. It was
the first plenary session of the Central Committee since the
death of our great leader and teacher Chairman Mao and since
our wise leader Chairman Hua took charge of the work of the
Central Committee. It consolidated and carried forward the
great victory of smashing the anti-Party "gang of four." Under
Chairman Hua's leadership, the session brought democracy

---

* English translation from *Peking Review,* July 29, 1977.

into full play, strengthened unity, drew upon all useful opinions, pooled the efforts of all, was lively and invigorating and made full preparations politically, ideologically and organizationally for the convening of the Eleventh National Congress of the Party.

The Third Plenary Session unanimously adopted the "Resolution Confirming the Appointment of Comrade Hua Kuo-feng as Chairman of the Central Committee of the Communist Party of China and Chairman of the Military Commission of the Central Committee of the Communist Party of China." At a critical moment in the Chinese revolution, Chairman Hua, carrying out Chairman Mao's behest, led the whole Party in shattering the anti-Party "gang of four," thus averting a major split and retrogression in our country. In the nine months and more following, Chairman Hua has set forth the strategic policy decision of grasping the key link of class struggle in running the country well, adopted a series of effective measures to eliminate the pernicious influence of the counter-revolutionary revisionist line of the "gang of four" in the political, economic, cultural and other fields, and resolutely implemented Chairman Mao's proletarian revolutionary line. All this has brought highly encouraging results. Experience in the struggle has proved that Chairman Hua is wise and resolute and good at both destruction and construction; it shows that the political line and the organizational line of the Party Central Committee headed by Chairman Hua and the policy decisions and measures it has adopted all are correct. In the course of the struggle, the 30 million Party members and the 800 million people have seen more and more clearly that Chairman Hua is worthy of being called Chairman Mao's good student and successor and our good leader and supreme commander. The Third Plenary Session's confirmation of Chairman Hua's status as leader of the Party and the army is the surest guarantee that our Party will hold aloft Chairman Mao's great banner and continue the revolution under the dictatorship of the proletariat.

The Third Plenary Session also adopted the "Resolution Restoring Comrade Teng Hsiao-ping to His Posts." Chairman Mao long ago made a clear and all-round assessment of Comrade Teng Hsiao-ping. At the central working conference held in March this year, Chairman Hua pointed out that the Wang-Chang-Chiang-Yao anti-Party clique's "attacks and false accusations against Comrade Teng Hsiao-ping were an important part of their scheme to usurp Party and state power" and that "all the slanders and unfounded charges made by the 'gang of four' against Comrade Teng Hsiao-ping should be repudiated." The plenary session's decision to restore Comrade Teng Hsiao-ping to all his posts both inside and outside the Party embodies the wishes of the mass of Party members and of the people. It is yet another proof that the Party Central Committee headed by Chairman Hua is of one heart with the masses.

Chairman Mao taught us: "It is reliance on the political experience and wisdom of the collective that can guarantee the correct leadership of the Party and the state and the unshakable unity of the ranks of the Party." With Chairman Hua as the leader of our Party and with Vice-Chairman Yeh, Vice-Chairman Teng and other central leading comrades working in concert with him, our Party now again has what Lenin described as a more or less stable group "composed of the most authoritative, influential and experienced members, who are elected to the most responsible positions, and are called leaders." Our Party has a bright future. The whole Party and the people throughout the country are even more confident of victory. . . .

11. NEW YEAR'S EDITORIAL LOOKS TO 1978

Peking's leading publications summed up 1977 and looked optimistically at 1978 in this joint editorial entitled "A Bright China."*

---

*English translation from *Peking Review,* January 6, 1978.

In the year 1977, all kinds of people round the world, including some of our friends and comrades as well as our enemies, kept an eye on China, wondering where the country was going after losing her great leader and teacher Chairman Mao Tsetung and her respected and beloved Premier Chou En-lai and Chairman of the National People's Congress Standing Committee Chu Teh and after smashing the "gang of four."

What did they see? They saw the Party Central Committee headed by the wise leader Chairman Hua hold aloft the great banner of Chairman Mao and the 800 million Chinese people rally closely round the successor chosen by Chairman Mao. They saw Chairman Hua lead us in grasping the key link of class struggle and bringing about great order across the land, resulting in stability and unity throughout the country and a vigorous development in production and construction. They saw that with the elimination of the "four pests," China's beautiful land became even more resplendent and the Chinese revolution went foraging ahead along the course charted by Chairman Mao!

Our struggle with the "gang of four" was another struggle between two possible destinies for China. Would there be a bright China or a dark China? The great decisive victory of October 1976 already gave the answer. But the development of the political and economic situation throughout the country was so splendid and so fast that it exceeded our expectations.

At the central working conference in March 1977, Chairman Hua proposed that initial success should be won in one year and marked success in three years in implementing the strategic decision of grasping the key link of class struggle and bringing about great order across the land. The year 1977 is now over and initial success has indeed been won in implementing the strategic decision. Following are the major indications:

One. The movement to expose and criticize the "gang of four" has advanced rapidly and healthily, the rights and wrongs concerning the line which were for a long time confused by the "gang of four" have been basically clarified, and Chairman Mao's proletarian revolutionary line can now be implemented quite smoothly on all fronts. After smashing the "gang of four," Chairman Hua and the Party Central Committee have time and again stressed the great significance of holding high and safeguarding the banner of Chairman Mao, made public a series of Chairman Mao's directives criticizing the "gang of four" and published Volume V of the *Selected Works of Mao Tsetung,* thus providing the cadres and masses with a powerful ideological weapon to master Mao Tsetung Thought comprehensively and accurately, to deepen the exposure and criticism of the "gang of four," and to carry on socialist revolution and construction. The central working conference in March, the Third Plenary Session of the Tenth Party Central Committee in July and particularly the Eleventh Party Congress achieved unity of thinking throughout the Party, made clear the orientation and rallied the whole Party still more closely round the Party Central Committee. This has enabled our struggle to overcome all forms of interference and advance triumphantly under the guidance of Mao Tsetung Thought.

Two. As far as the great majority of localities and departments are concerned, investigation of the individuals involved in and the incidents connected with the conspiracy of the "gang of four" to usurp Party and state power has in the main been completed and the class alignment has in the main become clear. The bourgeois factional setup of the "gang of four" and their followers have been dealt a crushing blow. The Party and people have taken back that portion of power which was usurped by them and have solved the problems of those departments and localities which were once under their tight control or seriously undermined by them. In a number of provinces, municipalities and autonomous regions as well as some departments under the Party Central Committee and the State Council, the leading bodies have been readjusted and strengthened.

Three. The oppressive situation in which "ten thousand horses stand mute" under the tyranny of the "gang of four" has ended, and the whole Party, the whole army, and the people of the whole country have become invigorated. The Party's fine tradition and style of work of seeking truth from facts and following the mass line are being revived and carried forward. Proletarian democratic centralism is being carried out in a better way. People's minds are at ease and lively. The political situation envisaged by Chairman Mao—*a political situation in which we have both centralism and democracy, both discipline and freedom, both unity of will and personal ease of mind and liveliness*—is taking shape.

Four. Forceful blows have been dealt at disrupters aided and abetted by the "gang of four"—smash-and-grabbers, criminals seriously undermining public security and landlords, rich peasants, counter-revolutionaries and bad elements who hated socialism and launched vengeful counterattacks. Public order has been greatly improved to the satisfaction of the people. This is especially true in those places which suffered the most.

Five. The conspiracy of the "gang of four" to oppose and disrupt the army and usurp its leadership has been exposed and criticized by commanders and fighters throughout the army. The army has conducted education in ideology and the Party line through a discussion of "ten should's or shouldn't's" to eliminate the pernicious influence of the "gang of four," correct unhealthy tendencies and restore and carry forward the spirit of the "Kutien Meeting." The Party's leadership over the army has been greatly strengthened. The movements to learn from Lei Feng and from the "Hard-Boned 6th Company" and military training are going full steam ahead.

Six. An encouraging new situation has appeared in the scientific, educational and cultural fields where the interference and sabotage by the "gang of four" were serious. Criticism of the "two estimates" has freed the intellectuals from mental shackles and fired them with greater enthusiasm for socialism. They are working hard to catch up with and surpass advanced world levels and enrich socialist culture, education, and science. The young people have shown unprecedented interest in acquiring general and scientific knowledge for the sake of the revolution. A new high tide in the development of socialist culture is in the offing.

Seven. The situation in the national economy has taken a turn for the better after a long period of stagnation or even backsliding, which resulted from interference and sabotage by the "gang of four." The mass movements to learn from Taching in industry and from Tachai in agriculture are developing vigorously. Despite serious natural adversities, we have reaped a fairly good grain harvest, increased the output of cotton, and made progress in forestry, animal husbandry, sideline production, and fishery. Farmland capital construction is being carried out on a big scale. Industrial production, which went up step by step in an all-round way, has rapidly reached or surpassed previous records. This started with the improvement in railway transportation. Coal production did well too. The output of petroleum rose steadily and that of chemical fertilizer soared. The output of iron and steel came up in the third and fourth quarters with a marked increase in daily output. The increase in total industrial output value is estimated at 14 percent, far exceeding the 8 percent target planned at the beginning of 1977. On the commercial front, both purchasing and marketing are brisk. There has been a marked increase in financial income which, however, failed to meet state plans for several years running. Revenue and expenditure are balanced, with a small surplus. Sixty percent of China's wage earners are getting more pay through wage increases made possible by the development of production. The year 1977 was truly a major turning point for China's national economy; it was a new starting point for a steady rise after stagnation, fluctuation, and back-sliding.

Eight. The disastrous effects on various fields of work caused by the "gang of four" through their frenzied sabotage of the Party's policies towards cadres, intellectuals, and minority nationalities are being eliminated step by step. The split caused by the gang in some areas and organizations has been cemented and the chaos overcome. Chairman Mao's principle of overall consideration and all-round arrangement is being carried out systematically. The unification of our country, the unity of our people and the unity of our various nationalities have been consolidated and strengthened. Our united front led by the working class, based on the worker–peasant alliance and including patriotic democratic parties, patriotic personages, compatriots in Taiwan, compatriots in Hongkong and Macao, and overseas Chinese is growing in strength and scope.

In foreign affairs, we have firmly adhered to Chairman Mao's strategic concept differentiating the three worlds and carried out his line, principles, and policies. We firmly support the world's people in their just struggle against imperialism, colonialism, and hegemonism, firmly support the people of various countries in opposing the superpowers' policies of aggression and war, and firmly support all revolutionary and progressive causes. Our country enjoys ever-growing international prestige and we have friends all over the world.

These are our achievements of the past year. One year is but a flash in the endless flow of history. Nevertheless in this fleeting year, the Party Central Committee headed by Chairman Hua has led us from victory to victory in grasping the key link of class struggle and running the country well. From their own experience the people of China have come to understand more and more deeply that socialist revolution and socialist construction in China have truly entered a new period of development, and that the Party Central Committee headed by Chairman Hua deserves to be called the vigorous fighting command of the proletariat which holds aloft the great banner of Chairman Mao. The whole Party, the whole army, and the people of all nationalities throughout the country are delighted to have such a wise leader and supreme commander as Chairman Hua. When drinking the water think of its source. Therefore we all the more cherish the memory of our great leader and teacher

Chairman Mao who showed great foresight in choosing such an excellent successor for us. And it is invincible Mao Tsetung Thought that has guided us to advance from victory to victory.

For the achievement of marked success in three years in grasping the key link of class struggle and bringing about great order across the land, 1978 counts as an important year. In the new year, the whole Party, the whole army, and the people of all nationalities throughout the country should continue to hold aloft the great banner of Chairman Mao, follow the line of the Eleventh Party Congress, fight in unity, and, taking the exposure and criticism of the "gang of four" as the key link, deepen the mass movements to learn from Taching in industry and from Tachai in agriculture, vigorously criticize capitalism and revisionism, go all out to build socialism and strive to fulfil the fighting tasks laid down by the Eleventh Party Congress; we should adhere to Chairman Mao's strategic concept differentiating the three worlds and abide by his revolutionary line in foreign affairs, so as to contribute to the development of the international situation in a direction favorable to the people of China and the world.

Carrying the great struggle against the "gang of four" through to the end is a task of first importance in grasping the key link of class struggle and running the country well. In the new year, we should continue to keep a firm hold on the key link of exposing and criticizing the "gang of four" and do a good job of it. Our struggle against the "gang of four" is a decisive battle of historic importance. Both in depth and breadth it is a battle of rare occurrence in the history of our Party. The victories we have won in this battle have tremendously changed the balance of class forces in our country in favor of the proletariat and brought profound changes to the political, economic, military, and cultural spheres. The reason underlying our initial success in the first year is that we have fought well in this battle to expose and criticize the "gang of four"; our fundamental guarantee for winning marked success in three years also lies in continuing to fight the battle well. It should be noted that the development of the movement is unbalanced. In a few areas and departments, the movement started a bit late, progress was not quite satisfactory, and investigation proceeded rather slowly. The work in these places should be stepped up according to the demands of the Eleventh Party Congress and under the unified leadership of the Party committees. In this struggle we must take a firm, clear-cut stand and not relent towards the "gang of four" and their followers and, at the same time, pay due attention to the Party's policies. This is a principle that combines firmness with prudence and thoroughgoing investigation with stabilization of the overall situation, a principle that will ensure complete success in carrying the investigation through to the end. We must conscientiously implement the policies formulated at the Eleventh Party Congress, strictly distinguish between the two different types of contradictions, do a really good job of helping more people by educating them and narrowing the target of attack, and must not mistake contradictions among the people for contradictions between ourselves and the enemy. Anyone who can be won over through education should not be pushed aside. Resolute blows should be aimed at the "gang of four" and the handful of their sworn followers who are guilty of serious crimes and unwilling to repent. Leadership should be strengthened particularly in those units which suffered seriously from interference by the "gang of four." Attention should be paid to the few units where problems are being covered up and the masses repressed; measures should be adopted to deal with the situation.

It is necessary to continue mobilizing the masses boldly and to fight resolutely for victory in the third campaign* for expos-

---

*The struggle to expose and criticize the "gang of four" has gone through two campaigns and the third campaign is now under way. The first campaign which took place from the winter of 1976 through the spring of 1977 was mainly devoted to exposing and criticizing the gang's conspiracies in usurping Party and state power. The second campaign which started in March 1977 centered on exposing and criticizing the gang's counter-revolutionary features and its members' past criminal records. The third campaign now under way concentrates on exposing and criticizing, from the theoretical plane of philosophy, political economy and scientific socialism, the ultra-Right essence of the gang's counter-revolutionary revisionist line and its manifestations in all fields.

ing and criticizing the "gang of four." This is a great campaign aimed at further distinguishing right from wrong, setting to rights things which were thrown into disorder by the gang, and emancipating the mind, a great campaign to ensure complete victory in the struggle to expose and criticize the "gang of four." The gang is a bunch of political swindlers who decked themselves out in Marxism–Leninism. They frenziedly opposed Mao Tsetung Thought, wantonly distorted, tampered with, and even forged Chairman Mao's directives. Wielding the power they had usurped, they tried in a thousand and one ways to inculcate slavishness and hoodwink the people, permitting them only to parrot what the gang had said and forbidding any form of dissent. The "gang of four" cooked up a counter-revolutionary political program which equated veteran cadres with "democrats" and "democrats" with "capitalist-roaders" and raised the counter-revolutionary slogan of "going against the way things were done in the seventeen years prior to the Cultural Revolution." With this they reversed the relationship of the people to the enemy, confused right and wrong, and attacked Chairman Mao's revolutionary line as "revisionist" and socialist principles and policies as "capitalist." Clearly the modernization of agriculture, industry, national defence, and science and technology is a grand goal set forth by Premier Chou in accordance with Chairman Mao's directives, yet the "gang of four" vilified it as "capitalist restoration"; "to each according to his work," which is clearly a socialist principle, was branded by the gang as "revisionist"; studying techniques for the sake of the revolution, a sure indication of the effort to become both Red and expert, was attacked by the gang as "the road of bourgeois specialists." Whoever disagreed with the gang's nonsense would be condemned as trying to bring about "restoration" and "retrogression," having "relapses" or being "counter-revolutionaries." Even to this day these accusations remain trammels shackling some comrades' minds and make them nervous. We should earnestly study works by Marx, Engels, Lenin, and Stalin and Chairman Mao's works, comprehend and grasp Mao Tsetung

Thought comprehensively and accurately as a system and, keeping a firm hold on the gang's counter-revolutionary political program, strip them of their "Leftist" guises, bare the ultra-Right essence of their counter-revolutionary revisionist line and all its manifestations, and conduct criticism from the theoretical plane of philosophy, political economy, and scientific socialism, so as to rectify what the gang turned upside down with regard to questions of right and wrong in line, ideology, and theory. At the same time we must earnestly and realistically sum up experience, both positive and negative, gained in the past twenty-eight years, make clear the specific line, principles, and policies guiding each field of work, and work out relevant rules, regulations, and methods. Only in this way can we smash the mental shackles imposed on us by the "gang of four," greatly emancipate our minds, sweep away all interference, achieve unity in thinking and action, and make determined, all-out efforts to build socialism, quicken the pace of construction, and push forward the national economy.

The speed of construction is not just an economic question, it is a serious political question. Why do we say the socialist system is superior? In the final analysis, it is because the socialist system can create higher labor productivity and make the national economy develop faster than capitalism. Why do we say the theory, line, policy, and ideology of the "gang of four," the media under their control and their bourgeois factional setup constitute an ultra-reactionary and rotten-to-the-core superstructure? At root, it is because this superstructure stands against the dictatorship of the proletariat, undermines the socialist economic base and impedes the development of the productive forces. In just a little over a year since the "gang of four" was smashed, we have already made a big stride forward. The question at present is that we must advance at high speed instead of resting content with what we have achieved. This is dictated by the need for the proletariat to vanquish the bourgeoisie and for socialism to defeat capitalism in the historical period of socialism, the need to strengthen the worker-peasant alliance on a new basis, to consolidate the dictatorship of the proletariat and steadily raise the people's standard of living, the need to build a powerful national defence, defend our socialist motherland and prepare for the liberation of our sacred territory Taiwan Province, and the need to attain the grand goal of four modernizations before the end of this century. In a word, quickening the pace of economic construction is dictated by the development of international and domestic class struggles; it is a glorious mission history has entrusted to us. Party committees at all levels must consider the question of speed and plan their work in the revolutionary spirit of seizing the day and seizing the hour, make it known among the masses, and mobilize them to contribute their talents and ability to the speedy development of the national economy.

A higher speed is not only necessary but possible. We are fully confident of our ability to accelerate the development of our national economy because we have Chairman Mao's proletarian revolutionary line and the strong leadership of the Party Central Committee headed by Chairman Hua, we have the superior socialist system and hundreds of millions of industrious, courageous, and ingenious workers, peasants, and intellectuals who have heightened their consciousness through education by positive and negative examples during the Great Cultural Revolution and in the Eleventh two-line struggle in particular, and we have rich natural resources and the material foundation built up in the past twenty-eight years. A higher speed in 1978 will make things easier in 1979. This will be vital to our efforts to "achieve marked success in three years." In the new year, the whole Party must vigorously grasp agriculture, the foundation of the national economy, and make it a success. All trades and professions must pay attention to agriculture, support it and do everything to further its development. A faster growth of agriculture is a prerequisite for a faster growth of industry and the national economy as a whole. In industry, particular attention must be paid to electricity, fuel, and transportation. With these "precursor departments" running in the van, the industries producing iron and steel and raw and semi-finished materials will follow up, so that the rate of growth can be greatly increased even on the basis of the existing industrial capacity alone and there will be a new and all-round leap forward in industry and the national economy as a whole. High speed involves not only quantity, but quality and cost. Our aim is to turn out more and better products at minimum cost, that is, to achieve greater, faster, better, and more economical results in fulfilling the state plan in an all-round way.

In 1978, China will convene the Fifth National People's Congress, the first session of the Fifth National Committee of the Chinese People's Political Consultative Conference and a national science conference. These will be major events in the political and cultural life of the Chinese people. The whole Party, the whole army, and the people of all nationalities in our country must fight in unity and greet these important events with new and outstanding successes in the three great revolutionary movements of class struggle, the struggle for production and scientific experiment.

The tasks ahead are great and arduous. It is crucial to strengthen Party leadership. All areas and departments must set up leading bodies which firmly adhere to Chairman Mao's revolutionary line and policies, conform to his five requirements for successors in the revolutionary cause and the principle of the combination of the old, middle-aged, and young, and enjoy the confidence and support of the masses. With such leading bodies, as Chairman Hua has said, the masses will rejoice and support them and feel encouraged as soon as the members are announced. We must win over all people who can be won over, unite with all people who can be united, mobilize all positive factors and turn negative factors into positive ones to serve the great cause of building socialism. In this way we will certainly be able to overcome all difficulties, vanquish all enemies, and work wonders.

The ice has been broken; the road is open. The revolutionary cause of the proletariat Chairman Mao pioneered in China must triumph and surely can triumph. A bright China surely can make a greater contribution to humanity.

ᘯ Index ᘯ

(Page numbers in italics refer to photographs.)

Ma Yu-chen, 31
middle class, emergence of, 10, 247
Middle Kingdom, China as, 3, 179, 239
mineral resources, exploitation of, 16–17
Ming Dynasty, Mao on, 103
modernization issue
Chou on, 42; Hua on, 75–76; Mao on, 180; priority of, 142–143, 169, 242; Teng on, 16–18, 50–53, 59–60, 240–241
multinational corporations, political effect of, 250

National Day, 209
Nationalists, *see* Taiwan
National People's Congress, *see* NPC
NATO (North Atlantic Treaty Organization), PRC and, 3
NBC poll (1974), 188–189
"new-born Socialist things," 55–56
New China News Agency, 79, 115
New Class, The (Djilas), 160–161
New York Times, 194
Nixon, Richard
China trip of, 1972: 181, 187, 188, 221 (*see also* Shanghai Communiqué); 1975: 185, 219; Chinese poems on, 296–297; Chou and, 28, 29; Mao on fall of, 222; Teng compared to, 134
NPC (National People's Congress), 29, 42, 53–54, 74, 78, 88, 113, 287–291
nuclear devices, PRC possession of, 11, 146, 166, 194, 234

oil
PRC supply of, 5, 16–17, 142, 251; Ta Ch'ing Oilfield, 150–151

Opium War of 1839–42, heritage of, 180, 241–242, 253

Pai Hsiang-kuo, 32
Pakistan, PRC and, 3
paramedics ("barefoot doctors"), 12, 50
party rhetoric, Teng on, 266, 269
Pathet Lao, 46
"peaceful coexistence," concept of, 224
Peking Construction Tool Plant, 175
Peking Review, 45
Peking Riot (April 1976), 10, 56–62, 64, 249, 259–266
P'eng Te-huai, 15, 53, 121, 215
People's Daily
on "capitulationists," 44–45, 56; on CCP anniversary, 31–32; on Gang of Four, 55, 109, 134–135; on Hua, 68, 134–135; on Lin Piao, 56; on Mao legacy, 109; on nuclear weapons, 166; on Peking Riot, 58, 61–62, 64, 259–265; on people-government relationship, 166; style of, 9, 84, 143, 203; on Teng, 45, 49, 58, 61–62, 219; on U.S.S.R., 45
"people's war," 246–247
personality politics, 65–67
PLA (People's Liberation Army—the PRC armed forces)
CCP and, 15, 31–32; Chiang Ch'ing and, 65; in Cultural Revolution, 19; foreign policy of, 52, 127, 214–216, 243–244; Gang of Four and, 16, 78–80, 99–101, 122, 127; Hua and, 15–16, 78–80, 99–101, 217; industrial growth and, 151, 153; influence of, 15–16, 249; Lin Piao and,

ROSS TERRILL

is the author of 800,000,000: *The Real China* and *Flowers on an Iron Tree,* among other books. Born in Melbourne, Australia, and educated at Melbourne and Harvard universities, he is Associate Professor of Government at Harvard and a contributing editor of the *Atlantic Monthly.* He visited China in 1964, 1971, 1973, and 1975.

DATE DUE	